Psychopharmacology:
Basic Mechanisms and Applied Interventions

Master Lectures in Psychology

Psychopharmacology:

Basic Mechanisms and Applied Interventions

Master Lecturers

Linda Dykstra

Chris-Ellyn Johanson

John R. Hughes

G. Alan Marlatt

Bernard Weiss

Edited by
John Grabowski
and Gary R. VandenBos

THE MASTER LECTURES

AMERICAN PSYCHOLOGICAL ASSOCIATION
WASHINGTON, DC 20002

First printing July 1992
Second printing July 1994

Published by the
American Psychological Association
750 First Street, NE
Washington, DC 20002

Copies may be ordered from
APA Order Department
P.O. Box 2710
Hyattsville, MD 20784

In the United Kingdom and Europe, copies may be ordered from
American Psychological Association
3 Henrietta Street
Covent Garden, London
WC2E 8LU England

Typeset in Cheltenham by Easton Publishing Services, Inc.,
Easton, MD

Printer: Kirby Lithographic Company, Inc., Arlington, VA
Technical editor and production coordinator: Linda J. Beverly

Library of Congress Cataloging-in-Publication Data

Psychopharmacology : basic mechanisms and applied
   interventions / edited by John Grabowski and Gary R.
   VandenBos.
        p.   cm.—(Master lectures)
   Includes bibliographical references.
    ISBN 1-55798-158-2 (acid-free paper)
       1. Psychopharmacology. 2. Mental illness—Chemotherapy.
   3. Behavioral toxicology. 4. Substance abuse. I. Grabowski,
   John. II. VandenBos, Gary R. III. Series.
       [DNLM: 1. Psychopharmacology.   QV 77 P972107]
   RC483.P77775   1992
   615'.78—dc20
   DNLM/DLC
   for Library of Congress   92-17732
                                                              CIP

Printed in the United States of America

CONTENTS

PREFACE

P sychologists are among the leaders in the laboratory and clinical investigation of drug–neurochemistry–behavior–environment interactions. Diagnosis and treatment of disorders requiring treatment with drugs, or resulting from drug abuse, are parallel critical areas of activity for psychologists. These two major areas are integral and complementary efforts of equal importance.

The following Master Lectures touch on several of these varied, often sensitive topics. Important issues and excellent science are described. The lectures necessarily do not fully address all of the science and the complexities that characterize these critical areas of research. Time and space constraints resulted in more being unsaid than said. However, the presentations admirably reflect the range of expertise of the work of psychologists, if not the entire scope and depth of these efforts.

Medications, "Drugs," Chemicals, and Problems

Issues in Therapeutics, Drug Abuse, and Chemical Toxicity

Drugs are used therapeutically with exemplary benefit. However, they may create problems for reasons ranging from chemical characteristics to inappropriate prescribing or patient noncompliance. A major focus of psychologists is the examination and understanding of the range of therapeutic agents used for the spectrum of behavioral and psychological disorders. Research in the area includes examination of behavioral and neurochemical mechanisms, actions, and interactions. Some drugs that are abused also have therapeutic benefit or represent categories that do. Research and discussion sensitive to commonalities permit research consumers to understand and relate areas that are often treated separately.

Teratology (the study of fetal effects), toxicology (the study of adverse effects), dose ranges, routes of administration, and interactions with other drugs are all considered in the evaluation of a new medication. These determinations lead to identification of an effective pharmacological regimen. When the drug is then administered to patients, complexity hinges in part on assuring compliance to an agent that may have unpleasant side effects, or adherence to the regimen by a patient with patently unrealistic fears that therapeutic medication taking is a route to drug dependence.

Drug self-administration characterized as drug abuse or dependence is often described as one problem, or at most, a few problems. In fact, the diversity of drugs, differences in doses, differences in patterns of use, several common routes of administration, great differences in availability, differences in social constraint, and, of course, differences in individual characteristics of the users all affect the result. Thus, the problems are not homogeneous or singular. Psychologists study the many facets and determinants of drug dependence and abuse to identify the antecedents, consequences, and strategies for treatment. There are commonalities in the range of biological and behavioral studies of therapeutics and drug abuse. Although there may be divergence at the level of specific treatment elements, parallels exist as well. Thus, for example, the problems of matching treatment strategies that exist with other psychological disorders also prevail in the area of treatment of drug abuse. Unfortunately, the data are only now beginning to emerge.

Behavioral toxicology is an area of study seemingly distinct and unrelated to other issues considered here. But in fact, it has many commonalities with research in therapeutic medication and drug dependence. It confronts many of the same issues, uses the same methods, and examines some of the same substances in its science. Behavioral toxicology is an essential discipline in the examination of the correlates of behavioral and biological effects not only of therapeutic medications and drugs of abuse and dependence but also of chemicals that permeate our work and living environments. Again, the focus is on the same continua: The routes of entry to the body may differ, the chemicals differ, the dose or "exposure" differ, and certainly short- and long-term effects may differ dramatically.

The endogenous neurochemistry, interacting neural systems, and behavior—a complex product of biological, behavioral, and environmental influences—act and interact with drugs and chemicals. Here reside the common links in all of these areas of study and practice that are the domain of psychologists.

Drugs, Chemicals, and Epidemiology

Medications are widely used in the treatment of psychological disorders. For example, there are 13 benzodiazepines available in the United States, most of which are used primarily in the treatment of behavioral and biobehavioral disorders. Furthermore, over the last decade, 10%–15% of the adult population was estimated to have had a benzodiazepine prescribed for therapeutics each year. Similarly, depression is a commonly diagnosed condition for which antidepressants are often effectively prescribed. Other conditions such as the major psychoses occur at lower frequency, but their treatments are often aided with psychoactive medications. This is also true, in a highly specific manner, for conditions such as bipolar disorders.

It is clear that new methods of drug discovery and biotechnology offer promise of medications that have highly specific neurochemical actions. However, they are no more likely to meet the criteria of "magic bullets" than other psychoactive medications available in the past. This is because many of the disorders reflect the complex interplay of biology, behavior, and environment. However, these new drugs can be expected to be more specific in action and, importantly, to provide greater relief with fewer of the side effects that are common deterrents to compliance. It follows that the epidemiology of therapeutic drug use will shift to a higher frequency of prescription, with perhaps a shorter course and more specialized treatments combined with appropriate cognitive and behavioral interventions.

The many faces of drugs and chemicals are the focus of scientific, social, economic, and political interest and concern. Drug use and abuse are periodically the center of political rhetoric focusing on treatment, prevention, and interdiction at the sites of production. There are often vastly differing interpretations of the data. The waves of social and political concern may outlast the particular problematic drug use from which the concern arose. As long as the focus is on any one drug, this particular strategy may repeatedly generate the unfortunate view of "too little, too late." The view stems from an entrenched crisis intervention mentality, at the policy and political levels, that demands breakthroughs and then moves on to the next crisis.

The major epidemiological studies, sponsored by the National Institute on Drug Abuse (combined with other data), reflect the shifting base of alcohol and drug dependence over the last decade. Epidemiological studies have generally indicated a decline in some forms of drug abuse, use, and "experimentation." Thus, for example, the High School Senior Survey has indicated declines in cocaine use since 1984 and declines in other drug use for more than a decade. Tobacco use within this population has decreased among males, increased among females, and remains unacceptably high overall. Similarly, alcohol use remains high in this underaged population, but it has been declining. There is evidence that most forms of drug use have declined to a greater extent among those high school seniors who plan to get a vocational or college education compared with those who plan to end their education with high school. Inferences from these data suggest that drug use is higher among the unsampled population of young people who drop out or who are forced out of school before reaching their senior year. The nationally conducted "Household Survey" provides a similar mix of encouraging and discouraging results, as does the Drug Abuse Warning Network, a national survey of emergency room admissions and medical examiners' results. The high rates of alcohol-related automobile fatalities has declined in the past decade, indicating changes in behavior. The data predict lower rates of alcohol use in the current high school population as it ages. These studies imply little of what might be expected in the next decade and beyond for young people who are at the highest risk for exposure to new drugs or reemergence of old drugs. It is reasonable to expect that other forms of drug use will emerge, some relatively benign and some with disastrous consequences.

It appears that in addition to national waves of drug use, there are periodic "localized" surges in use or abuse of one or another form of drug. Thus, phencyclidine (PCP) was common in Washington, DC, for a time in the mid-1980s. The use of volatile inhalants is common among some populations in the southwestern United States. Tobacco use, in both smoked and chewed forms, varies widely from one area and socioeconomic group of the United States to another, and the increasingly common use of the latter form among high school students presents an entirely different problem. Although the use of high-concentration alcoholic beverages has declined in the past decade, sales of a new product, the wine cooler, have burgeoned. The shifting sands of patterns of drug use and abuse can be viewed as objective data, with each new study, basic or applied, providing more information about drug use and its pharmacological, behavioral, and social underpinnings. All eventually contribute to a better understanding of primary, secondary, and tertiary prevention.

The problems confronting the field of behavioral toxicology become simultaneously more and less complex. There is continuing improvement in techniques and increased measurement sensitivity that permits us to determine previously undetectable but meaningful consequences of exposure to a host of chemicals. Thus, for example, we learn that more people than previously expected have been affected by lead. It is also clear, however, that changes in automobile fuel, including the elimination of lead as an octane agent, have had dramatic effects in reducing this toxin in the environment over the past two decades.

Specific Patterns of Drug Taking

The underlying issues of patterns of taking therapeutic pharmacological agents have similarities with other drug taking. Ironically, maladaptive patterns of drug taking exist here as well. "Drug-abusing" individuals self-administer to excess acutely or chronically, whereas patients treated for other disorders exhibit noncompliance in the direction of under-medication. Abusers may take more of a drug because of biology and perceived "good effect," whereas the patient on antidepressants exhibits improvement *because of the drug action*, fails to continue the regimen and then slides back into depression.

Establishing adherence to medication regimens is critical to assure maximum benefit from the drug. The pharmacology of a medication can be clearly delineated, but it is of little value if the drug is not appropriately taken by the patient. Ironically, psychologists, a group that does not currently have prescription privileges, represent a discipline that has generated the data, developed, and implemented strategies to enhance compliance and induce behavioral change. This suggests that psychologists should be actively involved in the development of medication regimens. It also suggests that with appropriate training in pharmacology, psychologists may be best equipped to use their expertise to engender compliance to medication regimens while providing excellent psychological and behavioral therapies.

Advances in behavioral techniques will permit enhanced compliance to therapeutic regimens. Advances in chemistry and pharmacology will permit development of agents that have longer therapeutic action, thereby decreasing the problems of noncompliance. Converging developments of both behavioral and pharmacological science will in the end benefit the patient and assure safe and effective patterns of medication use.

Self-administration of drugs for their behaviorally active effects are varied and manifold in appearance. These patterns are presumed to be important determinants of observed severity of problems. Smokers of crack cocaine engage in repeated use of the drug via a route that assures maximum effect and potential hazardous consequences. Occasional users of cocaine hydrochloride via the nasal route may have fewer problems, but more frequent use can generate severe dependence. Cigarette smokers, with continuous and uninterrupted patterns of low-dose nicotine intakes, run risks of lung disease and other disease despite the relative low risk inherent in nicotine, the drug that is now well documented to sustain the behavior of smoking. The use of alcohol and drugs together or combining drugs may present consistently greater risk to the user than any of the abused drugs alone, and this is reflected in emergency room data.

In the area of behavioral toxicology, the issue of patterns of intake are equally important and may be determined by both the inadvertent or intentional environmental exposure. The patterns of unintended exposure determine observed consequences; in the case of reports of workers using solvents who also intentionally expose themselves for behavioral effect, the complexity of the problems is multiplied. In all cases—drug-reinforced intake, unintended exposure, or therapeutic administration—the route and patterns of intake are critical.

Drug Abuse Prevention and Treatment

The problems of drug abuse, administration of medications, and assuring compliance converge in the treatment of drug abuse. The psychopharmacological literature on treatment warrants note. There are currently two remarkably effective treatments of long standing: methadone for opiate dependence and disulfiram for alcohol dependence. More recently, nicotine administration via patches and polacrilix, "gum," for tobacco dependence and the opiate antagonist naltrexone have been added to the list of recognized effective agents. Their effectiveness in resolving drug dependence can be altered by the confluence of other treatment elements and environmental factors. Thus, in some cases, or in some phases of treatment, pharmacological intervention may be the dominant feature, whereas in others, behavioral interventions in the form of individual psychotherapy or restructuring of life-styles may be paramount features. It should be noted that the same applies to treatment of other psychiatric disturbances. Unfortunately, in both cases, the emergence of schools of thought forcing one or another perspective deter from the goal of finding optimal treatment combinations and matching patients with treatment. For example, in some jurisdictions, courts mandate acupuncture treatments for drug abuse, although this is not warranted by the data (which are dismal). Scientifically based treatments of drug abuse are still rare in the field, but data pointing to more and less efficacious approaches are now emerging.

Alcohol and other drug taking are complex, multiply determined behaviors. This is true in therapeutic and socially acceptable forms as well as the extreme and potentially devastating forms characterized in the *DSM-III-R* as dependence and abuse. There is extensive literature examining strategies to modulate or prevent drug taking and treatment of drug taking that has become *abuse* or *dependence*. The need for delineating the biological and behavioral mechanisms of drug effects is clear. The myriad biological, behavioral, and environmental (including social) factors and their interactions become evident and often obscure the need for similarly well-controlled research in the domain of treatment. Clinical scientists and clinicians desperate to identify treatments overlook the need for precise examination of determinants when, as observed by Struve, their wish for success is magnified by the lens of desire. Nevertheless, excellent treatment research proceeds and advances and eventually contributes to widely available effective treatments for drug dependence. The wait is frustrating but is characteristic of all disciplines in clinical science. Some advances come in the form of pharmacotherapy, others will be improved behavioral interventions, and many will come in the form of judicious application of pharmacological and behavioral interventions in combination or in varied but effective sequences. All must also account for special problems such as complex associated medical disorders, HIV and TB, myriad social problems, and possible concurrent psychiatric conditions that are either antecedents or consequences of drug abuse.

The Master Lecture Chapters

The chapters in this book are diverse. Of necessity, they leave much unsaid. However, they provide an excellent sampling of selections from the study of drugs and behavior. The conceptual practice of psychopharmacology was the coming together of traditional pharmacology and "psychiatry." It continues to permeate developments such as behavioral pharmacology, which can be characterized as a joining of behavioral psychology. More recently, major contributions have been made in this area by psychologists focusing on the neurosciences. Currently, scientists with backgrounds in psychology, psychiatry, the neurosciences, and pharmacology are studying the relationships between drugs, the brain (often represented by receptors), and behavior, and the efforts to delineate the relationships between drug behavior and environment continue to be unraveled by behavioral pharmacologists. From behavioral pharmacology and toxicology, there also emerged the area of behavioral toxicology, where much of the seminal work was conducted by Laties and Weiss. Efforts devoted to the prevention of disease and disorders and the promotion of health have emerged from work in each of these areas.

Johanson has provided one anchor for this book: the examination of the basic principles of pharmacology and biochemical actions that underlie behavioral actions. She has described in a few pages the intricacies of a drug entering the body, being distributed to the sites at which it acts, and the factors that determine intensity and duration of the observed action. The drug, the dose, the route of administration, the pattern of drug taking, and the all-important sites of action influence the outcome that is then evidenced and described variously as drug abuse, dependence, therapeutics, or toxicity, regardless of whether the drug or chemical is illicit, therapeutic, or an environmental toxin. This chapter includes consideration of diverse fields such as neuroanatomy, physiology, and characteristics of nerve function and points to the greater complexity that results when treatment is the goal.

As Dykstra notes, the study of the effects of drugs on behavior has as interesting a history as it does a present. Early findings emerged from the laborings of the iconoclast or by serendipity as often as they did from rigorous science. Dykstra admirably notes the importance and benefits that have resulted from the systematic interdisciplinary effort that has emerged in the study of drugs and behavior. The importance of the findings is then characterized by consideration of basic behavioral and pharmacological principles in examining actions of several major groups of drugs. Dykstra notes the need to link the basic and applied animal and human laboratory studies to the clinical requirements for those drugs that are used as antidepressants or anxiolytics.

Hughes presents a circumscribed clinical psychopharmacology for the psychologist-practitioner. The issues that he raises represent the material on which clinical activity must focus. He simultaneously raises the questions to which research must respond. Psychopharmacological interventions for diverse disorders are well represented in the literature, yet much work needs to be done. Nevertheless, once the optimal dosing levels have been determined and the mechanisms of action are understood, the need for effective administration and patients' compliance to clinical regimens remains. Hughes describes the elements in this complex venue and points to the need for an integrated and educated effort.

Marlatt has been in the forefront of one conceptual perspective in examining the complex interrelations between behavior and environmental determinants in the treatment of drug abuse. Along with a detailed explication of his own perspectives, Marlatt also considers the problems that confront the rational study and treatment of drug abuse. Psychology, psychiatry, and behavioral science are generally often viewed as "every person's" domain. Thus, models based in all conceivable "truths" have emerged, and some have enjoyed great popularity among laypersons. Marlatt has advanced a theoretical framework that has as its core an important feature: It and its elements are testable. In this chapter, he considers both the scientific and societal perspectives that influence treatment and the development of new strategies for treatment.

Weiss, in a masterful chapter, guides the reader through the history, current science, and the future of behavioral toxicology. All too often in the past, the endpoint of exposure was determined by debilitating disease or death. Now, in great part because of the extraordinary efforts of Weiss, Laties, Woods, and many colleagues (along with the efforts of the APA itself), standards for consideration of behavioral-psychological function and dysfunction that may serve as sensitive early warning signs are incorporated into federally mandated testing of new compounds.

The utility of the research is extensive. The findings obviously can be applied to behavioral toxicology and to delineating toxic and safe levels of chemicals both for workers and in the general environment. However, the much broader view dictates that this work will permit better understanding of dosing with therapeutic agents where the balance of maximum therapeutic benefit countered with minimization of side effects is sought.

New Directions

These Master Lectures provide tantalizing glimpses of the complexities of drugs and chemicals in society. The benefits and hazards are both known and unknown. Each of the chapters bears on the future as well as the past and current effort in these interrelated fields. The need for delineating the systems on which agents have effects is clear, but this is not sufficient. Ultimately, the effects of chemicals and drugs are reflected in interactions between biology, behavior, and environmental factors. Examination of interactions is difficult, and all too often it is put aside for more examination of more pedestrian but readily manageable areas of study. Beyond this, there is a need for better diagnostic strategies in therapeutics and behavioral toxicology alike. Current treatments must be evaluated, not only to determine benefit, but also to exclude those that do harm and those that claim to offer improvement where none is apparent. The vulnerable populations that have suffered through the disorders of drug dependence or passive exposure to toxic chemicals, deserve more protection and better care than is likely found in putative cures that are ill-conceived, poorly applied, and in their application only deferring real opportunities for relief.

Beyond these issues, there is the continuing need to study our methods, study our society, study our health-care delivery systems, and generally broaden our understanding of the beneficial effects of drugs and chemicals. These Master Lectures present much that is positive and, as is often the case, point to how much more we must master.

JOHN GRABOWSKI, PhD
April 1992

CHRIS-ELLYN JOHANSON

BIOCHEMICAL MECHANISMS AND PHARMACOLOGICAL PRINCIPLES OF DRUG ACTION

C hris-Ellyn Johanson received her BS in psychology from the University of Illinois at Chicago Circle in 1968 and her PhD in biopsychology at the University of Chicago in 1972. After receiving her degree, she remained at the University of Chicago in the Department of Psychiatry until 1987 as a research associate and became the Associate Director of the Drug Abuse Research Center in 1982. During that time, she conducted animal and human experimental research on the behavioral effects of drugs. The primary emphasis of this research was on the behavioral effects of drugs that may contribute to the likelihood of their abuse. In 1987 Dr. Johanson took a position for a short time at the American Psychological Association as Director of Scientific Affairs and in 1988 joined the faculty in the Department of Psychiatry at the Uniformed Services University of the Health Science as an associate professor. She continues to conduct research in the area of behavioral pharmacology and is presently the principal investigator on two National Institute on Drug Abuse (NIDA)-funded grants. She has published over 90 articles in journals, 30 reviews, and numerous abstracts, and book entitled *Cocaine, The New Epidemic*. In addition, she is a reviewer for several journals (e.g., *Pharmacology, Biochemistry, and Behavior; Journal of the Experimental Analysis of Behavior; The Journal of Pharmacology and Experimental Therapeutics; Psychopharmacology;* and *Be-*

havioural Pharmacology) and is the editor of *Drug and Alcohol Dependence*. She is a member of the Society for the Stimulus Properties of Drugs, American Society of Pharmacology and Experimental Therapeutics, European Behavioral Pharmacology Society, a fellow in the American Psychological Association (Division 28) and American College of Neuropsychopharmacology, and current president of the Behavioral Pharmacology Society. She also serves on the Board of Directors of the Committee on Problems of Drug Dependence, Inc. and has been an ad hoc consultant for the World Health Organization. She is presently living in Kensington, MD with her spouse, Charles R. Schuster, and daughter, Alyson Schuster.

CHRIS-ELLYN JOHANSON

BIOCHEMICAL MECHANISMS AND PHARMACOLOGICAL PRINCIPLES OF DRUG ACTION

Introduction

Psychopharmacology is concerned with the development of new psychoactive drugs that ameliorate behavioral, psychological, or psychiatric disorders and the elucidation of their biochemical mechanisms of action in the central nervous system (CNS) through the application of pharmacological principles and techniques. However, drugs that act in the CNS include not only those that are used therapeutically for behavioral disorders (e.g., antidepressants) but those that are abused and produce dependence (e.g., cocaine). In addition, there are also toxic environmental agents (e.g., toluene) that produce profound behavioral changes because they act on the CNS.

The present chapter will introduce some basic principles of pharmacology and then focus on the potential biochemical actions that drugs may have within the CNS that underlie their behavioral effects. More specifically, this chapter will describe how drugs enter the body and reach their site of action, the types of mechanisms involved at the cellular level for effecting a specific action, and the means by which drug action is terminated and the drug or its metabolites are removed from the body. Concepts and principles of pharmacology that are needed for an adequate understanding of the drug's journey through the body will also be presented. Although specific drugs will be described in subsequent chapters, Table 1 lists the major psychopharmacological drug classes, examples of specific drug names, and therapeutic indications.

Pharmacokinetics

Although the main focus of this chapter will be on the cellular actions of psychopharmacological agents at their site of action, it is first necessary to describe how drug molecules reach these sites and how they are eliminated from the body (see also Benet, Mitchell, & Sheiner, 1990; Julien, 1988; McKim, 1986). This includes consideration of drug absorption, distribution, and clearance (Figure 1).

Transport of Drugs Across Tissues

All aspects of pharmacokinetics involve the basic principles of transport of drug molecules across tissues. To be absorbed into the blood stream from the gastrointestinal tract, drugs must cross a membrane of the stomach or small intestine. To reach certain molecular targets, drugs must cross cell membranes. Finally, to be excreted by the kidney, the breakdown products of the drug must be transported from the capillaries within the glomeruli into the tubules of nephrons.

The major factors that affect permeability are similar for all membranes. These include specific characteristics of the drug itself, the concentration gradient of the drug, and the acidity/alkalinity (pH) of the fluid in which the drug is dissolved. Drug molecules when dissolved in a fluid can exist in both ionized (charged) and un-ionized forms. Only the un-ionized form is fat-soluble (or lipid soluble) and therefore capable of crossing the lipophilic membranes of cells. The pH of the fluid as well as the particular characteristics of a drug determine the extent to which the drug is in the un-ionized form and thus available to cross a membrane. Different fluid compartments of the body (e.g., stomach, blood, urine) have different pHs that result in different relative amounts of the two forms. Although there are active transport processes, transfer across the membrane is largely a passive process which is dependent upon the concentration gradient of the un-ionized drug. As a result, the un-ionized drug is transported from areas of high concentration to areas of low concentration. The removal of un-ionized drug from one side of a membrane results in a conversion of some of the trapped ionized drug to its un-ionized form. Thus, although the system tends toward equilibrium, the processes are dynamic.

Table 1
Major Psychoactive Drug Classes

Drug class	Representative drugs	Therapeutic indications[a]	Typical effects
Alcohol	Beer Wine Spirits	None	Intoxication Disinhibition Ataxia Impaired judgement and memory Sedation
Antidepressants	Amitryptyline (Elavil) Fluoxetine (Prozac) Lithium	Depression	Dry mouth Dizziness Drowsiness
Antipsychotics-Neuroleptics	Haloperidol (Haldol) Chlorpromazine (Thorazine) Clozapine (Clozanil)	Schizophrenia	Sedation Motor depression Dysphoria Extrapyramidal reactions
Barbiturates	Pentobarbital Phenobarbital Secobarbital	Insomnia Seizure disorders	Sedation Ataxia Anesthesia
Benzodiazepines-Anxiolytics	Diazepam (Valium®) Alprazolam (Xanex®) Triazolam (Halcion®) Buspirone (Buspar®)	Anxiety Insomnia	Muscle relaxation Reduced anxiety Sedation
Cannabis	Marijuana Hashish	Nausea Glaucoma	Sedation Distorted perceptions, memory and thinking
Hallucinogens	LSD MDMA	None	Distorted perceptions and thinking
Opiates/Opioids	Morphine Heroin Codeine Meperidine	Analgesia Cough Diarrhea	Euphoria Nausea Drowsiness
Psychomotor Stimulants	Cocaine Amphetamine Methylphenidate (Ritalin®)	Obesity Attention disorder deficit Narcolepsy	Increased alertness-motor stimulation Loss of appetite Euphoria

[a]Not all representative drugs listed are used for each of the therapeutic indications. For instance, cocaine is a psychomotor stimulant but is only used as a local anesthetic. Heroin is an opiate, but it is not used therapeutically for any indication. These distinctions are not always due to the pharmacology of the drug but can also be due to legal constraints.

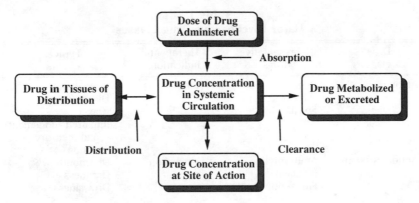

Figure 1. A representation of the relationships between absorption, distribution, and clearance of a drug at its site of action.

Administration and Absorption

The movement of a drug from its site of administration into the bloodstream, or its absorption, depends initially on how it is administered. Routes of administration include oral (p.o.), parenteral (intravenous, intramuscular, or subcutaneous), inhalation into the lungs, and absorption across mucous membranes (nose, mouth, rectal) as well as across the skin. The relative advantages and disadvantages of these various routes are listed in Table 2 (Benet et al., 1990) and a diagram of the principal ones is shown in Figure 2.

Most therapeutic drugs are given orally. The notable advantage of this route is its safety and convenience. Following oral administration, the drug enters the stomach and then passes to the small intestine which is the primary compartment where absorption takes place. One special feature of this route is that drugs administered in solid form (i.e., pills or capsules) must dissolve in the stomach before they can be absorbed. Dissolving can be influenced by the physicochemical characteristics of the drug (which determine extent of dissolution in the acid medium of the stomach), the contents of the stomach, and even the formulation of the drug. For instance, as originally formulated during clinical trials, temazepam, a benzodiazepine used in the treatment of insomnia, had a very slow onset of action. This resulted in variable effectiveness and was a decided disadvantage for reducing the latency of sleep onset if the drug was not taken well in advance of going to bed. However, when finally introduced onto the market, the company reformulated the compound so that it dissolved more rapidly. This resulted in a significantly faster onset of action and increased usefulness in the treatment of insomnia.

Table 2
Advantages and Disadvantages of Various Routes
of Drug Administration

Route	Advantages	Disadvantages
Oral (po)	Convenient	Solid forms must dissolve
	Safe	Gastric irritation, nausea
	Economical	Potential chemical change in stomach
		Metabolism in liver
		Variable absorption
		Delay in onset
		Requires patient cooperation
		Food interferes
Intravenous (iv)	Immediate onset	Overdosage
	Dose titration	Asepsis required
	No absorption	Skill required for injection
	Suitable for large volumes of substances irritating to other tissues	Can not be used with oily or insoluble drugs
Intramuscular (im)	Short onset	Asepsis required
	Can be used with some oily drugs	Absorption dependent on vascularity of injection site
Subcutaneous (sc)	Short onset	Asepsis required
	Can be used with insoluble substances and solid pellets	Cannot be used with large volumes
		Pain and necrosis at injection site
Smoked	Rapid onset	Requires patient cooperation
	No first pass effect in liver	Cumbersome to administer smoke
		Damage to lungs
		Not all drugs can be volatilized
Mucosal absorption (nose, mouth)	Short onset	Requires patient cooperation
	Convenient	
Transdermal	Short onset	Not possible for all drugs
	Convenient	Requires patient cooperation
	Safe	
	Sustained release	
Rectal	Useful for vomiting patient	Irritation
		Inconvenient

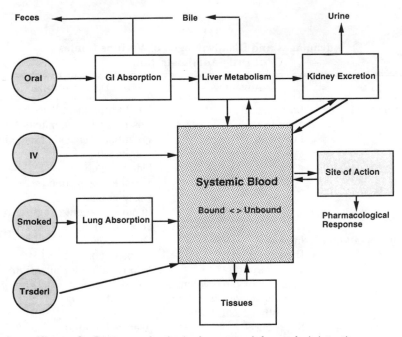

Figure 2. Diagram of principal routes of drug administration.

Although drugs are dissolved in the stomach, the small surface area of the stomach, its high acidity, its thick mucous membrane, and high electrical resistance limits absorption. In addition, because the stomach contains digestive enzymes, some drugs may be altered chemically and be inactivated, particularly if they remain in the stomach for a long time. Because most of the drug molecules are absorbed from the small intestine, the faster the stomach empties, the more rapid its absorption and less likely its degradation. For instance, if the stomach is filled with food, the rate and extent of absorption may decrease, which explains why many medications are taken before meals.

In the small intestine, which is thin and has a large surface area, the drug is absorbed into capillaries, collected into the portal vein and passed to the liver. Because the liver is the principal organ for drug metabolism (see the following section), some proportion of the drug may be inactivated during this "first pass." Furthermore, some drug is removed from the liver via the bile duct, which returns to the gastrointestinal (GI) tract to be eliminated in the feces. Whatever proportion of the drug enters the circulatory system, it is then available for distribution to target sites (Figure 1). However, some types of drugs are bound to proteins in the blood and thus become trapped and unavailable to reach a site of action.

Drugs, both therapeutic and recreational, also may be administered by injection (parenterally, by needle). Drugs administered intravenously (i.v.) directly enter the blood circulation so that absorption is not an issue and the effects of the drug occur almost immediately. However, drugs administered by this route are still subject to a first-pass effect and may also be bound to blood proteins. An important advantage of this route of administration is that it is possible to accurately administer a known dose and to titrate the amount of drug to produce the desired level of response. Although the immediate effect of administering a drug by this route can be an advantage in an emergency situation, it can also be a disadvantage if care is not taken to monitor the degree of drug effect (i.e., overdosage can occur). Other advantages and disadvantages are listed in Table 2. The other parenteral routes of administration are intramuscular (i.m.) and subcutaneous (s.c.). Absorption by both of these routes is usually more rapid than oral administration but is dependent upon the degree of blood flow to the muscle or subcutaneous area where the injection is given (Table 2).

Drugs that are smoked (i.e., inhaled into the lung after volatilization [igniting]) also immediately enter the blood stream. Unlike any other route of administration, drugs that enter the body through the lungs immediately enter the *arterial* circulatory system (after passing to left atrium and ventricle and leaving heart via the aorta; see Figure 3) and are more quickly distributed to target sites. This route of administration thus produces immediate effects, but also can produce damage to the respiratory system. Although some therapeutic drugs, particularly those for treating lung diseases, are delivered by this route, it is largely abused substances, such as nicotine, marijuana, cocaine and other stimulants, that are administered by this route, perhaps because of the rapid onset of action. Environmental toxins often enter the body by this route as well.

Drugs can also be absorbed from mucosal tissues of the mouth, nose, and rectum and pass directly into the blood stream (Table 2). Cocaine, for instance, is insufflated through the nose and has an almost immediate effect because of its rapid absorption through the highly vascular nasal mucosa. Like drugs administered orally, these routes are convenient but do not have the disadvantages associated with passage through the GI tract.

A route of administration that is receiving increasing attention in psychopharmacology is the transdermal route (i.e., absorption through the skin; Table 2). Technology is currently being developed to specially formulate drugs in sustained released preparations which attach to the skin like a bandage. This route has the advantage of the oral route in terms of convenience but may also have the advantage of a relatively fast onset of action. Furthermore, because the drugs are formulated into a sustained released preparation, constant blood levels can be attained for long periods of time. Examples of preparations available by this route include digoxin for the treatment of congestive heart failure, scopola-mine for the treatment of motion sickness, and nicotine for the treatment of nicotine dependence. As the technology necessary for formulating drugs to be delivered by this route advances, it is likely that increasing numbers of drugs which must be taken regularly will be delivered by this route. However, it is also important to point out that many envi-ronmental toxins, such as pesticides, produce behavioral effects because they can be absorbed through the skin (see Weiss, this volume).

Distribution

Once drugs reach the circulatory system after absorption, they are rap-idly distributed throughout the entire body. This rapidity is due to the fact that the blood circulates completely every minute. Drugs are ab-sorbed as described in the previous section into capillaries from the extracellular fluid where they are concentrated following ingestion or injection. The blood from the capillaries is collected into the venous system and transported to the right atrium of the heart (Figure 3). After being pumped out of the right ventricle, the blood goes to the lungs where oxygen and carbon dioxide are exchanged. This blood then re-turns to the left atrium via the pulmonary vein and is pumped out of the left ventricle to the arterial blood system. From the arteries, the

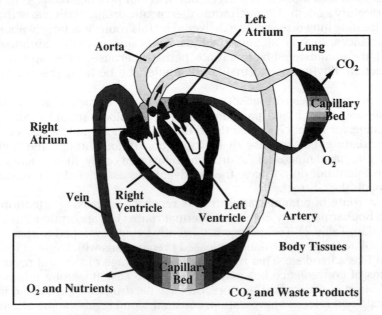

Figure 3. Diagram of the circulatory system.

blood is distributed to the capillaries throughout the entire body, where the transfer of drug molecules from the blood to tissues occurs. Transfer into extracellular fluid surrounding cells is through the walls of the capillaries which contain relatively large pores. Most drugs, whether or not they are water or fat soluble, are small enough to permeate these pores, although some drugs bind to the large blood proteins and are thus prevented from leaving the blood and exerting a biological effect. The flow of drug molecules across the capillaries is a passive process which is dependent upon the concentration gradient of the drug itself (see "Transport of Drugs Across Tissues," this chapter). Clearly the greater the supply of blood to a specific area, the greater the amount of drug that will reach a target cell in that area.

The focus of this chapter is on drugs that exert their effects in the CNS. Thus, it also may be useful to describe special features of the CNS that control the distribution of drugs into the brain (Benet et al., 1990; Julien, 1988). Although the brain is highly vascular and thus may be expected to receive a large share of drug, transfer of drugs into the CNS is retarded by the blood–brain–barrier (Figure 4). In the CNS, the pores in the capillary walls are relatively small and form tight junctions which restrict the transport of drug molecules. In addition, surrounding the capillaries is a dense network of glia cells. Thus the drug molecules must also pass through the membranes of the glia cells before reaching the neuronal cells of the CNS where they can finally exert their biological effect. Despite these barriers, drugs that are highly fat-soluble, or lipophilic, will enter the brain easily by transferring across the capillary and the glial membranes. However, less lipid soluble molecules do not gain access to the brain easily, although certain drugs may even enter the brain by an active carrier process. Differences in lipophilicity among drugs that exert almost identical effects at the receptor level can result in important differences in clinical utility. For instance, benzodiazepines, such as diazepam and triazolam, are extremely lipid soluble and therefore rapidly reach their site of action in the brain. However, other benzodiazepines, such as oxazepam, that have similar receptor mechanisms but are simply less lipophilic take up to 30 min to have an effect even after an intravenous injection (Benet et al., 1990; Julien, 1988).

After reaching the fluid surrounding the cells, drugs can then penetrate the cell itself via the cell membrane; this penetration is dependent upon the fat solubility of the drug. The cell membrane is composed of layers of lipids (fats) and proteins and drugs must be able to dissolve in this phospholipid structure in order to cross the membrane.

Clearance/Elimination

Although some drugs leave the body in their original form, typically drugs must be metabolized or transformed to other types of molecules,

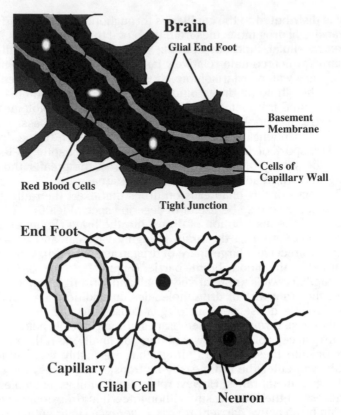

Figure 4. Diagrams of the blood–brain barrier.

or metabolites, in order to be eliminated from the body. The importance of metabolism is that drugs are converted from a more fat-soluble molecule to a less fat-soluble (and more water soluble) one in order to allow excretion. However, some drugs enter the body in an inactive form (the prodrug) which must be converted to an active form by metabolism. Most metabolism occurs in the liver as a result of an enzymatic reaction. The types of reactions that can occur between the drug and enzymes that are found in the liver include oxidation, reduction, and hydrolysis. In addition, by the process of conjugation, drugs or their metabolites may also form complexes with endogenous substances and in that manner be rendered inactive.

There are many factors that can greatly alter the rate or extent of metabolism. These include individual differences in the structure of liver enzymes (due to genetic factors) and the functioning of the liver enzymes, which can be altered by disease, age, and present and past administration of other drugs or environmental contaminants. Metabolites formed in the liver may pass into the blood stream, but they can also be sequestered in liver bile which is transferred to the intestine and eliminated in the feces.

Drugs and their metabolites are largely removed from the blood stream and excreted by the kidney (Figure 5). The kidney is made up of millions of filtering units called nephrons. Fluid from the blood enters the kidney via capillaries which form in groups called glomeruli and is forced by various types of active carrier systems into the nephrons at their opening, known as Bowman's capsule. This fluid contains not only drugs or their metabolites but also natural metabolites of body functioning (waste products) as well as electrolytes such as potassium and sodium. Products that are not needed by the body or are unwanted pass through a filtering system, are collected in the tubules of the nephron, and then transported via the ureters to the bladder where they are eliminated through urination. Depending on their fat solubility, however,

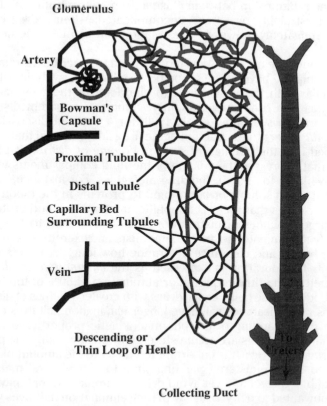

Figure 5. Diagram of the role of the kidney in drug clearance.

drug molecules may be reabsorbed into the blood stream from the tubules of the kidney. Thus to the extent that the liver has converted the parent compound to a more water soluble one, these metabolites will not be reabsorbed and will be excreted from the body.

Time Course of Effect

A major concern of the field of pharmacokinetics is the elucidation of the quantitative relationship between the concentration of a drug in the blood or plasma and time since administration, or the time course of absorption, distribution, and elimination. A major assumption of pharmacokinetics is that the concentration of drug at its site of action determines the level of its effect. Although it is not always true that the concentration of drug in plasma accurately estimates concentration at the site of action (particularly in the brain), in many cases, this estimate is accurate enough to have clinical utility. For acute administrations of drug, the relationship between plasma drug concentration and effect is relatively straightforward and uncomplicated. When a drug is administered repeatedly, however, this relationship can become quite complicated.

Although the mathematical models used to describe the quantitative relationship are beyond the scope of this chapter, psychologists should be familiar with the terms used to characterize the pharmacokinetic properties of a drug (bioavailability, volume of apparent distribution, and clearance; see Benet et al., 1990, for a detailed discussion). *Bioavailability* refers to the fraction of the drug administered that is actually absorbed into the circulatory system. *Volume of distribution* is a construct that expresses the volume of the fluid compartments within the body available to contain the drug molecules. For instance, drugs that are highly lipid soluble or fail to bind to proteins in the blood (relative to similar drugs that are less lipophilic and bind to blood proteins) will have larger volumes of distribution. *Clearance* refers to the ability of the body to eliminate the drug (metabolism and excretion). Both volume of distribution and clearance determine how long the effects of a drug will last. This duration is expressed as the *elimination half-life*, which is defined as the time required for elimination of 50% of the total drug in the body. All else being equal, drugs with greater volumes of distribution and less rapid clearance will have longer elimination half lives ($t_{1/2}$).

An understanding of the pharmacokinetic properties of a drug is essential when drugs are administered chronically. Using the principles of pharmacokinetics, it is important to calculate the amount of drug that needs to be administered per unit time to achieve and maintain the optimal blood level and yet avoid drug accumulation that may produce some unwanted toxicity. Drugs with long elimination half-lives will reach steady state levels at a much slower rate and the possibility that the blood level reached at this steady state exceeds that needed for optimal therapeutic effect is increased. On the other hand, drugs with very short elimination half-lives may have to be given frequently in order to maintain a steady state level.

The complexities of pharmacokinetics are multiplied by the extreme differences among individuals. The pharmacokinetics of a drug can be influenced by such factors as age, gender, fat content of the body, previous drug exposure, and disease state. For many drugs, this variability is so extreme that optimal dosing can only be achieved by periodic determinations of actual blood levels. For instance, the dose of a tricyclic antidepressant, such as imipramine, is constantly adjusted in order to achieve a blood level between 100–300 ng/ml. For some individuals, this requires an oral maintenance dose of only 30 mg whereas for other individuals, doses as high as 300 mg may be required.

Neuroanatomy

The principles of drug action that have been described clearly apply to any type of drug from penicillin to cocaine. Because the focus of this chapter is on agents that affect the nervous system, it may be useful to provide a brief overview of its function and structure (Bloom, 1990; Julien, 1988; McKim, 1986).

The nervous system functions as a receiver, transmitter, and integrator of information. This information includes stimuli from the outside world as well as information from within the body itself. The information is transmitted to the CNS (composed of the brain and spinal cord) with a resultant change in functioning which includes changes in behavior. It is this system that allows organisms to sense the world about and within them, compare and integrate the incoming information with past experience, and respond appropriately. Many have likened this function to that of a computer, but in reality, the complexity and adaptability of the system is much greater.

The nervous system is composed of the peripheral nervous system and the central nervous system (Figure 6). These integrated circuits are composed of cells called neurons whose structure and function will be described in more detail in a subsequent section. For the present, it is only necessary to appreciate that these cells transmit information and in most cases are physically separated from each other by gaps called synapses. Transmission across synapses is the result of the release of chemicals from the presynaptic neuron which bind to receptors located on the postsynaptic neuron.

The synapses of the peripheral nervous system occur outside the spinal cord. This system is divided into somatic, sensory, and autonomic components. The afferent (going into the CNS) sensory nervous system

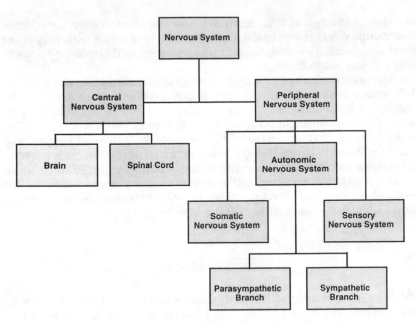

Figure 6. Diagram of major divisions of the nervous system.

consists of neurons that transmit sensory information (touch, pain, proprioception) from the environment via receptors in the skin into the CNS. These neurons enter the spinal cord at the level of the dorsal horn and initiate an immediate response (spinal reflex) and/or the information is channeled to the brain via fiber tracts in the spinal cord. Other types of sensory information (e.g., vision) arise from specialized cranial nerves. The efferent (leaving the CNS) somatic system regulates the activity of skeletal (striatal) muscles that are involved in voluntary muscle action. The neurons of this system leave the spinal cord at the level of the ventral horn. In both of these systems, there is only a single neuron between the sensory receptor or muscle (the latter is known as the neuromuscular junction or neuromotor endplate) and the spinal cord.

The autonomic nervous system (ANS; also called the visceral, vegetative, or involuntary nervous system) controls the functioning of the smooth muscle of various organs in the thoracic, abdominal, and pelvic cavities; of cardiac muscle; and of various glands. The constancy of physiological functioning of organisms (e.g., constant blood pressure, temperature) even in the face of changing internal conditions, is due to the ANS. There are both visceral afferent and efferent fiber tracts or nerve pathways. The afferent system mediates visceral sensation and provides feedback about the status of visceral functioning (e.g., stomach distension). The efferent system has two subdivisions, the sympathetic and parasympathetic, which control opposing actions on target organs. The parasympathetic system tends to conserve energy resources whereas the sympathetic system is an activator or user of energy. The actual level of activity of an organ, gland, or muscle is a function of the integration of inputs from the two reciprocal systems.

In both subdivisions of the ANS, the neurotransmitter (the chemical which crosses the synapse and is responsible for information transfer) in the ganglion is acetylcholine (ACh) which will be described in more detail in the following section. This neurotransmitter is released at the junction between neuron and target organ in the parasympathetic component. However, in the sympathetic component, norepinephrine (NE) is the primary transmitter between neuron and target organ. The neurotransmitters of the afferent ANS have not been clearly established but likely include Substance P and perhaps glutamate, which will be discussed in a later section.

In the sympathetic nervous system signals impinging upon any one postganglionic neuron may arise from many preganglionic neurons and there are interneurons within the ganglia that allow further modulation of incoming information. In addition, there is considerable branching of postganglionic neurons so that many effector cells can be affected by the activity of a single postsynaptic neuron. These attributes make it possible for a diffuse sympathetic discharge. This is less true for the parasympathetic system where activity occurs more discretely (single connections, little branching). As will be discussed in detail in the following paragraphs, drugs are capable of altering synaptic transmission at any of these sites within the sensory, somatic, and autonomic nervous system.

The CNS can be grossly divided into the brain and the spinal cord (Figure 6). The spinal cord is divided into four sections starting with the cervical region (nearest the brain), followed by the thoracic, lumbar, and sacral regions. The spinal cord is responsible for spinal reflexes as well as transmitting information to and from the brain. The former involves transmission of sensory stimuli to the spinal cord where neurons controlling motor activity are stimulated. The control of motor neurons also can be influenced by information emanating from the brain and, in addition, sensory information arriving at the spinal cord can be transmitted to the brain via the spinal cord. As with the peripheral nervous system, drugs may modify synaptic functions within the spinal cord.

The brain can be divided into the brain stem, cerebellum, diencephalon, and cerebral cortices (Figure 7 and Table 3), and drugs are capable of selectively modifying functioning in any of these areas or in certain neuronal systems within these areas. The part of the brain that connects with the spinal cord is the brain stem. All nerve tract fibers coming to and from the brain pass through this area. It consists of the medulla, pons, and midbrain. Above these structures is the cerebellum,

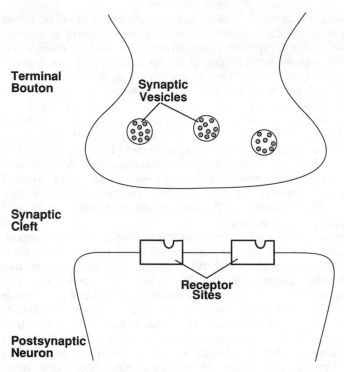

Terminal Bouton

Synaptic Vesicles

Synaptic Cleft

Receptor Sites

Postsynaptic Neuron

Figure 7. A stylized drawings of synaptic connection.

which is responsible for coordination of movement and maintenance of body posture. The medulla has nuclei or centers that control levels of arousal as well as respiration, blood pressure, heart rate, and gastrointestinal functioning. A major part of the medulla is the fiber tract known as the *reticular activating system* which extends to the thalamus and eventually to the cerebral cortex. This system is influenced by sensory input from the spinal cord and serves the function of arousing organisms and preparing them for incoming information. The pons, which is above the medulla, is largely a fiber tract area but it does play a special role in integrating the activity of the cerebellum and the rest of the brain. The midbrain is above the pons and is responsible for the control of vision and hearing among other functions. It connects to the diencephalon which is further divided into the thalamus, hypothalamus, and subthalamus. The thalamus is a primary relay station that receives sensory information and relays it to specific regions of the cerebrum. It also integrates information, projects to associative areas of the cerebrum, receives input from the reticular activating system, and is thus involved in arousal mechanisms. The subthalamus is also a major relay area for the coordination of the motor system, and the substantia nigra

Table 3
Divisions and Functions of the Brain

Brainstem	
Medulla	Arousal
Pons	Integrates cerebellum and brain
Midbrain	Sensory function
Cerebellum	Posture
Diencephalon	
Thalamus	Sensory relay, arousal
Subthalamus	Motor coordination
Hypothalamus	Homeostatic function
Pituitary	Endocrine function
Limbic	Emotion, learning, integrator
Cerebrum	Integration

is a well-known nucleus in this area that projects to areas in the cerebrum and limbic system. Finally, the hypothalamus is an area that regulates homeostatic functions such as water balance, carbohydrate and fat metabolism, temperature, sexual activity, blood pressure, sleep, and autonomic tone. It also influences, through the secretion of stimulating hormones, the production of trophic hormones by the pituitary gland and thus controls endocrine glands that reside in the periphery. The hypothalamus is also involved in mediating the action of events that are reinforcers (i.e., the reward system). Intimately connected to the hypothalamus are structures of the limbic system, such as the amygdala, hippocampus, septum, olfactory and pyriform lobes, and basal ganglia (caudate nucleus, putamen, and globus pallidus). These structures, which to some extent are under the control of the hypothalamus, subserve the expression of emotion as well as learning and memory and integrate emotional state with motor and visceral activities. The limbic system also is part of the extrapyramidal (involuntary) motor system. Not surprisingly, all of the areas of the diencephalon can be significantly influenced by drugs.

Finally, the largest area of the human brain is the cerebral cortex, which is divided into two hemispheres connected by the corpus collosum. It contains discrete regions (e.g., sensory cortex) that receive projections or information from lower brain areas as well as other areas of the cerebrum. These regions subserve specific functions, such as sensory perception, motor control, integration of sensory and motor systems, integration of the ANS, learning and memory, and motivation and emotion.

The complexity and intercommunications between different areas of the CNS is not possible to describe in the present chapter. For those interested in understanding more clearly the interrelationships between the various areas, most standard texts on physiological psychology can be consulted. Suffice it to say that the relationships are intricate and multiple and include hierarchical circuits, circuits localized within a specific area, and long, single neuronal projections from one area to a distant one. The relevance of this notion for understanding the actions of drugs is that regardless of how drugs may influence individual neurons, as will be described in the following section, the location of that neuron within the CNS and the nature of its connections can result in changes in functioning in many parts of the brain. Depending on which specific circuits are influenced, the actions of drugs can be diverse.

Electrical and Biochemical Properties of Nerve Cells

The Neuron

Drugs can affect cellular function in a number of ways. Drugs that have specific effects on the CNS generally do so because they modify the specialized characteristics of nerve cells. Therefore to understand the actions of psychoactive drugs it is necessary to understand the features of nerve cells that make them unique (Cooper, Bloom, & Roth, 1986; Julien, 1988). These features include the bioelectrical properties of the neuron, which allow signals to be promulgated along the neuron, and intercellular connections. Both of these features can be targets for drug action. The electrical properties of neurons are relatively comparable throughout the CNS but there is an enormous variety of intercellular connections (i.e., neurotransmitters and postsynaptic connections). Thus, to a large extent the effects of different classes of psychoactive drugs are a result of the release of chemical neurotransmitters and their activation or inhibition of the next neuron in the sequence.

Figure 7 shows a stylized drawing of a typical neuron (McKim, 1986). Although there are exceptions, the flow of information along neurons proceeds from the dendrites, to the cell body, down the axon and finally to its terminal where a neurotransmitter is released into the synaptic cleft. Neurons typically have many short dendrites that resemble a branching tree but there is usually only one axon that varies considerably in length within the CNS and spinal cord. However, at the terminal, branching may occur. Neurons do not actually come into physical contact with each other but interact across the synaptic cleft where axons of one neuron are in close proximity to dendrites of another neuron.

As was described before, neurons are organized into groups or circuits which form the basis of the anatomy of the brain and underlie its functioning. Groups of soma and dendrites are called nuclei and the axons emanating from these nuclei form fiber tracks which traverse from one area of the brain to other areas in order to relay information. The distance traversed can vary considerably. The CNS also contains another type of cell, the glia, the function of which is not completely understood (Cooper et al., 1986). Glia function as support cells and insulate neurons from each other. This provides a mechanism for organizing cells into units as discussed previously. Certain types of glia, the oligodendrocytes, form around certain axons in tight layers that make up a myelin sheath and these nerves are referred to as myelinated. There are gaps between oligodendrocytes, called nodes of Ranvier, which leave a portion of the axon uncovered or unprotected. As will be explained later, transmission of electrical activity is relatively rapid for myelinated nerves compared to transmission down unmyelinated fibers.

Neurotransmission and Action Potentials

In every cell, there is an electrical potential across the membrane separating the intracellular and extracellular space (Julien, 1988). This potential difference is due to an imbalance of ions differing in charge and ability to passively diffuse through tiny pores or channels on each side of the membrane (see Figure 8). Small ions such as potassium (K^+) and chloride (Cl^-) freely pass back and forth according to their concentration gradient. Large protein molecules within the cell, although negatively charged, cannot traverse the membrane under any condition. Thus Cl^- ions tend to be pushed outside the cell, but because of its own concentration gradient, not enough to balance the negative charge of the protein molecules. Sodium ions (Na^+), which are largely found ex-

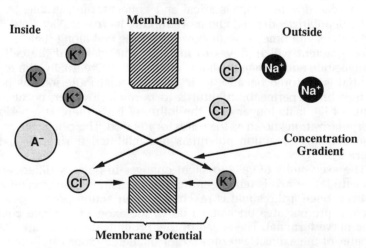

Figure 8. Distribution of ions at resting equilibrium.

tracellularly, do not readily permeate the cellular membrane; that is, the Na^+ channels are ordinarily closed and there is an active membrane process ("pump") that keeps Na^+ outside the cell. Thus K^+ ions tend to cluster intracellularly to balance electrical charge but against their own concentration gradient. As a result, there is a tendency for the extracellular space to be positively charged due to the distribution of Na^+ and K^+ and the intracellular space to be negatively charged due to the sequestering of negatively charged protein molecules and the distribution of Cl^-. Eventually the opposing electrical (due to charge) and chemical (due to concentration gradients) forces reach an equilibrium. The difference in electrical charge at equilibrium is about 50 to 70 mV and is known as the *polarized resting potential*. This polarization is a characteristic of all living cells. However, nerve cells have the additional unique electrical property of "excitability." This means that when the potential across the membrane is reduced (depolarized), the potential does not simply reduce gradually to zero. The change is so rapid that the inside of the membrane actually becomes more positive relative to the outside (i.e., it "overshoots"). This rapid change in polarity (lasting 0.2–0.5 ms) is known as the *action potential*. When a depolarization occurs in one local part of the axon, it spreads to adjacent areas and in this way the action potential (or the spread of depolarization) is propagated along the axon. Non-neuronal cells do not have this excitable property; that is, there is no rapid change in polarity with an actual overshoot in charge.

The mechanisms that initiate a slight change in polarity are complicated, but once this change occurs the events that result in an action potential are fairly well understood. As the membrane becomes more depolarized, its permeability to Na^+ ions increases and these ions rush into the cell due to their electrical and concentration gradients. This further depolarizes the cell and more rapidly increases Na^+ flow. However at the same time, K^+ ions flow out of the cell along their concentration gradient which serves to maintain the inside of the cell in a negative state and reduce the influx of Na^+ ions. Eventually, the resting potential is restored because ionic pumps redistribute ions as before and membrane permeability returns to normal. However, because the outflux of K^+ lasts longer than the influx of Na^+, there is a period of hyperpolarization known as the refractory period. The cell is in a resting phase and further action potentials are inhibited during this period (Figure 9).

The excitability of cells to slight changes in polarity differs across cells with larger axons tending to be more sensitive than smaller ones. However, once a threshold is reached and an action potential is generated, it promulgates unchanged down the axon to produce changes at the nerve terminal. The speed of this promulgation is related to the diameter of the axons (faster for larger diameter axons) and the length of the axon. Because ions can only enter and leave the axon where

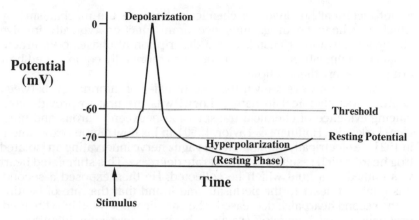

Figure 9. Diagram of action potential.

intracellular and extracellular spaces come into contact, promulgation is accelerated in myelinated nerves where this contact only occurs at the nodes of Ranvier.

Although the precise mechanisms that lead to an action potential are complicated and varied, they originate in the dendrites as a result of postsynaptic receptor activation. This activation results in depolarization of the dendrites in direct proportion to the frequency of receptor activation. The graded depolarization of the dendrites is known as an excitatory postsynaptic potential (EPSP). However, some types of receptor activation can also decrease excitability by hyperpolarizing the membrane, which is known as an inhibitory postsynaptic potential (IPSP).

Neurons can receive inputs from thousands of other neurons. As will be discussed later, the nature of the synaptic relationship between neurons is quite varied. As a result, some changes in the postsynaptic membrane generate EPSPs and others generate IPSPs. The role of the cell body is to integrate these various inputs. If the net effect of the algebraic summation of dendritic inputs is one of excitation, sufficient to reach a threshold, an action potential is generated. Likewise, if inhibitory influences predominate, an action potential will be prevented. Although some drugs, such as local anesthetics, prevent the generation of action potentials by influencing ionic conductance (preventing changes in Na^+ permeability), most psychoactive drugs produce changes by altering interneuronal communication.

Chemical Transmission

The unique bioelectrical properties maintaining the functioning of neuronal cells has been described. However, communication *between* cells is not electrical but involves chemicals. Because the mechanisms by which psychoactive drugs influence brain function typically involve changes in synaptic transmission, a description of phases of interneuronal communication is needed in order to more fully comprehend how drugs can exert their actions.

It was not always known that the transfer of information between neurons was chemical in nature. Loewi was the first to provide convincing evidence of chemical transmission between neurons and muscles (Lefkowitz, Hoffman, & Taylor, 1990). In his now famous experiment in 1921, he electrically stimulated the vagus nerve innervating an isolated frog heart, which resulted in a heart rate decrease. This stimulated heart was bathed in a fluid which he collected. He then exposed a second, unstimulated heart to the perfusate and found that the rate of beating of the second heart also decreased. The chemical liberated into the fluid, originally called *Vagusstoff* (vagus substance), was later identified as acetylcholine. Additional studies of communication between nerve cells themselves and studies demonstrating that there is a time delay between the production of the action potential and postsynaptic changes further supported the idea that chemical processes were involved in the transfer of information between neurons.

Although all neuronal cells have similar electrical properties, neurons differ in terms of their chemical properties. There are a variety of different types of neurotransmitters and receptors and they are differentially distributed within the CNS. Furthermore, the mechanism by which chemicals released from presynaptic terminals affect postsynaptic elements also varies. In addition, our understanding of the cascade of events that begins with the interaction of a neurotransmitter with its receptors on the postsynaptic membrane and results in the generation of an action potential (or its inhibition) is still evolving (Cooper et al., 1986). It is well beyond the scope of this chapter to describe the sequence of events from receptor to action potential in detail. However, the reader should appreciate the implication of this complex system—namely, drugs can affect the transfer of information anywhere along the chain of events. Furthermore, drugs do not always affect only a single aspect of the process and are likely to have different effects in different types of neurons, which in turn may be differentially distributed in different parts of the brain that control specific behavioral functions. Some released chemicals may not actually function as neurotransmitters in the classic sense but may affect the neuron's responsivity to true neurotransmitters (i.e., may serve a modulatory function or conditional effect). Cooper, Bloom, and Roth (1986) have eloquently summarized this complexity:

> Thus, it can be seen that there are abundant circuits, abundant transmitters and, for each, many classes of chemically coupled systems exist to transduce the effects of active transmitter receptors. These receptors can operate either actively or passively, condi-

tionally or unconditionally, over a wide range of time through non-specific, dependent, or independent metabolic events. Clearly neurons have a broad but finite and, as yet, incompletely characterized repertoire of molecular responses that messenger molecules (transmitters, hormones, and *drugs* [italics added]) can elicit. The power of the chemical vocabulary of such components is their combinatorial capacity to act conditionally and coordinatively and to integrate the temporal and spatial domains within the nervous system. (p. 31)

Neurotransmitter Release and Inactivation

The synthesis of chemicals that function as neurotransmitters generally takes place within the nerve terminal. After synthesis, neurotransmitters are believed to be stored in vesicles (see Figure 7) located in the axon terminal. Although the promulgation of the action potential is voltage-dependent (i.e., only occurs when depolarization exceeds a threshold) and largely due to changes in Na^+ conductance, the release of neurotransmitters from the axon terminal (called exocytosis) is dependent upon changes in calcium (Ca^{++}) conductance, or Ca^{++} influx into the terminal.

The neurotransmitter diffuses across the synaptic cleft and exerts its action on its postsynaptic membrane receptors as previously described. At this point, the neurotransmitter can undergo several fates which result in its functional deactivation. Some neurotransmitters are metabolized by enzymes that reside in the extracellular space. Alternatively, the presynaptic neuron may reabsorb the chemical (termed reuptake) into the terminal where it is either metabolized or re-stored into vesicles which protect it from degradation.

In summary, the steps involved in chemical transmission include synthesis of the neurotransmitter, its storage and release, action on pre- and postsynaptic receptors, and deactivation by reuptake or metabolism. One difficulty in precisely describing drug action arises from the important fact that drugs can affect neurotransmission at any of these steps. The possibilities are listed in Table 4 (see also Bloom, 1990; Cooper et al., 1986; Julien, 1988; Lefkowitz et al., 1990). For instance, drugs may interfere with synthesis, prevent storage or release (e.g., reserpine prevents storage of certain neurotransmitters). The net result of these alterations is decreased neuronal activity of postsynaptic elements. Drugs can also elicit the release of nerotransmitters from the intracellular space and at least temporally increase postsynaptic activity. For instance, amphetamines increase the release of several neurotransmitters. Furthermore, drugs can interfere with the deactivation of neurotransmitters by blocking the action of enzymes responsible for their breakdown. Because many neurotransmitters are largely taken

Table 4
**Potential Targets for Psychoactive Drugs on Synaptic
Interneuronal Communication**

Mechanism of action	Potential effect
Block synthesis	Depletion of transmitter
Prevent release	Decreased activity
Block reuptake	Increased activity
Block storage	Depletion of transmitter
Promote release	Increased activity
Inhibit enzymatic breakdown	Increased activity
Mimic action of NT[a] at postsynaptic receptor	Increased activity
Block action of NT at postsynaptic receptor	Decreased activity

[a]NT = neurotransmitter.

back up into the presynaptic element, it is possible to prolong neuronal activity by blocking this reuptake with drugs. Cocaine exerts its action by this mechanism. Drugs that alter synthesis, storage, release, metabolism, or reuptake are considered indirectly acting because they alter the effects of the neurotransmitter itself. Other drugs, however, exert more direct effects. For instance, they may mimic the effects of endogenous neurotransmitters by directly interacting with receptors (agonists; e.g., opiates). Likewise, other drugs may block the receptor and prevent the neurotransmitter from exerting its action (antagonists; e.g., naloxone for endogenous enkephalins, mecamylamine for nicotine).

In describing the interactions of drugs and receptors, it should be appreciated that these effects can change with repeated application of drugs. This is because receptors are themselves subject to regulatory and homeostatic control. Since most psychopharmacological agents are taken repeatedly, these changes with repeated administration can be significant. Continued stimulation of receptors with agonists (direct or indirect) can result in the decrease in the sensitivity of the receptors. This desensitization or down regulation of the receptors results in a decrease in the effect of the drug. Likewise, repeated administration of antagonists that reduce receptor stimulation can result in an increase in sensitivity to receptor agonists. Even in the absence of the drug, the effect of the endogenous neurotransmitter itself can be reduced or augmented by the repeated administration of a drug.

Drugs can have multiple effects and these effects may vary in different neurons depending upon the neurotransmitter present, the nature of the receptor, and the mechanism for translating receptor activation into changes in the excitability of the postsynaptic neuron. Furthermore, the nature of these modulatory influences can change with repeated administration of a drug or other drugs. Thus, it should not be surprising that the precise mechanisms of action of even extensively studied psychoactive drugs are only beginning to be understood (see Hughes and Dykstra, this volume). These actions will be better understood with additional delineation of the complexities of the nervous system resulting from the tremendous progress in molecular biology. However, even a rudimentary description of the effects of a particular drug permits it to serve as a tool for understanding brain processes.

Receptors and Receptor Theory

A major area of research in pharmacology, pharmacodynamics, is devoted to understanding the relationship between the magnitude of a drug effect and its interaction at the receptor (Ross, 1990; Ruffolo, 1982). Receptors, which primarily reside on the surface of cells have been identified for all known neurotransmitters. In some cases, these receptors have been isolated and the sequence of amino acids composing them determined. Likewise, it has been discovered that specific neurotransmitters can interact with different forms of a receptor, called *receptor subtypes*. Receptor subtypes are often differentially distributed throughout the CNS and may have different consequences when activated.

Receptor theory began with the simple notion that the degree of effect is mathematically related to the extent of receptor occupation, which is governed by the law of mass action. That is, the more receptors that are occupied, the greater the response. It was also assumed that the maximum effect is only obtained when all receptors controlling the response are occupied. Hence this theory was called the occupancy theory of drug action. This theory implies that the measure of affinity (the ability of a drug to bind to the receptor), or the dissociation constant, is directly related to the ED_{50} (effective dose that produces a half-maximal or 50% response) since at that dose it is presumed that half of the receptors are occupied. The smaller a drug's ED_{50}, the greater its ability to bind (i.e., the greater its affinity).

However, in the 1950s, research indicated that even though a series of chemically related compounds could all be shown to completely saturate the receptor population, there were differences in maximum effect, with some compounds producing a smaller effect no matter how much drug was present. This led to the delineation of two independent features of receptor interaction: (a) *affinity*, which refers to the ability of a molecule to bind to a receptor and (b) *intrinsic activity*, which refers to the ability of the molecule to produce an effect once it is bound. Drugs that bind and have activity are termed agonists. Drugs with intermediate levels of intrinsic activity are classified as partial agonists whereas drugs that are capable of producing the maximal response are full agonists. Drugs that bind but produce no activity are termed antagonists. Since the binding of an antagonist interferes with or prevents the binding of agonists (as well as the endogenous neurotransmitter), antagonists block (i.e., antagonize) the activity of agonists.

Receptor theory as described by Ariëns (1954) assumed that the proportion of total receptors occupied would be equal to the percentage of maximal response and furthermore that all receptors of a particular population needed to be occupied for maximal response. However, more recent experiments have demonstrated that certain agonists can produce a maximal effect even in the presence of an antagonist that is known to occupy a proportion of the receptors. More specifically, the function relating dose of the agonist drug to the effect is shifted to the right in the presence of the antagonist but the maximal response is still obtained albeit at a higher dose of the agonist (Figure 10A). Only at higher doses of the antagonist is the effect reduced.

These findings required an alteration in the occupancy theory. It was postulated that a maximal response did not require the occupation of the entire receptor population, that is, some receptors were "spares." Drugs might produce a maximal response but they were able to do so by occupying different proportions of the available receptors. Those that occupied fewer receptors when producing the maximal were considered more efficacious. This modification in the theory explained the results obtained when full agonists were given in combination with antagonists. That is, the effect of the antagonist could be overcome by efficacious compounds that do not require a large proportion of receptors to be occupied to produce maximum effect. Eventually, however, the antagonist blocks enough of the receptors to prevent a full effect, that is, there are no spare receptors left (Figure 10A).

In revising receptor theory to explain the observed phenomena, it was assumed that the tissue in question is by some means limited to the observed maximal response. Occupation of additional receptors may produce responses in those receptors but the tissue is not capable of making a greater response. To the extent that there are no spare receptors (receptor reserve) and thus a linear relationship exists between occupancy and effect, the ED_{50} will approach being an accurate measure of affinity. But to the extent that they diverge, the ED_{50} cannot be used to assess the affinity of a compound. If one then adds the notion that different tissues have different concentrations of receptors, it becomes possible to relate the terms of intrinsic activity and efficacy. Intrinsic activity is dependent upon the characteristics of the drug and receptor with which it interacts. Efficacy, on the other hand, is a function of intrinsic activity *and* the concentration of the receptor population in a particular tissue. Because efficacy thus depends upon the degree of receptor reserve, the efficacy of a particular drug can differ across tissues.

Although we have described the terms intrinsic activity and efficacy in relationship to a single compound, these terms are usually used to describe the activity of compounds relative to a prototypic full agonist. In this case, *relative* intrinsic activity is defined as the ratio of the

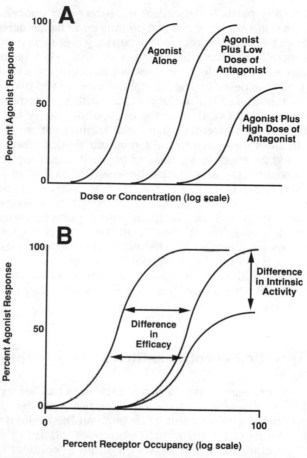

Figure 10. The dose-response functions of an agonist given in combination with an antagonist at a low and high dose is shown in Figure 10A. Figure 10B shows the comparison of relative intrinsic activity and relative efficacy.

maximum response of the compound to the maximum response of the full agonist and can be determined directly from the dose-response function (Figure 10B). In contrast, *relative efficacy* is the ratio of the percent receptor occupancy of the compound required to produce a specified response to the percent receptor occupancy of the full agonist required to produce that same degree of effect. Compounds that both produce the same maximum effect and thus have the same relative intrinsic activity might very well differ in relative efficacy with the less efficacious compound needing to occupy more receptors to produce the same effect. Because efficacy is dependent upon receptor reserve, which in turn is partially dependent upon receptor concentration (or density), the relative efficacy of compounds can change across tissues. Although the modified receptor occupancy theory as described previously generally accounts for the quantitative relationship between many drugs and their effects, it does not account for all interactions. Ruffolo (1982) has described additional theories that involve events that occur after the interaction of the receptor with the membrane. These other theories do not contradict the occupation theory but add to its complexity and the range of changes that administration of a drug can produce. In all of these theories, the relationship described is between drug dose and an effect on an *isolated tissue*. It should be obvious that when we consider the relationship between the action of a drug at a receptor and larger units of analysis, such as behavioral effects in the intact organism, a number of other factors which intervene between receptor activation in a specific brain region and a behavioral change must be understood. Nevertheless, with the tools of modern-day molecular biology *combined* with state-of-the-art behavioral analyses, there is hope that we will be able to account at a molecular biological level for how drugs produce their behavioral effects. As will be illustrated thoroughly in the chapter by Dykstra (this volume), there is increasing evidence of our ability to do so.

Specific Neurotransmitters and Receptors

A description of neurotransmitters and receptors has been provided in general terms. Although electrical conductance from dendrites to the axonal terminal is generally similar throughout the brain, there is wide diversity in terms of interneuronal communication. It is this diversity and resultant complexity that allows the brain to conduct its complex affairs. Table 5 lists the commonly accepted neurotransmitters and receptors subtypes that have been identified in the CNS. This list is not exhaustive but includes those most important for understanding the actions of psychoactive drugs and those that will be discussed more extensively in subsequent chapters. Furthermore, new transmitters and receptor types are constantly being discovered and this list will undoubtedly grow.

Acetylcholine

The first transmitter identified in the periphery was acetylcholine (ACh) and subsequently it has also been isolated from the brain (Lefkowitz et al., 1990). There are two types of receptors that react to ACh within the CNS, the nicotinic and muscarinic, identified and named because nic-

Table 5
Selected Neurotransmitters and Receptor Subtypes

Neurotransmitter/neuromodulator	Receptor subtype
Acetylcholine (ACh)	Muscarinic
	Nicotinic
Norepinephrine (NE)	Alpha$_1$
	Alpha$_2$
	Beta$_1$
	Beta$_2$
Dopamine (DA)	D$_1$
	D$_2$
Serotonin (5-HT)	5-HT$_{1A-E}$
	5-HT$_2$
	5-HT$_3$
	5-HT$_4$
Gamma-aminobutyric acid	GABA$_A$
	GABA$_B$
Endogeneous Opioid Neuropeptides	mu
	delta
	kappa

otine and muscarine are agonists at these receptors, respectively. Because ACh is believed to be a flexible molecule, it is likely that its conformation changes when it binds to these two different types of receptors. These two types of receptors are differentially distributed within the CNS and there also appears to be multiple forms (subtypes) of both types.

ACh is synthesized within the axon or its terminal from acetyl CoA and choline, in the presence of the enzyme choline acetyltransferase, and is stored in vesicles within the terminal of axons (Figure 11). Axons containing ACh are located throughout the brain but there are high concentrations in specific areas such as the caudate nucleus and cerebral cortex. Concentrations of available choline appear to be the rate-limiting step in the synthesis of ACh and ACh is rapidly hydrolyzed by the enzyme acetylcholinesterase. Thus drugs that interfere with either enzyme, choline acetyltransferase or acetylcholinesterase, can influence levels of ACh. Since release of ACh (or lowered concentrations of ACh in the terminal) appears to activate further synthesis, concentrations of ACh remain relatively constant for resting and stimulated nerves. Therefore, the amount of ACh found within a brain area does not indicate its degree of activity.

Peripherally, it is well known that ACh is an important transmitter at certain autonomic effector sites, sympathetic and parasympathetic ganglion cells, and motor end-plates on skeletal muscles (Lefkowitz et al., 1990). However, within the CNS, its function is less clear (Cooper et al., 1986). There are even areas of high ACh concentration which contain no ACh receptors. Because cholinergic mechanisms are prominent in the peripheral nervous system, the mechanisms of action of particular drugs on cholinergic transmission are well known and serve as models of the ways that a drug can affect interneuronal communication within the CNS.

Figure 11 depicts a typical ACh synaptic junction and illustrates the steps in interneuronal communication where drugs can potentially alter function (Cooper et al., 1986). The most important target of cholinergic

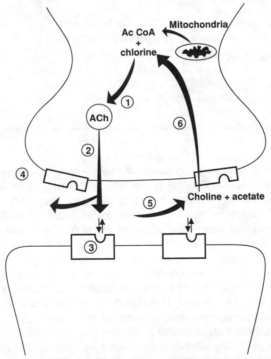

Figure 11. Acetylcholine (ACh) synaptic connection and potential sites of action of psychoactive drugs. At site 1, ACh synthesis is blocked. At site 2, release of ACh is prevented or promoted. At site 3, the postsynaptic nicotinic or muscarinic receptor is activated or blocked. At site 4, nicotinic or muscarinic presynaptic receptor is activated or blocked. At site 5, acetylcholinesterase is inhibited. Finally, at site 6, ACh reuptake is blocked.

Note. From *Biochemical Basis of Neuropharmacology* (5th ed.) (p. 197) by J. R. Cooper, F. E. Bloom, and R. H. Roth, 1986, New York: Oxford University Press. Copyright 1986 by Oxford University Press. Adapted by permission.

neurotransmission involves binding to the postsynaptic receptors (either nicotinic or muscarinic) on the effector cell. Pilocarpine and arecoline are drugs that are agonists (cholinomimetics) at muscarinic and nicotinic sites, respectively. They each have effects that represent a subset of effects of cholinergic activation since each selectively binds to only one type of cholinergic receptor. Likewise, the effects of pilocarpine at muscarinic sites can be blocked by atropine and the effects of arecoline at nicotinic sites can be blocked by hexamethonium. Thus, these two drugs are designated as anticholinergics and can be used to block the effects of cholinergic activation. In addition to directly interacting with receptors, drugs can also influence cholinergic transmission by interfering with the metabolism of ACh. For instance, physostigmine enhances the effects of ACh because it interferes with acetylcholinesterase activity. This anticholinesterase effect leads to an increase in ACh in the synaptic cleft. Other targets where cholinergic transmission can be altered include interfering with ACh synthesis, displacing ACh from the terminal, and preventing its release.

ACh does not have a well-understood role in behavioral disorders nor are agents that interact with this system used therapeutically to any great extent for the treatment of behavioral disorders. Nevertheless, ACh is involved in behavioral events in a variety of ways. The administration of physostigmine causes increases in anxiety, depression, and motor retardation, effects that are blocked by atropine. Drugs that act as anticholinesterases, particularly the organophosphorus compounds that have irreversible effects, are well known toxins. For instance, diisopropyl phosphorofluoridate (DFP), a compound commonly found in pesticides, is particularly toxic because its volatility makes inhalation and absorption from the skin relatively easy. Another well-known anticholinesterase is parathion which is used as an insecticide in agriculture and its use has frequently resulted in accidental poisonings. Certain ACh agonists such as oxetremorine produce tremors and antimuscarinics such as atropine and scopolamine produce amnestic effects. Scopolamine also reduces motion sickness and is particularly beneficial when administered via a skin patch (transdermally). It is clear that cholinergic mechanisms are important in certain diseases such as myasthenia gravis and suggestions that it may be important in Alzheimer's disease. In addition, some of the significant side effects of neuroleptic agents, such as tardive dyskinesias, may be due to increases in cholinergic receptor sensitivity. ACh also appears to be related to mechanisms of pain because it is found in areas of the brain that subserve this function.

Catecholamine Neurotransmitters

Relative to ACh, far more is known about the actions of catecholamine (CA) neurotransmitters in the brain and these endogenous neurotransmitters play major roles in behavior (Cooper et al., 1986; Julien, 1988; Lefkowitz et al., 1990). Furthermore, many drugs that are used to treat behavioral disorders or produce profound changes in behavior appear to do so because of their modification of these systems. CAs include dopamine (DA), norepinephrine (NE), and epinephrine, the latter of which is found primarily in the peripheral nervous system with only minor amounts present in the CNS. Within the CNS, NE and DA are differentially located in distinct fiber tracts. There are two major groups of NE cell bodies, each of which sends fiber tracts to other parts of the brain. Five major tracts emanate from the first of these, the locus coeruleus, which is located in the midbrain. Three of these tracts ascend to innervate neurons in the cerebral cortex, thalamus, hypothalamus, and olfactory bulb. A fourth tract ascends to innervate the cerebellum whereas the fifth tract descends into the brain stem and spinal cord. In general, the synaptic connections involve inhibition of ongoing spontaneous activity. The second major group of NE fibers arise from neurons in the lateral tegmental area and these fibers are often intermixed with those from the locus coeruleus.

The anatomy of DA-containing neurons is relatively complex and the fibers of these neurons vary considerably in length. Of particular relevance for the mediation of behavior are the long-length systems, that is, circuits with cell bodies in one location and terminals in distant regions. These include the nigrostriatal pathway which traverses from the substantia nigra to the neostriatum (caudate and putamen), the mesocortical pathway connecting the ventral tegmental area to the limbic cortex, and the mesolimbic pathway which goes from the ventral tegmental area to limbic structures such as the septum and nucleus accumbens. There are a variety of receptor types in the various regions of the brain mediating the effects of CAs pre- and postsynaptically (see Table 5). For NE there are four types of receptors, designated as α_1-, α_2-, β_1-, β_2-adrenergic receptors. While there is considerable activity in the area of classifying dopamine receptors at the present, D_1 and D_2 are the most completely understood. Finally, the intense study of CA systems has revealed each neuron contains more than one neurotransmitter. For instance, CA neurons can also contain certain neuropeptides that may function as neurotransmitters (see Table 6; Cooper et al., 1986). Some DA terminals contain cholecystokinin and some NE terminals contain the endogenous opiate peptide, enkephalin. Although the importance of coexisting neurotransmitters and the mechanism by which they function together (e.g., one may function as a neuromodulator) are only beginning to be understood, their coexistence clearly increases the possible complexities of the CNS interneuronal communication and increases the types of effects that drugs can have on normal functioning.

The synthesis of NE and DA begins with the compound tyrosine, which is converted to DOPA and then dopamine (Figure 12). Tyrosine is not synthesized within the terminal but is taken up into CA neurons

Table 6
Coexistence of Selected Neurotransmitters and Selected Neuropeptides

Transmitter	Peptide
Acetylcholine	Substance P
Norepinephrine	Enkephalin
	Neurotensin
Dopamine	Cholecystokinin
	Neurotensin
Serotonin	Substance P
	Enkephalin
GABA	Somatostatin
	Cholecystokinin

Note. From *The Biochemical Basis of Neuropharmacology* (5th ed.) (p. 359) by J. R. Cooper, F. E. Bloom, and R. H. Roth, 1986, New York: Oxford University Press. Copyright 1986 by Oxford University Press. Adapted by permission.

from other parts of the organism. The rate-limiting enzyme, tyrosine hydroxylase, controls the conversion of tyrosine to DOPA. There are inhibitors of this enzyme, such as α-methy-ρ-tyrosine (AMPT), which can be used to decrease CA synthesis. NE neurons contain the enzyme, dopamine-β-hydroxylase, which converts DA to NE. Both this enzyme and the one mediating the conversion of DOPA to dopamine are so abundant that their inhibition has little or no effect on CA levels. The synthesis of CAs appears to be controlled by a feedback loop that accelerates tyrosine hydroxylase activity when the catecholamine are depleted from the terminal through a removal of a disinhibitory influence. Alternatively, there is also evidence that enzymatic activity is modified through a change in the physical properties of the enzyme resulting from increased impulse flow. Clearly the latter mechanism provides a faster adjustment to CA release since it occurs before (in milliseconds, however) the CA is actually released and is depleted from the terminal. Regardless of the mechanism, however, increases in impulse flow, such as might occur as a reaction to stress, increase CA synthesis.

After CAs are released into the synapse, they are taken back up by the terminal where they are either metabolized by monoamine oxidase (MAO) or are stored in specialized vesicles or granules that protect them from degradation and are thus available for re-release. There is some evidence to suggest that there is more than one type of vesicle in the terminal that stores CAs, with newly synthesized molecules in vesicles separate from those filled by the reuptake mechanism. In addition, there are drugs such as reserpine that interfere with granular storage, exposing the CA to MAO and thus decreasing concentrations in the terminal. There are also drugs, such as cocaine, that block the reuptake of CAs and functionally increase their levels within the synapse.

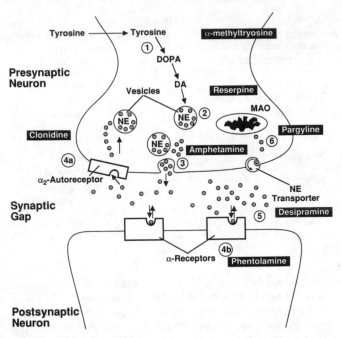

Figure 12. Norepinephrine (NE) synaptic connection and sites of action of selected psychoactive drugs. At site 1, synthesis of NE is blocked by inhibiting tyrosine hydroxylase (e.g., α-methyltyrosine) or dopamine-β-hydroxylase. At site 2, NE uptake-storage mechanism (e.g., reserpine) is blocked. At site 3, release of NE (e.g., amphetamine) is promoted. A site 4, presynaptic α₂-autoreceptors (e.g., 4A; clonidine) and postsynaptic α-receptors (e.g., 4b; phentolamine) interact with NE receptors. At site 5, reuptake of NE (e.g., desipramine) is blocked. Finally, at site 6, monoamine oxidase (MAO) (e.g., pargyline) is blocked.
Note. From *Biochemical Basis of Neuropharmacology* (5th ed.) (p. 290) by J. R. Cooper, F. E. Bloom, and R. H. Roth, 1986, New York: Oxford University Press. Copyright 1986 by Oxford University Press. Adapted by permission.

In addition to deactivation by a reuptake mechanism, a portion of transmitter is metabolized extraneuronally by MAO or catechol-O-methyltransferase (COMT). However, relative to ACh, the importance of this enzymatic mechanism of deactivation is not as great.

Many drugs that influence behavior or are used in various psychiatric disorders are believed to exert their effects through catecholaminergic mechanisms (Figure 12). Such drugs may either influence the synthesis (e.g., AMPT), release (e.g., amphetamine), storage of CAs (e.g., reserpine), and reuptake (e.g., cocaine) or interact with CA receptors and either mimic the effects of NE or DA (i.e., act as agonists) or block their effects (i.e., act as antagonists). In addition to the different receptor types previously described for CAs, it is also important to distinguish between autoreceptors and postsynaptic receptors. Autoreceptors are those receptors on a neuron that are sensitive to the CAs released by the same neuron and are usually located on the cell body, axon, or terminal. In general, for NE these receptors are of the α_2 type and for DA they are D_2 receptors. Activation of these receptors on the terminals decreases the release of NE and DA and with DA there is also a decrease in its synthesis, a type of negative feedback loop. Autoreceptors on the cell bodies, on the other hand, appear to decrease release and synthesis of CAs by actually decreasing neuronal excitability. Blockade of auto-receptors has opposite effects (i.e., an increase in synthesis or release). It is also interesting to note that some DA neurons (e.g., in the meso-cortical tracts) do not have autoreceptors so synthesis and release are controlled by a neuronal feedback as well as the concentration of DA in the terminal, as previously described. Many drugs that activate or block autoreceptors also activate postsynaptic receptors and thus can exert opposing actions. However, in many cases, there are differences in efficacy, with autoreceptors being more sensitive. Thus at low doses, the activation of autoreceptors may predominate. Since this suggests that the coupling mechanism for these receptors differs, it offers a pos-sibility of finding drugs with specific actions on only one receptor type.

DA agonist drugs in the nigrostriatal and mesolimbic tracts can produce effects that mimic the actions of DA in those areas. Upon post-synaptic receptor activation, there is a compensatory decrease in DA synthesis and release. These decreases are due to both an end-product feedback mechanism as well as an activation of autoreceptors. Likewise, if the breakdown of DA is prevented by an MAO inhibitor (MAOI), the amounts of DA both extracellularly and intracellularly increase and syn-thesis is decreased. Receptor blockers have effects that are opposite to those of agonists, increasing synthesis and release. However, if drugs such as the phenothiazine antipsychotics (DA antagonists) are given repeatedly, tolerance develops to the activation of synthesis and release so that the net effect is one of decreased DA activity in the presence of the antipsychotic drug.

As previously discussed, psychoactive drugs, both those used ther-apeutically and recreationally, produce their actions by modifying neu-ronal activity. Although the mechanisms involved (e.g., interfering with reuptake) apply to all types of neurotransmitter systems, the interest in CAs is due to the fact that many drugs of interest to psychologists interact in some way with this system. As noted previously, this is certainly true for the antipsychotic drugs that appear to function as DA receptor antagonists. These drugs (see Table 1) include the phe-nothiazines (e.g., chlorpromazine), thioxanthenes (e.g., flupenthixol), and butyrophenones (e.g., haloperidol). Although stimulant drugs are only used therapeutically in a few disorders (e.g., Ritalin [methylphenidate] and amphetamine in attention disorder deficit), their actions appear to be related to increased CA activity due to causing either a release of

CAs or a blockade of reuptake. Cocaine, which has only limited therapeutic use as a local anesthetic (and functions thus by preventing the generation of action potentials in a local area), does not appear to release DA or NE but blocks their reuptake. This can result in an increase level of DA or NE in the synaptic cleft, which consequently causes increased postsynaptic activity. Interestingly certain types of antidepressants also block CA reuptake and thus function to increase synaptic levels of CAs. As with cocaine, both DA and NE uptake are blocked but it is believed that drugs such as desipramine are more potent as NE uptake blockers. MAOIs are also used as antidepressants and they too, by blocking CA metabolism, can increase synaptic levels of both NE and DA.

As will be discussed later, certain antidepressants primarily block the reuptake of serotonin (as does cocaine) so it has been postulated that this mechanism is also related to antidepressant activity. However, it should be remembered that antidepressants do not appear to have true therapeutic effects until after several weeks of chronic treatment. Therefore, it is unlikely that these acute or immediate effects of blockade of reuptake are the major mechanisms underlying their therapeutic action. Much research is presently being devoted to to determining the neurochemical sequellae of reuptake blockade after repeated drug administration in an attempt to understand antidepressant activity and to design drugs with more specific actions.

Finally, both antianxiety agents and opiates also appear to interact with CA systems. Antianxiety agents, for instance, perhaps through a facilitation of γ-aminobutyric acid (GABA) transmission (discussed in the following section) appear to decrease noradrenergic activity in the locus coeruleus and may even decrease activity of the mesoprefrontal dopamine system. Morphine and morphine-like endogenous peptides also decrease locus coeruleus activity and this activity is blocked by naloxone (a specific opiate receptor antagonist) but not α_2-antagonists (which block NE autoreceptors). Interestingly, during morphine withdrawal, locus coeruleus firing is increased and α_2-agonists, such as clonidine, which stimulate NE autoreceptors and thereby decrease locus coeruleus firing rates, also reverse the manifestation of the withdrawal syndrome.

It should be no surprise from the description of potential mechanisms of action of antidepressants and antipsychotics that it has been repeatedly postulated that some type of dysfunction in CA systems may play a role in the pathophysiology of depression and schizophrenia. This will be discussed more thoroughly in subsequent chapters. In the case of depression, a decrease in CA activity has been hypothesized to cause depression. This theory is largely based upon the therapeutic efficacy of drugs that increase synaptic levels of CAs in treating depression. Amphetamines do this by a variety of mechanisms such as blockade of reuptake, release, MAO inhibitory activity, and there is even some evidence that amphetamine is a partial agonist at NE receptors. But eventually tolerance develops to these effects of amphetamine due to either a depletion of CAs or decreased CA neuronal activity. Thus as antidepressants, they are not useful for long-term administration. Furthermore, when chronic administration is stopped, the decreased CA sensitivity results in a condition that is opposite to activation. Tricyclic antidepressants and MAOI, by either increasing synaptic levels of CAs (tricyclics) or increasing the availability of CAs within the neuron (MAOIs) might increase CA activity which presumably is deficient in depressed individuals. Likewise, since lithium produces opposite effects, it is understandable why it is effective in manic disorders which are hypothesized to be due to excessive CA activity. In addition to the evidence from drug studies, more direct evidence of decreased NE activity in depressed patients has been obtained by measuring urinary MHPG (3-methoxy-4-hydroxyphenethyleneglycol, a metabolite of NE) in cerebrospinal fluid (CSF). These studies have shown that certain types of depressed patients have low MHPG levels and that in bipolar patients, levels fluctuate appropriately (see Cooper et al., 1986).

While the catecholamine theory of affective disorders is attractive, there are many anomalies that cannot be explained. For instance, cocaine does not act as an effective antidepressant despite that fact that it blocks the reuptake of CAs. Conversely, antidepressants do not have any notable therapeutic effects until after several weeks of chronic treatment although the effect of modifying CA levels occurs immediately. Eventually the repeated treatment with tricyclic antidepressants produces a decreased post-synaptic sensitivity (reduced number of the postsynaptic β receptors and decreased intrinsic activity) and increased sensitivity of α_2 autoreceptors. Yet antidepressants unlike stimulants continue to exert therapeutic effects, that is, tolerance does not occur. Another discrepancy in the catecholamine theory of depression is that while lithium is clearly useful in manic disorders, it is also used in bipolar disorders where periods of depression alternate with periods of mania. Finally, the development of new drugs such as fluoxetine (Prozac®) that primarily act by blocking the reuptake of serotonin, also makes it clear that depression is not caused by one single mechanism. It is likely that a combination of mechanisms is involved and even just as likely that individuals differ in the relative proportion of involvement of individual mechanisms. There is currently no satisfactory inclusive theory that accounts for all current data.

Abnormalities in CA functioning have also been implicated in schizophrenia although like mania, the hypothesized deficit involves an overactive CA system. The theory largely evolved because drugs that were found effective in treating schizophrenia were drugs that blocked dopamine receptors. Haloperidol, for instance, is a postsynaptic DA receptor antagonist that is an effective antipsychotic. Although levels of HVA (homovanillic acid, a metabolite of DA) in the cerebrospinal fluid change when schizophrenics are treated with drugs such as haloperidol, and these changes appear to be specific to certain regions of the brain, there is no evidence, comparable to that found with depressives and MHPG, that HVA levels are different in schizophrenics compared to normals. There is more recent evidence, however, that there are differences in numbers of DA receptors in schizophrenics but this research is only suggestive at this time. Once, again, however, it is not likely that schizophrenia, with all its many variations and variety of positive and negative symptoms, is due to an aberration in a single neurochemical system. Further, it can be expected that aberrant behaviors may be modulated by social and environmental factors. These interactions complicate description by neurochemical factors alone. Indeed much of the work and expertise of psychologists is directed at induced change in these behaviors.

Serotonin

Serotonin (5-HT) is distributed throughout the body and only a small proportion of total body amounts are found in the brain (Cooper et al., 1986). The existence of 5-HT has been known for sometime but only recently has it been accepted as a true neurotransmitter. Within the brain, 5-HT nuclei are located near the midline and raphe regions of the pons and upper brainstem. These nuclei project both back to lower brain stem regions as well as forward and in general the projections tend to be diffuse. One nucleus, the raphe medianus innervates the limbic system and the dorsal raphe innervates the neostriatum, cerebral cortex, cerebellum, and thalamus. In these pathways, the primary action of 5-HT is inhibitory, caused by an increase in K^+ conductance.

Because 5-HT cannot cross the blood–brain barrier, it is synthesized within the CNS. An important precursor of 5-HT is tryptophan. Tryptophan is not synthesized by the body but is obtained from dietary sources. Thus, maintenance of an adequate intake of this amino acid is essential for optimal 5-HT functioning. The amount of tryptophan that is actively taken up into the brain is not only a function of the amounts in the blood (after being extracted and absorbed from dietary sources) but also the amounts of other amino acids which compete with tryptophan for uptake. Once in the brain, it is converted to 5-hydroxytryptophan by the enzyme tryptophan hydroxylase. Like tryrosine hyroxylase, tryptophan hydroxylase is the rate-limiting enzyme so inhibition of its activity can greatly influence the levels of 5-HT in the brain. A drug that is capable of inhibiting this enzyme is called p-chlorophenylalanine (PCPA) and this inhibition is long-lasting, requiring the synthesis of new supplies of the enzyme. During this inhibition, animals given PCPA do not sleep, indicating the importance of the 5-HT system in sleep processes and perhaps sleep disorders.

In the next step of synthesis, 5-hydroxytryptophan is converted to 5-HT by a decarboxylation enzyme. Finally, 5-HT is metabolized by MAO as was also true for NE and DA. However, the control of synthesis and release of 5-HT is somewhat different than for CAs. For instance, increased levels of 5-HT within the synapse that occur as a result of the administration of MAOI do not decrease synthesis nor does blockade of 5-HT receptors or removal of 5-HT metabolic products have any influence on synthesis. However, as with CAs, it appears that neuronal activity itself influences the activity of the rate-limiting enzyme, tryptophan hydroxylase, with the resultant regulation of synthesis.

Within the past few years, the delineation and characterization of 5-HT receptors has received increasing attention. Thus, it is likely that a description of these receptor types will soon become outdated and it is also true that their functional significance is not completely understood. Nevertheless Table 5 lists the currently accepted putative 5-HT receptors based upon studies of selective agonists and antagonists. Although there is disagreement among experts in terms of the methods used for deriving this classification system (Martin, 1990), at present four subtypes of 5-HT, 5-HT_1 to 5-HT_4, are commonly considered. Within the 5-HT_1 designation, there are further subdivisions ranging from A to E (e.g., 5-HT_{1A}). The 5-HT_{1A} subtype is believed to occur primarily presynaptically and function as an autoreceptor, decreasing the synthesis and release of 5-HT.

Research is now focused upon the functional significance of the different receptor subtypes and there is evidence that some of them mediate certain types of disorders, such as anxiety, depression, schizophrenia, and alcoholism (Murphy, 1990). Drugs that are 5-HT_{1A} receptors agonists, such as buspirone, are being used in the treatment of anxiety whereas certain 5-HT reuptake blockers such as fluoxetine (Prozac®), are used in the treatment of depression. There are also indications that buspirone and fluoxetine are useful in the treatment of alcoholism but the mechanism of their effects is still unknown. What can be said, however, is that in terms of the development of drugs, compounds that act upon the serotonin system are receiving intensive evaluation for their possible therapeutic effect in a variety of behavioral disorders. With the development of more specific agonist and antagonist drugs, our understanding of the dynamics of the serotonin system will increase.

Of particular interest because of its hallucinatory properties was the discovery that LSD had effects on the 5-HT system and as well was similar to 5-HT in structure. LSD and related hallucinogenic drugs appear to decrease raphe activity and thus disinhibit the responsivity of the postsynaptic neuron. However, this purported action is not completely supported by a variety of experimental findings. For instance, destruction of the raphe (and subsequent disinhibition) does not produce effects that are comparable to LSD. Despite extensive research directed at understanding the basis of hallucinatory activity, the undoubtedly complex mechanism still eludes us.

Neuropeptides

General considerations. Numerous peptides have been identified in both the periphery and CNS in recent years (Cooper et al., 1986). This was spurred to some extent by the discovery of endogenous opioid peptides (Hughes et al., 1975) which followed the discovery of discrete types of opioid receptors (Pert & Synder, 1973; Simon, Hiller, & Edelman, 1973; Terenius, 1973). There is increasing evidence that neuropeptides can function as neurotransmitters but also as neuromodulators or neurohormones. For instance, neuropeptides are commonly found in neurons containing amino acid or monoamine transmitters (see Table 6) and at least in the peripheral nervous system, there is little evidence that they exist in their own separate neurons. Thus, when a neuron is activated, it is likely that there is a co-release of different neurotransmitters. The potential of co-release greatly augments the complex signals that can be transmitted to adjacent neurons.

Compared to amino acid and monoamine neurotransmitter substances, the origin of peptides is different. These peptides are synthesized in the cell body and dendrites under the "direction" of messenger ribonucleic acid (RNA). Initially, a larger molecule is expressed that appears to have little biological activity. Active peptides are then formed by cleavage of the larger molecule by ribosomal peptidases. The neuropeptides are then stored in vesicles which migrate to the axon terminal where release can occur, perhaps in combination with other neurotransmitters. Whether or not the activation of a postsynaptic receptor always occurs in the immediate vicinity of the presynaptic neuron is not known (i.e., peptides may also exert their effects as neurohormones).

The numerous neuropeptides can be classified into groups or families based upon similarities in structure or their origin from the same propeptide molecule (Cooper et al., 1986). As stated before, these neuropeptides co-exist in neurons with other transmitters (Table 6). Several neuropeptide families have pronounced behavioral effects. The family consisting of vasopressin and oxytocin has effects on learning and memory and the tachykinin peptides, which include Substance P, may be transmitters for primary afferent sensory tracts. Other peptides found in the CNS include neurotensin, glucagon-related peptides (e.g., vasoactive intestinal polypeptide and growth hormone releasing hormone), the pancreatic polypeptide-related peptides, somatostatin, cholecystokinin, angiotension, corticotropin releasing factor with many more being discovered at a rapid pace. The distribution, life cycle, and exact function of these neurotransmitters–neuromodulators–neurohormones are not completely understood at the present time but research in this area is proceeding at a rapid pace.

Opioid neuropeptides and receptors. The rapidly advancing field of neuropeptides was stimulated by the discovery of peptides that function as endogenous opioids and interact with the various types of opioid receptors that have been identified. An understanding of this system will be extremely helpful for understanding the mechanisms of action of opioids, in particular those effects involved with the amelioration of pain (analgesia). The cellular mechanisms underlying analgesia will be thoroughly explored in the chapter by Dykstra (this volume). Furthermore, given that opiate drugs, such as heroin, are extensively abused, a complete understanding of endogenous opioid neuropeptides and their receptors may also be helpful in understanding the etiology of addiction.

There are several different types of endogenous opioid peptides which are differentially distributed within the CNS (Cooper et al., 1986). The isolation of these peptides began with the observation that certain extracts from the brain produced an effect on the guinea pig ilium (a part of its GI system) that was similar to that produced by morphine (i.e., inhibition of intestinal contractions). Further, this action, like the action of morphine, was reversed by the co-administration of naloxone, an opiate antagonist. It was found that this extract contained two pentapeptides (a five amino acid sequence) called met- and leu-enkephalin. Since that early discovery in the 1970s, many more naturally occurring opioid-like peptides have been identified. These are classified into three groups based upon the propeptide from which they are derived. Met- and leu-enkephalin are expressed in separate areas of the CNS and derive from the precursor proenkephalin. β-endorphin is a 31 amino acid sequence that is expressed in specific areas of the brain by cleavage from the precursor, proopiomelanocortin. Leu-enkephalin also arises from the precursor prodynorphin as do various forms of dynorphin. All of these precursors also produce important non-opioid peptides.

Opiate receptors are found in several regions of the brain, although their distribution does not appear to coincide very closely with the distribution of endogenous opioid peptides. These receptors not only mediate the activity of the endogenous peptides but are believed to mediate the effects of opioid drugs (e.g., analgesia, respiratory depression, GI motility, cough reflex, euphoria, and addiction). The areas where opioid receptors are found include the brain stem in nuclei mediating analgesia; nuclei mediating cough, nausea, and vomiting; and nuclei controlling the maintenance of blood pressure. Deep pain, which has an affective component, appears to be mediated by opiate receptors in the thalamus. Opiate receptors that are in the spinal cord may function to integrate incoming information related to pain. Finally, there are high concentrations of opiate receptors in the limbic system that probably do not mediate analgesia but have an influence on affective behavior.

As with the peptides, there are multiple types of opiate receptors that have been designated on the basis of their differential responses to different opioid agonists and antagonists (Martin, Eades, Thompson,

Huppler, & Gilbert, 1976). At present three types of receptors, mu (μ), kappa (κ), and delta (δ), are generally recognized. These receptors are differentially distributed within the brain. Mu receptors are named for the prototypic agent morphine, and it is believed that analgesia, respiratory depression, decreased gastric motility, and euphoria are mediated by these receptors (there may also be subtypes that allow a separation of these effects). The largest concentration of these receptors is in the brain stem and thalamic areas. Kappa receptors, which are primarily located in the spinal cord, also mediate analgesia. Their activation produces dysphoric rather than euphoric mood alterations, which can limit their therapeutic utility. The function of delta receptors is less well understood but many of its effects are comparable to those produced by activation of mu receptors. The opioid antagonist naloxone has activity at all three types of receptors. Opioid drugs differ in their relative affinity for different receptors and many possess actions at more than one receptor type. These mixed actions can vary from full agonist effects, partial agonist effects, and antagonist effects. Further repeated administration of particular drugs can alter relative activity (e.g., decrease sensitivity of one receptor type while increasing sensitivity of another). Drugs may even possess both agonist and antagonist activity at the same receptor depending upon dosage. Clearly these variations make it possible to develop opioid-like drugs with varying profiles of activity.

Amino Acids

It has only recently been appreciated that amino acids, which were thought to be primarily involved in cell metabolism, can function as neurotransmitters within the CNS (Cooper et al., 1986). Ironically, these neurotransmitters are quantitatively the most abundant in the CNS and are almost nonexistent outside the CNS. Although there are several types of both excitatory (e.g., glutamate) and inhibitory (e.g. glycine) amino acids, γ-aminobutyric acid (GABA), an inhibitory amino acid, has received the most attention in part because of the role of GABA receptors in the actions of benzodiazepines (Haefely, 1990). GABA and GABA receptors are diffusely located in great abundance over the entire CNS. While there are distinct GABAergic systems that project from one area to another (the Purkinje cells of the cerebellum and projections to vestibular and cerebellar nuclei and neurons in the striatum which project to the substantia nigra), in general, the GABA neurons primarily function as interneurons in many local areas of the brain. There are two types of GABA receptors, $GABA_A$ and $GABA_B$. Within the CNS, the most important receptor is the $GABA_A$, which is directly coupled with a chloride ion channel, which in the absence of GABA is impermeable to chloride ions. Activation of the receptor opens this channel allowing the influx of chloride ions. Thus, its activation hyperpolarizes the post-synaptic neuron or inhibits its potential for activation by excitatory influences; that is, GABA has inhibitory effects. Investigations of the actions of benzodiazepines demonstrated that their binding sites or receptors occurred in close proximity to the $GABA_A$ receptor. It has now been shown that there is a molecular association between these two receptors and that activation of the benzodiazepine receptor can both increase and decrease the binding of GABA. In the former case, this results in enhanced inhibition which appears to account for the actions of benzodiazepines. Likewise other types of compounds, known as "inverse" agonists, can have opposite effects and decrease the inhibitory effects of GABA. Clearly, this mechanism is somewhat different than those previously described and is known as allosteric modulation because the activation of one receptor alters the steric configuration of a second receptor ($GABA_A$) or the ion channel itself. This modulation of the receptor-channel complex renders it more or less sensitive to GABA. The role of this conformational change in anxiety and the actions of anxiolytic drugs will be discussed in the chapter by Dykstra (this volume).

Summary

The purpose of this chapter has been to acquaint the reader with basic pharmacological principles that are needed to appreciate the mechanisms of action of psychoactive drugs. The topics covered included pharmacokinetics, which describes the processes by which drugs enter the body, are distributed to their cellular sites of action and how their actions are terminated. A brief overview of the anatomy of the nervous system was also described. The most important aspects of this chapter were the delineation of the special properties of neuronal cells that account for the ability of the nervous system to function as a receiver, integrator, and transmitter of information. In addition to the bioelectrical properties of neurons, the process involved in transmitting information across synapses was also described. Interneuronal communication involving neurotransmitters/neuromodulators and receptors was emphasized because the modification of this process largely accounts for the actions of drugs, including behavioral effects.

References

Ariëns, E. J. (1954). Affinity and intrinsic activity in the theory of competitive inhibition: I. Problems and theory. *Archives Internationales de Pharmaco-dynamie et de Therapie, 99,* 32–49.

Benet, L. Z., Mitchell, J. R., & Sheiner, L. B. (1990). Pharmacokinetics: The dynamics of drug absorption, distribution, and elimination. In A. G. Gilman, T. W. Rall, A. S. Nies, & P. Taylor (Eds.), *Goodman and Gilman's the pharmacological basis of therapeutics* (pp. 3–32). New York: Pergamon Press.

Bloom, F. E. (1990). Neurohumoral transmission and the central nervous system. In A. G. Gilman, T. W. Rall, A. S. Nies, & P. Taylor (Eds.), *Goodman and Gilman's the pharmacological basis of therapeutics* (pp. 244–268). New York: Pergamon Press.

Cooper, J. R., Bloom, F. E., & Roth, R. H. (1986). *The biochemical basis of neuropharmacology* (5th ed.). New York: Oxford University Press.

Haefely, W. (1990). Benzodiazepine receptor and ligands: Structural and functional differences. In I. Hindmarch, G. Beaumont, S. Brandon, & B. E. Leonard (Eds.), *Benzodiazepines: Current concepts* (pp. 1–18). New York: Wiley.

Hughes, J., Smith, T. W., Kosterlitz, H. W., Fothergill, L. A., Morgan, B. A., & Morris, H. R. (1975). Identification of two related pentapeptides from the brain with potent opiate agonist activity. *Nature, 258*, 577–579.

Julien, R. M. (1988). *A primer of drug action* (5th ed.). New York: W. H. Freeman and Company.

Lefkowitz, R. J., Hoffman, B. B., & Taylor, P. (1990). Neurohumoral transmission: The autonomic and somatic motor nervous systems. In A. G. Gilman, T. W. Rall, A. S. Nies, & P. Taylor (Eds.), *Goodman and Gilman's the pharmacological basis of therapeutics* (pp. 84–121). New York: Pergamon Press.

Martin, G. R. (1990). Current problems and future requirements for 5-hydroxytrytamine receptor classification. *Neuropsychopharmacology, 3*, 321–333.

Martin, W. R., Eades, C. G., Thompson, J. A., Huppler, R. E., & Gilbert, P. E. (1976). The effects of morphine and nalorphine-like drugs in the nondependent and morphine-dependent spinal dog. *The Journal of Pharmacology and Experimental Therapeutics, 197*, 517–532.

McKim, W. A. (1986). *Drugs and behavior: An introduction to behavioral pharmacology.* Englewood Cliffs, NJ: Prentice-Hall.

Murphy, D. L. (1990). Neuropsychiatric disorders and the multiple human brain serotonin receptor subtypes and subsystems. *Neuropsychopharmacology, 3*, 457–471.

Pert, C. B., & Synder, S. H. (1973). Properties of opiate-receptor binding in rat brain. *Proceedings of the National Academy of Sciences of the United States of America, 70*, 2243–2247.

Ross, E. M. (1990). Pharmacodynamics: Mechanisms of drug action and the relationship between drug concentration and effect. In A. G. Gilman, T. W. Rall, A. S. Nies, & P. Taylor (Eds.), *Goodman and Gilman's the pharmacological basis of therapeutics* (pp. 33–48). New York: Pergamon Press.

Ruffolo, R. R. (1982). Review: Important concepts in receptor theory. *Journal of Autonomic Pharmacology, 2*, 277–295.

Simon, E. J., Hiller, J. M., & Edelman, I. (1973). Stereospecific binding of the potent narcotic analgesic [^{3}H]etorphine to rat-brain homogenate. *Proceedings of the National Academy of Sciences of the United States of America, 70*, 1947–1949.

Terenius, L. (1973). Characteristics of the "receptor" for narcotic analgesics in synaptic plasma membrane fraction from rat brain. *Acta Pharmacologica et Toxicologica, 33*, 377–384.

LINDA DYKSTRA

DRUG ACTION

L inda Dykstra received her BA in mathematics and psychology from Hope College in Holland, Michigan in 1966 and her PhD in psychology from the University of Chicago in 1972. After receiving her degree, she moved to the University of North Carolina where she did postdoctoral work in the Pharmacology Department and in 1973 was appointed assistant professor in the Departments of Psychology and Pharmacology. Currently, she is a William Rand Kenan, Jr. professor of psychology and pharmacology at the University of North Carolina as well as a member of the Neurobiology Faculty. She is the director of a training grant from the National Institute on Drug Abuse and conducts research in the area of behavioral pharmacology. She also teaches both undergraduate and graduate courses in drugs and behavior, psychopharmacology, and in the biological basis of behavior. She is presently the principal investigator on a research grant investigating the behavioral and pharmacological determinants of opioid analgesia and recipient of a Research Scientist Award, both from the National Institute on Drug Abuse. She has published over 70 articles in journals and a book entitled *Psychopharmacology: A Biochemical and Behavioral Approach*. In addition, she is a reviewer for several journals and field editor for the *Journal of Pharmacology and Experimental Therapeutics*. She is a member of the Society for Neuroscience, American Society of Pharmacology and Ex-

perimental Therapeutics, European Behavioral Pharmacology Society,
American Association of Science, the American College of Neuropsychopharmacology, as well as a fellow of the American Psychological
Association (APA; Division 28) and a member of the Board of Advisors
of the North Carolina Center for Alcohol Studies. She is also a past
president of the Psychopharmacology Division of APA and has served
on several APA committees, including the Committee on Research Support, which she chaired in 1985, and the Board of Scientific Affairs.
Presently she lives in Durham, North Carolina with her spouse, William
Hylander, and her two children, Grayson and Rebecca.

LINDA DYKSTRA

DRUG ACTION

Introduction

A n understanding of how drugs alter behavior requires knowledge
from a variety of fields including pharmacology, physiology, neurochemistry, and, of course, psychology. Chapter 1 (Johanson, this volume) provides an introduction to pharmacology and neurochemistry,
with particular emphasis on how drugs enter the body, reach their site
of action, and culminate in pharmacological action. The purpose of the
present chapter is to add behavior to this equation and thereby move
toward an understanding of the mechanisms whereby drugs alter behavior. In order to illustrate the relationship between a drug and its
behavioral effect, four different classes of behaviorally active drugs will
be considered, namely, the opioids, the antianxiety agents, the antidepressants, and the antipsychotics. The basic pharmacology of each class
of drugs will be discussed, followed by an introduction to those neurochemical systems thought to play a prominent role in the effects of
a particular class of drugs. Then, the prominent behavioral effects of
each drug class will be discussed with emphasis on the way in which
these behavioral effects are examined in the laboratory. Finally, relationships between a drug's behavioral effects and underlying mechanism
of action will be discussed. This knowledge of the pharmacological and

behavioral principles of drug action will provide the background for Chapter 3 (Hughes, this volume) in which the responsible and appropriate use of these drugs in clinical settings is discussed.

History

Although interest in the relationship between the brain and the mediation of behavior dates back to the eighteenth century, scientific investigations of the relationship between behaviorally active substances and brain function did not really begin until the end of the last century. Probably one of the first investigators in this area was Sigmund Freud who examined the behavioral effects of cocaine by administering it to himself and carefully noting its effects. On the basis of these observations, Freud suggested that cocaine might have therapeutic potential as a cure for depressed moods and for alcohol or morphine dependence (Jones, 1953).

At the turn of the century, anthropologists working in Mexico and the southwestern part of the United States noted that certain groups of people used peyote in their religious ceremonies. When chewed, or dissolved in hot water and consumed in tea, peyote buttons produced visual and auditory hallucinations thought to be similar to the acute psychotic episodes associated with schizophrenia. The isolation of mescaline in 1896 as the active substance in peyote generated further interest in behaviorally active substances and their relationship to brain function and the possibility that schizophrenia had a biochemical basis.

In 1943 Hofmann discovered that lysergic acid diethylamide (LSD) produced effects very similar to those of mescaline. Hofmann accidentally ingested LSD while working with a series of indole derivatives. Shortly after ingesting the LSD, he experienced unusual sensations of vertigo and restlessness; his perception of size and shape was distorted and his ability to concentrate was reduced. Subsequent discoveries that the chemical structure of LSD was similar to that of the naturally occurring neurotransmitter serotonin further reinforced interest and speculation about a chemical basis for schizophrenia and advanced the notion that chemical agents might be useful tools in understanding brain function and behavior (Seiden & Dykstra, 1977).

Currently, the investigation of drug-induced alterations in behavior and of the biochemical mechanisms that underlie these alterations is a very productive and interactive discipline. A clear understanding of the role of naturally occurring substances located in brain and other nervous tissue can facilitate our understanding of drug-induced alterations in behavior, and also advance our understanding of the important biochemical and physiological processes that play a role in behavior.

Measuring Behavior

In order to examine drug–behavior interactions, the first task is to define and measure behavior. Although the distinction is not an absolute one, the term *behavior* traditionally has been reserved for integrated processes within the central nervous system, such as locomotor activity, food intake, sleep, perception, communication, attention, memory, and emotion. Nevertheless, drugs that alter behavior also alter other ongoing functions such as heart rate, gastrointestinal (GI) function, and respiration. For example, a drug may reduce anxiety and thereby alter behavior; however, it also alters many of the autonomic signs that accompany anxiety such as increased heart rate and blood pressure.

It is also important to note that behavior itself can influence the drug effect. Indeed, the ongoing behavioral state of the organism as well as the organism's past history contribute as much to the final drug effect as do pharmacokinetic variables such as the dose of drug and its duration of action. Figure 1 illustrates this interchange. Drugs that alter behavior produce their effects by altering brain chemistry, thereby leading to a change in behavior. Note that this interaction also goes in the other direction, with behavior and environment influencing each other as well as ongoing neurochemical events (Seiden, MacPhail, & Oglesby, 1975).

The reliable measurement of behavior is crucial to the examination of drug-behavior interactions. Given the complexity and multifaceted nature of human behavior and the difficulties encountered when at-

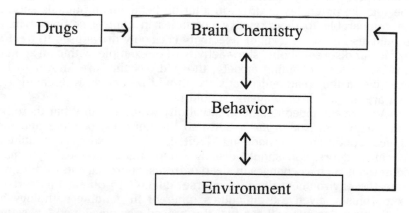

Figure 1. Modification of behavior through internal and external events, including drug-induced alterations in brain chemistry, environmental events, and environmentally-induced alterations in brain chemistry. Adapted from *Psychopharmacology: A Biochemical and Behavioral Approach* (p. 158) by L. S. Seiden and L. A. Dykstra, 1977, New York: Van Nostrand Reinhold Company. Copyright 1977 by Van Nostrand Reinhold Company. Adapted by permission.

tempting to bring it under experimental control in a clinical context, many investigations of drug–behavior–neurochemical interactions are carried out in animals. By using animals, investigators are better able to control the conditions under which the behavior occurs and thereby examine the numerous behavioral and pharmacological variables that determine the drug effect as well as investigate accompanying changes in neurochemical events. Moreover, by using animals, investigations that require large numbers of subjects with the same genetic make-up, age, or previous history can be carried out.

The procedures used to examine drug–behavior interactions in animals are evaluated by the same standards that are used to evaluate any body of scientific data, that is, *reliability* and *generality*. Reliability is synonymous with repeatability—"Will the experiment, if repeated, yield the same results?" This question can be approached through a variety of techniques, either statistical or by careful control over the experimental conditions. One of the best ways to insure reliability is to employ a well-defined behavioral measure that can be operationally defined and easily quantified. Generality refers to the representativeness of a single subject within a group of subjects as well as the interspecies generality of the finding (Sidman, 1960).

Although reliability and generality are extremely important in evaluating drug-induced alterations in behavior, more concern has been focused on the predictiveness of these procedures, that is, the extent to which drug-induced alterations in animal behavior correlate with the clinical effects of a given drug (Johanson, Woolverton, & Schuster, 1987). This type of validity is often referred to as *predictive validity*. Ideally, the relative potencies of drugs in altering behavior in animals should be comparable to their relative potencies in clinical settings. There should also be some level of selectivity (i.e., only drugs used to treat a particular disorder should show activity). For example, within an animal procedure for examining anxiety, those drugs that are known to be effective in the treatment of anxiety should be active, whereas drugs that are not antianxiety agents should not be active.

A more expanded definition of validity would require that there be some degree of *isomorphism* between the animal procedure and the clinical condition it is modeling (Treit, 1985). For example, an animal model of depression should display symptoms analogous to human depression such as changes in sleep patterns, anorexia, and withdrawal from the environment. It is, of course, difficult to obtain this sort of isomorphism, given the difficulties inherent in defining pathology in another species. We will see that the procedures developed for examining behaviorally-active drugs in animals vary widely. Some are best for screening (i.e., for quickly predicting what drugs might be useful in the treatment of a particular behavior disorder). Other procedures are best for identifying the behavioral and environmental variables important in the development of behavior disorders and finally, still others are useful for drawing correlations between neurobiological events and behavior.

Finally, because research on the behavioral effects of drugs often employs animals, it is important to consider the ethical guidelines for the care and use of animals. Presently, all animal research is reviewed by a committee that includes a veterinarian experienced in laboratory animal care. This committee inspects animal research areas and reviews the design of proposed experiments to ensure that animals are used humanely. In addition, professional societies such as the American Psychological Association have prepared guidelines for incorporating the animal's well-being into the design and conduct of all experiments.

Examining Mechanism of Action

The next task is to review briefly the mechanisms by which psychoactive drugs produce their effects. As described in the previous chapter, the majority of psychoactive drugs are thought to produce their effects by interacting with specific neurotransmitter or neuromodulator systems.

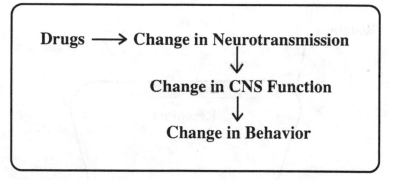

There are a variety of neurotransmitter systems with which drugs interact. These include: (a) the amino acid neurotransmitters such as GABA (gamma-aminobutyric acid), (b) the neuropeptides such as the enkephalins, and (c) the monoamines (dopamine, norepinephrine, and serotonin). There are also a variety of ways in which drugs can interact with these neurotransmitter systems and a quick review of these will provide some guidance in understanding drug action. As with all neurotransmitter systems, activity within a given system is regulated by a number of different processes, many of which relate to activity at the synapse. This activity can occur either presynaptically, within the synapse, or postsynaptically. Each of these synaptic processes—from presynaptic through postsynaptic—can be modified by drug administration as illustrated by the norepinephrine system (Figure 2).

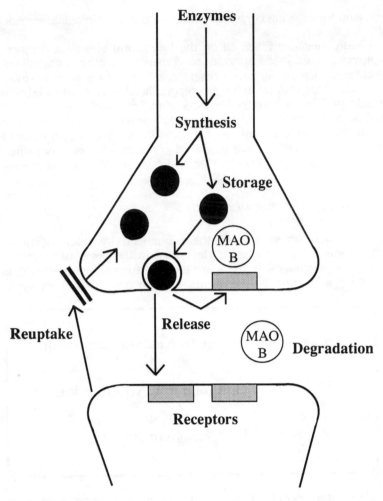

Figure 2. Possible sites of drug action at the synapse illustrating synthesis, storage in granules, release, and inactivation through reuptake and enzymatic degradation, and interaction at the receptor.
Note. MAO/B = monoamine oxidase B.

Norepinephrine is *synthesized* and *stored* in presynaptic elements. Then it is *released* in discrete quantities into the synaptic cleft where it interacts with postsynaptic receptors located on specific effector cells. This interaction is, in turn, followed by a cascade of secondary events that lead to a response termed *the drug effect*. Processes related to termination of the transmitter also play a role in drug action. For example, termination of norepinephrine's effect can be accomplished in several ways. Norepinephrine can be *degraded* enzymatically, *diffused* away from the receptor site, or taken back up into the presynaptic nerve endings (i.e., *reuptake*). The important point is that drugs can alter central nervous system function in numerous ways.

Drugs can alter presynaptic processes, including synthesis, storage, and release of neurotransmitter. The most important clinical drugs in this group are probably those that promote release of neurotransmitter, also called *indirect receptor agonists*. Indirect receptor agonists promote the release of a variety of neurotransmitters, leading to the activation of postsynaptic receptors. For example, in the norepinephrine system, these effects would include the typical spectrum of effects seen with indirect receptor agonists such as amphetamine. These include peripherally mediated events such as dilation of the pupil, relaxation of the bronchials, drying of the nasal mucous, and an increase in blood pressure as well as centrally mediated events such as increases in locomotor activity, decreases in food intake, heightened attention, and perhaps a sense of euphoria.

The second group consists of drugs that act predominately within the synapse. These drugs interfere with the termination of transmitter function, either by interfering with *degradation* of neurotransmitters or by *blocking the reuptake* of these transmitters. It is interesting that two major classes of antidepressants alter transmitter function in this manner—first, the monoamine oxidase (MAO) inhibitors interfere with degradation of norepinephrine, dopamine, and serotonin; and second, the tricyclic antidepressants interfere with reuptake of these neurotransmitters.

Yet another point at which drugs have been shown to act is postsynaptically, as *receptor agonists* or *receptor antagonists*. As receptor agonists, they interact directly at the receptor, producing the classic signs of receptor activation. As receptor antagonists, drugs interfere with (block or reverse) the activity of other drugs or neurotransmitters. The best known example of this type of interaction is the antipsychotics which are thought to produce their effects by blocking dopamine receptors. Some drugs produce long-term changes in receptor function, either by *sensitizing the receptor* or by *altering the number of receptors*.

Although the elucidation of drug-induced alterations in neurotransmission is crucial to our understanding of drug action, this information alone does not reveal how a drug, having interacted with some ongoing biochemical processes within the organism, results in an alteration in behavior. Thus it is necessary to delineate both chemical and behavioral mechanisms of action in order to understand how a drug might alter food intake, pain perception, the sense of well-being, anxiety, or the recall of thoughts. This chapter will focus on the answers to questions such as these and in order to do so, behavioral as well as neurochemical events will be examined.

The Opioids

Perhaps the best way to illustrate the techniques and theories employed to investigate drug–behavior–neurochemical interactions is with a success story. Among all the psychoactive drugs, the opioids provide one of the most interesting and complete examples of how a drug can alter behavior. Moreover, the approach employed to investigate opioid-induced alterations in behavior is not unique to the opioid system. The same techniques that are used to investigate opioid-induced alterations in behavior can be used to investigate interactions between other drugs and the systems presumed to subserve them, including the antianxiety agents and the GABA system, the antipsychotics and the dopamine system as well as the antidepressants and noradrenergic or serotonergic systems.

Pharmacology of the Opioids

Every drug class has a prototypic example, a drug that embodies in its pharmacology, the distinguishing characteristics of that drug class. For the opioids that drug is morphine. There are a number of related drugs in the opioid class that have effects that are qualitatively similar to those of morphine, varying either in potency or in pharmacokinetic properties such as rate of absorption and duration of action. The opioids are used primarily in the treatment of severe pain and are vastly superior to all other drugs as strong analgesics since they relieve pain without altering sensory modalities such as vision and touch. In addition to altering pain perception, the opioids produce a number of other physiological effects, including decreases in respiration, suppression of the cough reflex, decreases in gastric motility, and reduction of gastric and intestinal secretion. The opioids are also well-known for their ability to serve as reinforcers, which underlies their abuse liability, and to produce a withdrawal syndrome following termination of long-term usage.

The Opioid System

One of the most exciting pharmacological events of this century was the discovery in the early 1970s of binding sites (now called opiate receptors) on neuronal membranes in the central nervous system that were specific for morphine-like drugs and associated with synaptic regions. Large numbers of these opiate receptor sites were found to be located in the amygdala of the limbic system as well as in pathways associated with the perception of pain. This exciting discovery was followed by the finding that the brain itself synthesized molecules, the enkephalins and endorphins, that possess morphine-like properties. These naturally occurring substances were capable of producing analgesia and their effects were blocked by an opiate antagonist. Today, the enkephalins are thought to function as neurotransmitters in the brain, mediating the integration of sensory information related to pain. (See Snyder, 1977 or Watkins & Mayer, 1982 for a review.) These discoveries were followed in turn by a very productive and fascinating period of investigation in which many of the effects of exogenously-administered opioids, such as morphine, were shown to be mediated by interaction with endogenous opioid systems.

Several aspects of opioid action suggest that these drugs exert their clinical effects via a system of receptors, highly selective for the opioids. First of all, the opioids have similar molecular structures which suggests that they interact with a complementary receptor site. Additional evidence for receptor-mediated action comes from the existence of opioid antagonists which can reverse the effects of the opioids while producing no effects themselves. Finally, there is a good correlation between the potency of various opioids for binding to opioid receptors and their numerous effects (see Pasternak, 1987; Snyder, 1977).

Measuring Analgesia

In order to examine interactions between morphine, analgesia, and the opioid system, it is necessary, first of all, to develop a measure of pain perception and analgesia. As noted in the previous section, the behavioral measure selected must be sensitive, reliable, and repeatable. It will need to be brought under experimental control so that the variables that affect the behavior of interest can be explored. Finally, given a reliable measure of pain perception, its predictive validity must be examined in order to determine whether analgesics other than morphine also alter responding in this procedure and conversely, whether drugs that are not thought to have analgesic properties are active.

There are a number of different behavioral procedures for assessing analgesia (see Dykstra, 1985, for a review of these). In most, a potentially painful stimulus is presented to an organism and the time it takes the organism to respond to that stimulus is observed. Once baseline levels of responding are determined and considered to be reliable, a drug is administered. If the time it takes the organism to respond to the stimulus is prolonged following drug administration and if it can be determined that the prolongation is not simply due to general sedation, then it is presumed that the drug has analgesic properties.

One of the most reliable, repeatable, and predictive assays for opioid analgesia is the shock titration procedure in which an electric shock is presented to an animal's tail in intensities which increase from undetectable levels (near zero) to intensities which are potentially painful. In the typical titration procedure, the shock intensity begins at zero and then increases by some small amount every 15 s until it reaches some peak intensity (Dykstra, 1990; Dykstra & Massie, 1988). The animal controls the intensity of the shock by responding on a lever. For example, if the shock increases up to a level that becomes uncomfortable, the animal has the option of responding on a lever in order to decrease the shock intensity to a lower, presumably less uncomfortable level. The intensity at which responding occurs is said to reflect the animal's pain threshold. Thus, the experiment begins with information about the animal's baseline level of responding which defines the animal's normal pain threshold. Subsequently, when morphine is administered, the level at which the animal maintains the shock increases. Moreover, these increases in shock level are related to how much morphine is administered (i.e., small amounts of morphine produce small increases in shock level; larger amounts produce larger increases). Presumably, morphine has increased the animal's pain threshold, and as with all pharmacological substances, it has done it in a manner that depends on the amount or dose of drug administered. It is important to emphasize that this effect is *dose-dependent* since evidence such as this supports the notion that these alterations in behavior are due to drug administration (see Chapter 1, this volume).

Thus, analgesia has been *defined operationally* as an increase in the intensity at which a shock is maintained. The model is reliable because the behavior has been placed under experimental control and the conditions under which the behavior occurs have been explored. To verify the model further, it could be *repeated* within the same animal or across several different animals. The procedure is *predictive* because a known analgesic, morphine, increases the level at which the shock was maintained. In order to expand the generality of that prediction, other analgesics should be examined as well as drugs that are not analgesics (such as amphetamine, diazepam, chlorpromazine).

Given then a reliable, repeatable, and predictive procedure for measuring pain and analgesia, how can this model be used to examine the mechanism whereby opioids alter pain sensitivity? This question can only be answered through a variety of empirical, inferential, and somewhat theoretical approaches. It is a question that requires knowledge of the pharmacology and biochemistry of the opioid system, and of drug-induced alterations in the behavior of interest.

The Opioid System and Analgesia

The opioid system has been discussed briefly in the previous chapter and more detailed information also can be obtained from Akil, Mayer, and Liebeskind (1984) and Jaffe and Martin (1990). Briefly, the opioids are thought to produce their effects by interacting with both spinal and supraspinal opioid receptors which produce their effects through a number of different neurotransmitter systems. Evidence that these effects are receptor-mediated comes from a series of studies showing that morphine's analgesic effects are dose-dependent, stereoselective, shared by other mu opioids and reversible by the opioid antagonist naloxone. Indeed, the opioids satisfy the usual criteria for establishing receptor-mediated phenomenon.

The next task is to determine whether there is a relationship between morphine's action at the opioid receptor and its analgesic effects. For example, do drugs that share morphine's receptor binding profile also alter pain perception? The answer, of course, is yes. A variety of morphine-like opioids, all of which bind to the opioid receptor, produce analgesia in the shock titration procedure as well as in other procedures used to measure analgesia. Moreover, the order of potency with which these drugs produce analgesia within this procedure generally parallels their order of potency in binding to the mu opioid receptor. Importantly, drugs which are structurally similar to opioids, but inactive at the opioid receptor due to their chemical configuration, do not produce analgesia. Additional evidence to support the hypothesis that morphine-like opioids produce analgesia by interacting with mu opioid receptors comes from antagonism studies that have shown that the analgesic effects of morphine and other morphine-like opioids can be antagonized by the opioid antagonist, naloxone.

Support for the view that morphine's analgesic effects are mediated by activity within the opioid system also comes from studies that have shown that the endogenous opioids are involved in the control of pain. First of all, early studies have shown that electrical stimulation of specific sites in the brain lead to a reduction in responsiveness to pain (Mayer, Wolfe, Akil, Carder, & Liebeskind, 1971). Moreover, this type of analgesia can be reversible by naloxone and shows cross-tolerance with morphine, suggesting that endogenous opioid systems are involved in the regulation of pain as well as in the expression of analgesia following the administration of an opioid (Akil et al., 1976; Mayer & Hayes, 1975).

The approach described here to investigate the opioid system can be extended to examine other psychoactive drugs and their behavioral mechanisms of action. In the sections that follow, drug action will be examined by first exploring the prominent behavioral effects of a particular class of drugs and then examining what is presently known about their neurochemical mechanism of action. In order to bring these two lines of inquiry together, we will examine data from studies that draw correlations between the behavioral and the neurochemical effects of a drug. Few of the procedures for examining behavioral disorders are as well-developed as the analgesia procedures are for evaluating opioid analgesics; however, they still have been very useful for investigating the action of several psychoactive drugs. Finally, an attempt will be made to apply knowledge gained from these investigations to advance our understanding of the neurobiology of particular behavioral disorders.

The Antianxiety Agents

Recent estimates indicate that approximately 7% of the U.S. population suffers from an anxiety disorder in any one month (Katz, 1990). Anxiety is also an integral part of human emotions, not just a symptom of behavioral disorders. In its simplest form anxiety includes a sensation of dread or uneasiness which is often accompanied by physiological symptoms such as restlessness, tension, and tachycardia. Anxiety can result from medical procedures, stress from daily events, or psychosomatic complaints. In some cases, the term *anxiety* has been expanded to include behavioral disorders such as panic attacks, phobias, and obsessive-compulsive disorders. Although anxiety accompanies many of life's events, anxiety per se does not constitute a disorder. Anxiety is considered a disorder when it occurs with no known cause, when it is out of proportion to danger, or when it becomes debilitating.

Pharmacology of the Antianxiety Agents

Prior to the early 1960s, ethanol and the barbiturates were the most widely used antianxiety agents. With the introduction of chlordiazepoxide (Librium®) in 1961 and diazepam (Valium®) shortly thereafter, the treatment of anxiety changed markedly. These two drugs, and a host of others which were to follow, all come from a class of drugs called the benzodiazepines.

Virtually all the effects of the benzodiazepines result from actions on the central nervous system. The most prominent of these effects are decreased anxiety, sedation, muscle relaxation, and anticonvulsant activity. The benzodiazepines have a tremendous advantage over the barbiturates since they produce antianxiety effects at doses appreciably lower than those that produce marked sedation. Moreover, although drowsiness is often reported upon initial benzodiazepine administration, this effect usually wanes after a few days. It is important to note, however, that the benzodiazepines do produce sedation. As the dose of any benzodiazepine is increased, sedation can progress to hypnosis and ultimately to stupor. Indeed, one of the major goals of drug development among the antianxiety agents is the discovery of compounds that produce antianxiety effects with less sedation.

The benzodiazepines include a wide range of compounds, all differing in pharmacokinetic properties such as onset and duration of action. Although our discussion will center around the benzodiazepine antianxiety agents, it is important to mention that some of the more recently developed antianxiety agents may produce their effects through different mechanisms than those of the benzodiazepine antianxiety agents (Sanger, Perrault, Morel, Joly, & Zivkovic, 1987; Taylor, 1988).

The benzodiazepines are used effectively to treat insomnia, epilepsy, muscle spasms, panic disorders, and short term anxiety as well as more severe generalized anxiety disorders. They are absorbed well after being taken orally, and they have a relatively low incidence of toxic reactions. They produce only minor alterations in respiration and cardiovascular function. Physical dependence and withdrawal upon termination of long term administration in the therapeutic range is generally very mild. Even after high dosages, withdrawal is usually mild because the benzodiaze- pines generally have a long duration of action and thus are eliminated gradually. The overwhelming majority of patients use the benzodiaze- pines appropriately and do not reveal patterns indicative of abuse (Woods, Katz, & Winger, 1987). Nevertheless, the benzodiazepines should be used with caution since they can produce substantial memory impairment, motor incoordination, ataxia, confusion, and, in some individuals, they do produce signs of mild withdrawal upon termination; however, these effects differ greatly among the various antianxiety agents. When com- bined with other central nervous system (CNS) depressants such as ethanol, sedation can be a problem.

The GABA System

Several of the mechanisms by which the benzodiazepines produce their effects were described in the previous chapter. It is generally agreed that most, if not all, of the actions of the benzodiazepines are mediated by the inhibitory neurotransmitter gamma-aminobutyric acid (GABA). The benzodiazepines bind to high affinity, stereospecific sites associated with GABA receptors. These sites are probably restricted to the central nervous system and appear to mediate the main clinically relevant ac- tions of benzodiazepines (Baldessarini, 1990; Haefely, 1983; Mohler & Okada, 1977; Squires & Braestrup, 1977).

The mechanism whereby the benzodiazepines are thought to inter- act with the GABA system is different, however, than that of most drug- receptor interactions. Rather than binding directly to the GABA receptor and affecting a response, the benzodiazepines potentiate the effects of GABA by increasing the ability of GABA itself to bind to its receptor. This interaction takes place due to the close molecular association between sites of action for GABA and the benzodiazepines as shown in Figure 3. Thus, the benzodiazepines increase the potency of GABA by enhancing its ability to bind to the GABA receptor, but do not alter GABA's maximal response.

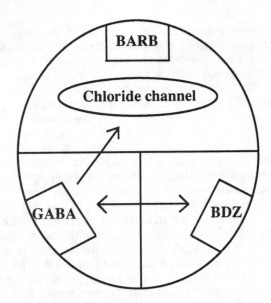

Figure 3. Schematic of the GABA receptor complex illustrating possible sites of GABA receptors, benzodiazepine receptors (BDZ), barbiturate receptors (BARB) and their relationship to the chloride channel.

It is well known that some parts of the GABA system produce their effects through interaction with chloride channels. Recall (Chapter 1) that GABA receptors have been classified into two major subtypes: $GABA_A$ and $GABA_B$ receptors. The $GABA_A$ receptor is a large complex of proteins, containing GABA binding sites, benzodiazepine binding sites, the chloride channel, and the chloride channel regulator binding site. $GABA_B$ receptors are not linked to the chloride channel. Since the effects of the benzodiazepines are thought to be due to interaction with $GABA_A$ receptors, discussion will focus on that system.

Briefly then, $GABA_A$ receptors are thought to trigger the opening of chloride channels. Benzodiazepines themselves produce little or no effects on the chloride channel, but in the presence of GABA they potentiate GABA's effects on the chloride channel. This enhancement of GABA's effects leads to a decrease in the firing rate of critical neurons in many parts of the central nervous system. Interestingly, the barbiturates are also thought to produce their effects through interaction with the GABA system, however, they generally act directly on chloride channels, rather than by indirectly altering GABA's effects on the chloride channel.

In addition to activation of the GABA complex through benzodiazepine binding sites, several other types of drugs can act as agonists for the $GABA_A$ receptor. The most common of these is muscimol. These agents are effective in mimicking the effects of GABA on chloride conductance and cell activity. Like GABA and the benzodiazepines, these drugs produce sedation and are potent anticonvulsants. Antagonists for the GABA receptor include bicuculline which competitively displaces GABA from its binding sites and blocks its action on the chloride channel. Other classes of antagonists include picrotoxin which is thought to work directly at the chloride channel and flumazenil which is an antagonist at the benzodiazepine binding site.

Given this information about the neuropharmacological mechanisms whereby the benzodiazepines produce their effects, we can move on to consider whether the behavioral effects of the benzodiazepines can be explained through this mechanism. Specifically, we can ask whether the benzodiazepine's antianxiety effects relate to facilitation of GABA-ergic synaptic transmission. To consider this question further, a behavioral measure of anxiety is required.

Measuring Anxiety

As with the opioids and analgesia, there are numerous behavioral procedures that attempt to assess anxiety and its alteration by antianxiety agents. They include situations in which rats are socially isolated and exploratory behavior is examined or situations in which animals are treated first with drugs that are thought to produce anxiety-like responses and the effects of antianxiety agents on these behaviors are examined (Crawley, 1985; Parker & Morinan, 1986). Naturally occurring anxiety-like behaviors that have been examined include aggressive behaviors, defensive burying, and distress vocalizations following separation of pups from their mother. (See Bignami, 1988; Lader, 1989, and Treit, 1985 for a review of these.)

One procedure that has some intuitive appeal is the social interaction test (File, 1985). In this procedure, pairs of rats are placed in a neutral area and the time they spend in active social interaction (sniffing, following, grooming) is scored under different conditions. In one condition, the rat is placed in a familiar environment; in another condition the environment is unfamiliar. These two conditions are then varied by the addition of either low or bright light. Briefly, it has been shown that rats engage in more social interaction when they are in a familiar area and the light is low, than when they are in an unfamiliar area with high intensity lighting.

In order to verify this procedure as a measure of anxiety, investigators have shown that the behavior observed in the unfamiliar, bright light condition is characterized by symptoms of anxiety such as defecation and increased levels of stress hormones. Finally, since the benzodiazepines increase interaction in the unfamiliar, bright light condition but do not alter interaction in the familiar, dim light condition, the procedure has been used to predict whether novel compounds have anxiolytic properties.

Although the procedures described above meet many of the criteria necessary to establish them as valid measures of anxiety, none have been as well-characterized as procedures that involve conflict situations. There are many variations on the conflict procedure; however, punishment procedures are the most widely used (Barrett, Brady, & Witkin, 1985; Cook & Davidson, 1973). In a typical punishment procedure, responding is first maintained by a schedule of food delivery. Brief periods are then added during which responding is both reinforced by food and also punished by an unpleasant event. As a result, responding occurs at a lower rate during periods in which responding is punished than during unpunished periods. Figure 4 shows the design of a typical punishment procedure. First, note in the first panel that responding maintained by food alone occurs at a high rate. In the second panel, responding is punished by the addition of an unpleasant event and, as a result, rate of responding is decreased during the punishment period. The third panel shows that an antianxiety agent such as chlordiazepoxide selectively affects responding during the punishment period by restoring rates of responding to their baseline level. Because these increases in punished responding occur following a number of other antianxiety agents, but not following drugs such as morphine or amphet-

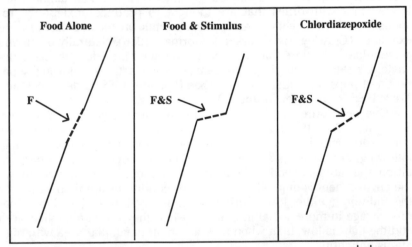

Figure 4. Diagram of a typical conflict procedure. In the first panel, responding is maintained by food alone. The second panel shows responding maintained by food as well as responding during a period in which responding is suppressed by punishment. The third panel shows the restoration of responding by chlordiazepoxide. (Adapted from Cook & Davidson, 1973.)

Note. F = food; S = stimulus.

amine, increases in punished responding are said to reflect the antianxiety properties of these drugs. It might be argued that this procedure models situations encountered by humans in which generally positive circumstances are interspersed with unpleasant or punishing events, leading to a suppression in behavior. Indeed, the punishment procedure is used by a number of pharmaceutical companies to predict whether a drug might be useful in treating anxiety. The interesting aspect of the conflict procedure is that antianxiety agents restore responding that has been suppressed by punishment.

The conflict procedure provides patterns of responding that are quantifiable, consistent over time and repeatable both within animals and across large numbers of animals. Therefore, it has been used extensively to examine antianxiety agents. To date, all the benzodiazepines that have been examined restore responding that has been suppressed by the delivery of punishment. Several points are important. First, increases in punished responding occur at doses that do not alter unpunished responding as illustrated in Figure 5. Second, the barbiturates also restore responding that has been suppressed by punishment as does ethanol (Barrett, Brady, & Witkin, 1985; Koob, Braestrup, & Britton, 1986). Third, drugs that are not known for their antianxiety effects such as the antidepressants and the antipsychotics do not alter responding

Chlordiazepoxide

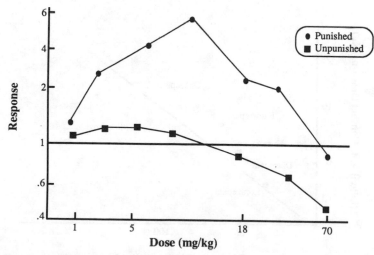

Figure 5. Effects of doses of chlordiazepoxide on punished and unpunished responding in a conflict procedure. Note that doses of chlordiazepoxide that increase punished responding, either do not alter or decrease unpunished responding. (Data adapted from Cook & Davidson, 1973.)

under this procedure. Given these findings, it is not surprising that the conflict procedure is recognized as an effective screening test for uncovering new anxiolytics.

The GABA System and Anxiety

Given a valid behavioral procedure for examining anxiety and some knowledge about the pharmacological mechanism of action of the benzodiazepines, the correspondence between the anxiolytic effects of these drugs and their proposed mechanism of action can be examined. The first task is to determine whether there is a correlation between the ability of various antianxiety agents to bind to the benzodiazepine receptor and the extent to which they restore responding that has been suppressed by punishment. Figure 6 illustrates this relationship. The dose of a benzodiazepine that restores punished responding in a conflict procedure is shown as a function of the amount of benzodiazepine that interferes with the binding of diazepam to the benzodiazepine binding site. (See Chapter 1 this volume for a discussion of receptor binding techniques.)

Benzodiazepine Receptors

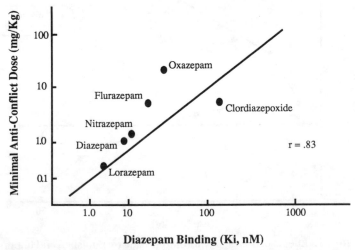

Figure 6. Correlation between the dose of various benzodiazepines that restore punished responding in a conflict procedure and the dose that displaces diazepam from its binding site. (Data adapted from Lippa et al., 1978.)

Given these findings, we might ask whether other compounds that facilitate GABAergic neurotransmission produce behavioral effects similar to those of classic benzodiazepines. Current research in this area has provided some evidence to support this hypothesis; however, not all data converge upon a common conclusion. Because many of the studies are limited methodologically in that thorough dose-effect curves have not always been employed, definitive answers may emerge as the field matures and more data are collected.

Support for the benzodiazepine/GABA hypothesis has been provided by experiments in which the benzodiazepine antagonist flumazenil reversed the effects of benzodiazepine antianxiety agents on punished responding; however, the effects of nonbenzodiazepine antianxiety agents such as pentobarbital and ethanol were not reversed by a benzodiazepine antagonist (Barrett et al., 1985; Koob, et al., 1986). This evidence indicates that the benzodiazepines produce their effects via interaction with benzodiazepine receptors whereas other antianxiety agents probably produce their effects via other mechanisms.

Yet another line of evidence implicating the GABA system as the major mechanism underlying antianxiety effects of the benzodiazepines arises from data indicating that the GABA system itself plays a role in the expression of anxiety. Evidence to support such involvement comes from the demonstration that the ethyl ester of β-carboline-3-carboxylic acid (β-CCE), which possesses a high affinity for the benzodiazepine receptor (Braestrup, Nielsen, & Olsen, 1980), elicits a profound behavioral and physiological syndrome reminiscent of anxiety, including agitation, increases in heart rate and blood pressure as well as increases in stress hormones. Moreover, both the behavioral and physiologic effects of β-CCE are blocked by prior treatment with the specific benzodiazepine receptor antagonists flumazenil (Insel, et al., 1984; Ninan et al., 1982) and by the administration of an antianxiety agent. Recently, investigators have administered a drug which is very similar to β-CCE to human volunteers and found that it resulted in symptoms of apprehension and hyperactivity (Dorow, Horowski, Paschelke, Amin, & Braestrup, 1983). Other compounds that produce effects via the GABA receptor complex have also been shown to produce anxiety in humans. Thus, these data suggest that the benzodiazepine receptor plays a role in the expression of anxiety (see review by Hommer, Skolnick, & Paul, 1987).

A final complexity to the GABA/anxiety theory lies in the recent discovery of drugs that appear to have antianxiety effects in clinical situations, but which do not act on the GABA receptor. One compound of particular interest is buspirone which is thought to produce its antianxiety effects through serotonergic systems (Mansbach & Barrett, 1987; Witkin et al., 1987). These findings, which have led to a resurgence of interest in the role of serotonergic systems and anxiety, emphasize the complexity involved in investigating the underlying mechanisms of action of behaviorally-active drugs.

The Antidepressants

The two most common affective disorders, mania and depression, are characterized by extreme and inappropriate changes of mood. Mania is characterized by elation, hyperactivity, and uncontrollable thought and speech and is generally treated with lithium and/or antipsychotic drugs. Depression is manifested by feelings of worry or intense sadness, agitation, and self-deprecation and is often accompanied by physical signs, including loss of libido, insomnia, and anorexia. Depression is treated with a variety of interventions, including nonpharmacological treatment such as electroconvulsive therapy and a host of pharmacological interventions such as the tricyclic antidepressants, monoamine oxidase (MAO) inhibitors, and the more recently developed atypical antidepressants.

Pharmacology of the Antidepressants

In general, the tricyclic antidepressants, MAO inhibitors, and atypical antidepressants do not have stimulating or mood-elevating effects in nondepressed individuals. Indeed, nondepressed individuals often feel sleepy and light-headed due to decreased blood pressure. In contrast, when antidepressants are given to depressed individuals over a period of several weeks, their mood is elevated, sleep disturbances are reduced, appetite improves, and suicidal thinking disappears.

The tricyclic antidepressants, which are so-named because of their three-ring molecular core, are well-absorbed when taken orally and, due to their relatively long half-life, generally can be administered once a day. In addition to alleviating symptoms of depression, the tricyclics produce drowsiness, hypotension, and a variety of anticholinergic effects such as dry mouth and blurred vision. With continued use, tolerance develops to these effects, whereas their antidepressant effects remain unchanged.

The MAO inhibitors were actually developed for the treatment of tuberculosis (TB); however, when their mood-elevating effects in TB patients were discovered, investigations of their antidepressant action began. Today, the use of MAO inhibitors is limited because of their severe and often unpredictable side effects involving interactions with foods containing high amounts of tyramine such as aged cheeses, beer, and wine. The MAO inhibitors also interfere with various enzymes and thereby prolong and intensify the effects of other drugs by interfering with their metabolism.

The atypical, or second-generation antidepressants, were developed in the search for more effective, less toxic antidepressants with a more rapid onset of clinical effectiveness. Because many of these drugs appear to produce their antidepressant effects through mechanisms different from those of the tricyclic antidepressants or the MAO inhibitors, they have been designated atypical antidepressants. Given marked differences between the compounds in this group, it is difficult to make any general statements about their pharmacology, except to note that although some produce their clinical effects more rapidly than the tricyclic antidepressants or MAO inhibitors, they still require some time to reach clinical efficacy (see Baldessarini, 1990, for more information about these drugs).

Noradrenergic and Serotonergic Systems

The mechanism of action of tricyclic antidepressants, MAO inhibitors, and other agents used clinically to treat depression is far from clear. The biogenic amine theory of depression was developed over 25 years ago and was based on the observation that reserpine, which decreased levels of the monoamines, norepinephrine, dopamine, and serotonin, also produced sedation in animals and depression in some people. The tricyclic antidepressants increased the concentration of monoamines by blocking their reuptake back into the presynaptic element, thereby increasing the level of monoamines at the synapse; the monoamine oxidase inhibitors also increased the concentration of monoamines by blocking their enzymatic destruction. In summary, depression was thought to be due to a deficiency of monoamines and the antidepressants were thought to produce their clinical effects by increasing the concentration of monoamines at the synapse (Schildkraut, 1965). Conversely, manic disorders were thought to be due to excessive catecholamine activity and lithium was thought to reverse this effect.

Despite the parsimony of this hypothesis, subsequent evidence made this explanation unsatisfactory. First of all, investigators have been unable to substantiate this hypothesis within depressed individuals. It is still questionable whether levels of monoamines as measured in the urine and cerebrospinal fluid are different in depressed and nondepressed individuals (Jimerson, 1987; Siever, 1987). In addition, neither cocaine nor amphetamine, both of which increase levels of monoamines, are effective as clinical antidepressants.

The most serious difficulty with the hypothesis, however, relates to the time course of the effects of antidepressant drugs. Although the antidepressants elevate monoamine concentrations almost immediately, their clinical effects are only apparent after several weeks of administration. The fact that there is a delay in clinical response to antidepressants suggests that antidepressants may produce an adaptive change in neurotransmission—referred to as down regulation or receptor desensitization. Thus, more recent hypotheses about antidepressant action have emphasized long-term adaptations in the ongoing responsiveness of noradrenergic and serotonergic systems (Heninger & Charney, 1987).

Specifically, it has been hypothesized that chronic treatment with antidepressants results in a reduction in density of both β-adrenergic and serotonergic receptors as well as an increase in α-adrenergic sensitivity as illustrated in Figure 7. Receptor binding studies have confirmed the fact that chronic, but not acute, treatment with clinically effective antidepressants induces a decrease in β-adrenergic and serotonergic binding. The temporal relationship between alterations in receptor binding and clinical improvement suggest that these changes may be critical to the attenuation of depressive behavior (Heninger & Charney, 1987; Sulser, 1978; Wolfe, Harden, Sport, & Molinoff, 1978). Because receptor binding studies alone reveal little about the functional consequences of antidepressant treatment, the next step is to show that changes in receptor sensitivity are correlated with drug-induced changes in behavior.

Measuring Depression

One of the most prominent signs of depression is retarded motor activity, an effect that can be easily observed in animals. Accordingly, one of the

Receptor Desensitization

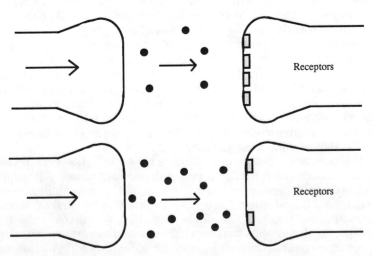

Figure 7. Diagram illustrating alteration in receptor number following repeated administration of an antidepressant.

screens for antidepressant activity involves treating animals with reserpine or tetrabenazine, drugs that are known to produce sedation in animals, and determining whether this effect can be reversed with an antidepressant. Although the reversal procedure has been somewhat successful in detecting certain types of antidepressants, it has missed some of the atypical antidepressants and is not specific for antidepressants. Thus, other procedures have been developed to examine the antidepressants. Of the many procedures that have been developed, the most common are the separation model, the learned helplessness model, and the forced swim test (see Henn & McKinney, 1987 and Wilner, 1984 for a review of these). An additional model employs responding under a schedule of food presentation. It should be emphasized that none of these procedures can provide a complete model of something as complex and diverse as depression. Nevertheless, each of these procedures has been successful in representing some of the elements of depression.

In separation models of depression, an animal is separated from its mother or its peers at an early age (McKinney, 1977). As the result of this period of separation, investigators have noted the occurrence of behaviors such as agitation and withdrawal, decreased food and water intake, and huddling. In theory, separation models would be ideal procedures for examining some forms of depression since many of the behaviors observed following separation are analogous to those observed in depressed individuals; however, there are only a few investigations demonstrating reversal of these effects with antidepressants.

The learned helplessness model is considered by many to provide one of the best measures of depression. In this procedure animals are exposed to an aversive event under circumstances in which they cannot control or predict its occurrence. This experience leads to a long-lasting deficit in escape performance, weight loss, decreased activity, and sleep disturbance, symptoms analogous to some aspects of human depression. Reports indicate that tricyclic antidepressants, monoamine oxidase inhibitors, several atypical antidepressants as well as electroconvulsive therapy all reverse learned helplessness whereas stimulants, sedatives, and antipsychotics do not (Sherman, Sacquitne, & Petty, 1982). Despite its predictability, the learned helplessness model has been used less often to explore the relationship between behavioral and neurochemical effects of antidepressants.

Another procedure that has been particularly useful for examining the activity of novel antidepressants is the DRL (differential reinforcement of low rate) schedule of food presentation. In this procedure rats are required to make responses at a specified interval in order to receive food. Rates and patterns of responding generated by this schedule are remarkably consistent over time, providing a stable baseline for examining drug effects. Under control conditions, rats tend to space many of their responses close together (called bursts of responses) and thus reinforcement frequency is not optimal. When antidepressants are administered, responding becomes more efficient and the animals gain more reinforcers. This effect occurs with a variety of antidepressants, MAO inhibitors as well as a number of the newly developed atypical antidepressants. Other treatments for depression, such as electroconvulsive therapy, also improve performance under this procedure, whereas the antipsychotics, psychomotor stimulants, antianxiety agents, and alcohol do not (O'Donnell & Seiden, 1983; Seiden, Dahms, & Shaughnessy, 1985).

To summarize, it appears that there are no universally valid animal models for depression or for any other behavioral disorder, all of which are exceedingly complex, and multiply determined. Perhaps a compromise is to use different models to ask different questions. Some procedures may be best for screening, for quickly predicting what drugs have potential as antidepressants, others might identify the behavioral and environmental variables that are important in the development of depression, and finally, still others might be used to draw correlations between neurobiological events and behavior.

Receptor Desensitization and Depression

Presently, understanding of the behavioral effects and presumed mechanism of action of the antidepressants is just beginning to unravel. Although several animal procedures have been developed that can be used to assess antidepressant activity, for the most part, research examining underlying neurochemical mechanisms of action is limited. On the neurochemical side, there is substantial evidence to suggest that chronic administration of the antidepressants produces long-term alterations in adrenergic and serotonergic receptor function which might be related to their clinical efficacy. What is missing are data relating changes in receptor mechanisms to alterations in animal behavior. Duncan et al. (1985) have noted a correlation between the effects of antidepressants on the forced swim test and down-regulation of brain β-adrenergic receptors. More recently, Seiden and colleagues have shown that serotonin plays a major role in the effects of antidepressant on the DRL schedule described above (Marek, Li, & Seiden, 1989). These findings are in keeping with the recent development of antidepressants with serotonergic activity. Future research efforts are needed to confirm these findings as well as determine whether altered monoamine sensitivity plays a role in the pathogenesis of depression.

The Antipsychotics

The psychoses are among the most severe of psychiatric disorders. Although they represent a very heterogeneous group of disorders, they can be distinguished by the presence of disorganized behavior, and an inability to think coherently and to comprehend reality. In the case of schizophrenia, delusions and hallucinations are often present. Antipsychotic drugs exert beneficial effects in virtually all classes of psychotic illness, and are not necessarily selective for schizophrenia. Because of the numerous disorders that can be treated with the antipsychotics, the terms used to describe them are varied, including antipsychotics, neuroleptics, antischizophrenics, and at one time, major tranquilizers.

Pharmacology of the Antipsychotics

Chlorpromazine was introduced as an antipsychotic in the early 1950s. Prior to its introduction, effective drugs for the treatment of psychosis were virtually nonexistent and patients were usually permanently hospitalized. Following its introduction and remarkable success, pharmaceutical companies began a search that still goes on today for more efficacious antipsychotics with fewer side effects. This search has yielded drugs from a number of different chemical classes, including the phenothiazines of which chlorpromazine is the prototype, the thioxanthenes and the butyrophenones of which haloperidol is the prototype. More recently, compounds such as clozapine and sulpiride, both extremely effective antipsychotic with minimal neurological effects, have been developed.

In general, the antipsychotics reduce psychotic displays of emotion or affect. Patients become less agitated and restless. Aggressive and impulsive behavior diminishes and in time, hallucinations, delusions, and disorganized or incoherent thinking tend to disappear. The antipsychotics also reduce initiative and interest in the environment. They are extremely safe due to their high therapeutic index, and although some tolerance develops to their sedative effects, very little tolerance develops to their antipsychotic effects. In general, patients do not abuse the antipsychotics. Indeed, a bigger problem with the antipsychotics is insuring patient compliance.

Like the tricyclic antidepressants, the antipsychotics produce anticholinergic effects, including dry mouth, dilated pupils leading to blurred vision, and constipation. They also dilate blood vessels, resulting in decreased blood pressure, but have very little effect on respiratory function. They are used widely as antiemetics. The antipsychotics also produce a variety of movement disturbances such as muscle dystonia, restlessness, and the parkinsonian-like symptoms, which include dulled facial expression, slow movements, rigidity, and tremor of the limbs. Another common motor disturbance is tardive dyskinesia, which often persist for prolonged periods after the antipsychotics are discontinued. Thus, although the use of antipsychotic agents is very widespread as evidenced by the millions of patients that have been treated with them, they are not without a number of unwanted effects.

The Dopamine System

In 1963, Carlsson and Linqvist found that the antipsychotics increased the turnover of dopamine and suggested that they did so by blocking dopamine receptors. Their hypothesis was subsequently confirmed by studies which showed that the antipsychotics bound to dopamine receptors (Creese, Burt, & Snyder, 1976). Virtually all of the antipsychotics in use today exert activity within the dopamine system, with the dominant mechanisms of action being blockade of dopamine receptors.

On the basis of these pharmacological findings, the dopamine hypothesis of schizophrenia was advanced. Thus, it was proposed that schizophrenic individuals suffer from an overactivity of dopamine systems in critical cell groups. This overactivity might be due either to increased sensitivity of dopamine receptors within the brain or perhaps to an increased number of dopamine receptors.

Evidence to support the dopamine hypothesis of schizophrenia comes from several sources; however, the pharmacological evidence is the strongest. First of all, it has been shown that drugs that act as dopamine agonists and stimulate the release of dopamine produce a state that closely resembles schizophrenia. For example, amphetamine, an indirect dopamine agonist, provides the best available model of acute, paranoid schizophrenia. Second, the antipsychotics themselves can reverse the effects of drugs which increase dopamine activity. Third, the antipsychotics often produce many of the symptoms of Parkinson's disease. Since Parkinson's disease is known to be due to dopamine deficiency, this provides more evidence that the antipsychotics are linked to dopamine systems. Fourth, the antipsychotics inhibit the binding of radiolabeled dopamine in a stereospecific, saturable manner, indicating that dopamine receptor blockade is indeed a common pharmacological property of this class of drugs (see Chapter 1 this volume for a discussion of receptor binding techniques). More recent evidence suggests that this effect is linked to activity at the D_2 subtype of the dopamine receptor (Carlsson, 1988). Finally, as illustrated in Figure 8, the strongest evidence for the dopamine hypothesis of schizophrenia is the fact that the potencies of the antipsychotics in displacing the binding of a D_2 dopamine agonist (e.g., spiroperidol) from dopamine receptors closely parallels their clinical effectiveness. Although this correlation suggests that the effects of the antipsychotics are linked to D_2 dopamine receptors, more recent evidence suggests that both D_1 and D_2 receptor systems are required for this effect and that full effect may require an interaction between both receptor subtypes (Carlsson, 1988).

Dopamine Receptors

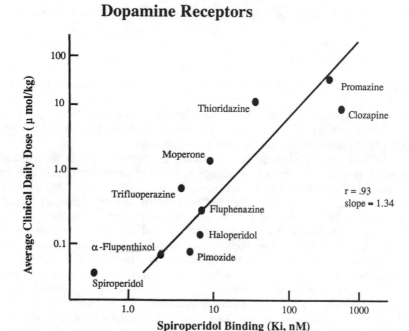

Figure 8. Correlation between the average clinical daily dose of various antipsychotics and the dose that displaces the D_2 dopamine agonist, spiroperidol from its binding site. (Data adapted from Peroutka & Snyder, 1980.)

Despite the strength of the evidence in favor of the dopamine hypothesis of schizophrenia, it is important to note that although antipsychotics act as dopamine antagonists upon initial administration it usually take weeks before clinical improvement occurs. As a result, hypotheses about the effects of the antipsychotics have been adjusted to include alterations in long term receptor sensitivity and/or number. Indeed, it appears that repeated administration of the antipsychotics leads to a decrease in dopamine cells in specific areas of the midbrain and the time-course changes matches the emergence of their therapeutic effects (Bunney, 1984; White & Wang, 1983).

Efforts to obtain more direct evidence in support of the dopamine theory of schizophrenia have been less successful. Studies of dopamine levels in the cerebrospinal fluid of schizophrenics are not always consistent. Postmortem investigations of the brains of schizophrenics provide some support that dopamine D_2 receptors are elevated in schizophrenics, however, these findings may be confounded by chronic antipsychotic administration. More recent developments in positron-emission topography (PET scan) and other neuroimaging techniques may provide evidence along these lines (Losonczy, Davidson, & Davis, 1987).

Measuring Psychosis

Among all the behavior disorders discussed here, providing a quantifiable measure of schizophrenia is perhaps the most difficult. The primary symptoms of schizophrenia are thought disorder, affect disorder, and social withdrawal. Thus, it is understandable why it would be difficult to measure this type of effect in animals.

An alternative strategy for examining disorders such as schizophrenia has been to examine drugs known to produce psychoses in humans. If the drug-induced psychoses mimic schizophrenic symptoms, then a drug that antagonizes these effects might be a good antipsychotic. During the 1950s LSD-induced hallucinations were compared to the hallucinations that occur in schizophrenia and thus used as a model of psychosis. Numerous difficulties with this model led to its disfavor and researchers today use frequent, high doses of amphetamine as a model of psychoses. Indeed, in humans high doses of amphetamine often produce paranoid delusions, stereotyped, compulsive behavior, and both visual and auditory hallucinations. Importantly, these symptoms can be alleviated by antipsychotics. Moreover, when amphetamine is administered to schizophrenics, many of the symptoms of schizophrenia are exacerbated. As an extension of these observations in humans, the stereotyped sniffing, licking, and gnawing that occur in animals following high doses of amphetamine or the direct acting dopamine agonist, apomorphine, has been used as a quantifiable behavior that parallels the compulsive, repetitive behavior seen in schizophrenia. These effects are reversed by antipsychotics as well as by the destruction of dopamine-containing neurons (see Creese & Iversen, 1973; Seiden & Dykstra, 1977 for a review of these findings).

The behavioral effects of the antipsychotics have also been demonstrated in animals trained to avoid an aversive stimulus. It has been shown that if an aversive stimulus is proceeded by a signalling stimulus (or conditioned stimulus), rats will learn to avoid the presentation of the aversive stimulus by responding during the conditioned stimulus. When administered an antipsychotic, rats no longer avoid the aversive stimulus, however, they are still able to escape it once it has been presented. Interestingly, most antipsychotics block these conditioned avoidance responses, whereas the antianxiety agents do not (see Seiden & Dykstra, 1977 for a review).

The Dopamine System and Psychosis

Early investigations of the effects of the antipsychotics on conditioned avoidance behavior established the role of the dopamine system in this effect. Indeed in an intriguing series of studies, Seiden and Carlsson (1963) showed that the effects of antipsychotics on avoidance behavior could be reversed with l-dopa, a precursor in the synthesis of dopamine and norepinephrine, but not by serotonin precursors. Interestingly, l-dopa is now used clinically to treat Parkinson's disease, which is thought to be due to a deficiency of dopamine. In addition, it has been shown that when the normal development of catecholamines is prevented with the neurotoxin, 6-HDA, conditioned avoidance responding is permanently suppressed (see Seiden & Dykstra, 1977 for a review of these early studies).

In brief, although the animal measures that have been used to investigate the mechanism of action of the antipsychotics in ameliorating the signs of schizophrenia may not model the most distinguishing features of schizophrenia such as thought disorder, they still have provided data to suggest that some of the behavioral effects of these drugs involve the dopamine system. And so, approximately 40 years after the introduction of chlorpromazine for the treatment of schizophrenia, there are still many questions left unanswered. Indeed it has been stated that "If you put everything that is known about schizophrenia into a pot and boiled it down you would come up with three things—it seems to run in families, . . . [antipsychotics] make it better, and there may be something structurally abnormal in the brains of schizophrenics" (Barnes, 1987).

Summary

In summary, we have examined four different classes of behaviorally active drugs, the opioids, the antianxiety agents, the antidepressants, and the antipsychotics. The opioids were examined as a model system, as a way to illustrate techniques and approaches used to investigate drug-behavior interactions. Although the opioid story appears complete and consistent in terms of the mediation of analgesia through opioid receptors, the expression of analgesia is very complex and involves a number of different neural systems. The link between the effects of the antianxiety agents and the GABA system also seems relatively consistent; however, the recent development of antianxiety agents with unique mechanisms of action indicate that this story will become far more complex as investigations continue. Understanding of the mechanism of action of the antidepressants and antipsychotics is still advancing as unique compounds are introduced and the technology for understanding brain function develops.

Progress in understanding drug–behavior interactions has relied heavily on the integration of neurochemical, behavioral, and pharmacological data. Sometimes it is difficult to imagine that a rat's responding in a conflict procedure can reveal information about the mechanisms of action of a drug in a disorder as complex as anxiety or that DRL responding can have anything to do with depression. Nevertheless, the combination of solid behavioral techniques with current knowledge in pharmacology has (a) yielded important information about the behavioral as well as the pharmacological factors that play a role in drug effect, (b) advanced our understanding of the biochemical basis of behavior, and (c) in a more practical sense, aided in the development of new drugs for the treatment of behavior disorders.

References

Akil, H., Mayer, D. J., & Liebeskind, J. C. (1976). Antagonism of stimulation-produced analgesia by naloxone, a narcotic antagonist. *Science, 191*, 961–962.

Akil, H., Watson, S. J., Young, E., Lewis, M. E., Khachaturian, H., & Walker, J. M. (1984). Endogenous opioids: Biology and function. *Annual Review of Neuroscience, 7*, 223–255.

Baldessarini, R. J. (1990). Drugs and the treatment of psychiatric disorders. In A. G. Gilman, T. W. Rall, A. S. Nies, & P. Taylor (Eds.), *Goodman and Gilman's the pharmacological basis of therapeutics* (pp. 383–435). New York: Pergamon Press.

Barnes, D. M. (1987). Biological issues in schizophrenia. *Science, 235*, 430–433.

Barrett, J. E., Brady, L. S., & Witkin, J. M. (1985). Behavioral studies with anxiolytic drugs. I. Interactions of the benzodiazepine antagonist Ro 15-1788 with chloridazepoxide, pentobarbital, and ethanol. *Journal of Pharmacology and Experimental Therapeutics, 233*, 554–559.

Bignami, G. (1988). Pharmacology and anxiety: Inadequacies of current experimental approaches and working models. *Pharmacology Biochemistry and Behavior, 29*, 771–774.

Braestrup, C., Nielsen, M., & Olsen, C. (1980). Urinary and brain β-carboline-3-carboxylates as potent inhibitors of brain benzodiazepine receptors. *Proceedings of the National Academy of Science, 77*, 2288–2292.

Bunney, B. S. (1984). Antipsychotic drug effects on the electrical activity of dopaminergic neurons. *Trends in NeuroSciences, 7*, 212–215.

Carlsson, A. (1988). The current status of the dopamine hypothesis of schizophrenia. *Neuropsychopharmacology 1*, 179–186.

Carlsson, A., & Lindqvist, J. (1963). Effect of chlorpromazine and haloperidol on formation of 3-methoxytyramine and normetanephrine in mouse brain. *Acta Pharmacol, 20*, 140–144.

Cook, L., & Davidson, A. B. (1973). Effects of behaviorally active drugs in a conflict-punishment procedure in rats. In S. Garattini, E. Mussini, & L. O. Randall (Eds.), *The benzodiazepines* (pp. 327–345). New York: Raven Press.

Crawley, J. N. (1985). Exploratory behavior models of anxiety in mice. *Neuroscience and Biobehavioral Reviews, 9*, 37–44.

Creese, I., Burt, D. R., & Snyder, S. H. (1976). Dopamine receptor binding predicts clinical and pharmacological potencies of antischizophrenic drugs. *Science 192*, 481–483.

Creese, I., & Iversen, S. D. (1973). Blockade of amphetamine induced motor stimulation and stereotypy in the adult following neonatal treatment with 6-hydroxydopamine. *Brain Research, 55*, 369–382.

Dorow, R., Horowski, R., Paschelke, G., Amin, M., & Braestrup, C. (1983). Severe anxiety induced by FG 7142, a beta-carboline ligand for benzodiazepine receptors. *Lancet, 2*, 98–99.

Duncan, G. E., Paul, I. A., Harden, T. K., Mueller, R. A., Stumpf, W. E., & Breese, G. R. (1985). Rapid down regulation of beta adrenergic receptors by combining antidepressant drugs with forced swim: A model of antidepressant-induced neural adaptation. *Journal of Pharmacology and Experimental Therapeutics, 234*, 402–408.

Dykstra, L. A. (1985). Behavioral and pharmacological factors in opioid analgesia. In S. Leiden & R. L. Balster (Eds.), *Behavioral pharmacology: The current status* (pp. 111–129) New York: Alan R. Liss, Inc.

Dykstra, L. A. (1990). Butorphanol, levallorphan, nalbuphine, and nalorphine as antagonists in the squirrel monkey. *Journal of Pharmacology and Experimental Therapeutics, 254*, 245–252.

Dykstra, L. A., & Massie, C. A. (1988). Antagonism of the analgesic effects of mu and kappa opioid agonists in the squirrel monkey. *Journal of Pharmacology and Experimental Therapeutics, 246*, 813–821.

File, S. E. (1985). Animal models for predicting clinical efficacy of anxiolytic drugs: Social behavior. *Neuropsychobiology, 13*, 55–62.

Haefely, W. (1983). The biological basis of benzodiazepine actions. *Journal of Psychoactive Drugs, 15*, 19–39.

Heninger, G. R., & Charney, D. S. (1987). Mechanism of action of antidepressant treatments: Implications for the etiology and treatment of depressive disorders. In H. Y. Meltzer (Ed.), *Psychopharmacology: The third generation of progress* (pp. 513–526). New York: Raven Press.

Henn, F. A., & McKinney, W. T. (1987). Animal models in psychiatry. In H. Y. Meltzer (Ed.), *Psychopharmacology: The third generation of progress* (pp. 687–695). New York: Raven Press.

Hommer, D. W., Skolnick, P., & Paul, S. M. (1987). The benzodiazepine/GABA receptor complex and anxiety. In H. Y. Meltzer (Ed.), *Psychopharmacology: The third generation of progress* (pp. 977–983). New York: Raven Press.

Insel, T. R., Ninan, P. T., Aloi, J., Jimerson, D. C., Skolnick, P., & Paul, S. M. (1984). A benzodiazepine receptor-mediated model of anxiety. *Archives of General Psychiatry, 41*, 741–750.

Jaffe, J. H., & Martin, W. R. (1990). Opioid analgesics and antagonists. In A. G. Gilman, T. W. Rall, A. S. Nies, & P. Taylor (Eds.), *Goodman and Gilman's the pharmacological basis of therapeutics* (pp. 485–521). New York: Pergamon Press.

Jimerson, D. C. (1987). Role of dopamine mechanisms in the affective disorders. In H. Y. Meltzer (Ed.), *Psychopharmacology: The third generation of progress* (pp. 505–512). New York: Raven Press.

Johanson, C., Woolverton, W. L., & Schuster, C. R. (1987). Evaluating laboratory models of drug dependence. In H. Y. Meltzer (Ed.), *Psychopharmacology: The third generation of progress* (pp. 1617–1626) New York: Raven Press.

Jones, E. (1953). *The life and work of Sigmund Freud, Vol. I (1856–1900)*. New York: Basic Books.

Katz, J. L. (1990). Testimony to Maryland Governor's Prescription Drug Commission, taken from *Consensus Panel J, American Medical Association, 251*, 2410–2414, 1984.

Koob, G. F., Braestrup, C., & Britton, K. T. (1986). The effects of FG 7142 and RO 15-1788 on the release of punished responding produced by chlordiazepoxide and ethanol in the rat. *Psychopharmacology, 90*, 173–178.

Lader, M. (1989). Drug treatment of anxiety: Implications for animal models. *Behavioral Pharmacology, 1*, 95–100.

Lippa, A. S., Klepner, C. A., Yunger, L., Sano, M. C., Smith, W. V., & Beer, B. (1978). Relationship between benzodiazepine receptors and experimental anxiety in rats. *Pharmacology Biochemistry & Behavior, 9*, 853–856.

Losonczy, M. F., Davidson, M., & Davis, K. L. (1987). The dopamine hypothesis of schizophrenia. In H. Y. Meltzer (Ed.), *Psychopharmacology: The third generation of progress* (pp. 715–726). New York: Raven Press.

Mansbach, R. S., & Barrett, J. E. (1987). Discriminative stimulus properties of buspirone in the pigeon. *Journal of Pharmacology and Experimental Therapeutics, 240*, 364–369.

Marek, G. J., Li, A. A., & Seiden, L. S. (1989). Selective 5-hydroxytryptamine[2] antagonists have antidepressant-like effects on differential-reinforcement-of-low-rate 72-second schedule. *The Journal of Pharmacology and Experimental Therapeutics, 250*, 52–59.

Mayer, D. J., & Hayes, R. L. (1975). Stimulation-produced analgesia: Development of tolerance and cross-tolerance to morphine. *Science, 188*, 941–943.

Mayer, D. J., Wolfe, T. L., Akil, H. Carder, B., & Liebeskind, J. C. (1971). Analgesia from electrical stimulation in the brainstem of the rat. *Science, 174*, 1351–1354.

McKinney, W. T. (1977). Behavioral models of depression in monkeys. In I. Hanin & E. Usdin (Eds.), *Animal models in psychiatry and neurology* (pp. 117–126). New York: Pergamon Press.

Mohler, H., & Okada, T. (1977). Benzodiazepine receptor: Demonstration in the central nervous system. *Science, 198*, 848–851.

Ninan, P. T., Insel, T. M., Cohen, R. M., Cook, J. M., Skolnick, P., & Paul, S. M. (1982). Benzodiazepine receptor-mediated experimental "anxiety" in primates. *Science, 218*, 1332–1334.

O'Donnell, J. M., & Seiden, L. S. (1983). Differential-reinforcement-of-low-rate 72-second schedule: Selective effects of antidepressant drugs. *The Journal of Pharmacology and Experimental Therapeutics, 224*, 80–88.

Parker, V., & Morinan, A. (1986). The socially-isolated rat as a model for anxiety. *Neuropharmacology, 25*, 663–664.

Pasternak, G. W. (1987). Opioid receptors. In H. Y. Meltzer (Ed.), *Psychopharmacology: The third generation of progress* (pp. 281–288). New York: Raven Press.

Peroutka, S. J., & Snyder, S. H. (1980). Relationship of neuroleptic drug effects at brain dopamine, serotonin, α-adrenergic, and histamine receptors to clinical potency. *American Journal of Psychiatry, 137*, 1518–1522.

Sanger, D. J., Perrault, G., Morel, E., Joly, D., & Zivkovic, B. (1987). The behavioral profile of zolpidem, a novel hypnotic drug of imidazopyridine structure. *Pharmacology Biochemistry & Behavior, 41*, 235–240.

Schildkraut, J. J. (1965). The catecholamine hypothesis of affective disorders: A review of supporting evidence. *American Journal of Psychiatry, 122*, 509–522.

Seiden, L. S., & Carlsson, A. (1963). Temporary and partial antagonists by L-Dopa of reserpine induced suppression of a conditioned avoidance response. *Psychopharmacologia, 4*, 418–423.

Seiden, L. S., Dahms, J. L., & Shaughnessy, R. A. (1985). Behavioral screen for antidepressants: The effects of drugs and electroconvulsive shock on performance under a differential-reinforcement-of-low-rate schedule. *Psychopharmacology, 86*, 55–60.

Seiden, L. S., & Dykstra, L. A. (1977). *Psychopharmacology: A biochemical and behavioral approach*. New York: Van Nostrand Reinhold Company.

Seiden, L. S., MacPhail, R. C., & Oglesby, M. W. (1975). Catecholamines and drug-behavior interactions. *Federation Proceedings, 34*, 1823–1831.

Sherman, A. D., Sacquitne, J. L., & Petty, F. (1982). Specificity of the learned helplessness model of depression. *Pharmacology Biochemistry and Behavior, 16*, 449–454.

Sidman, M. (1960). *Tactics of scientific research*. New York: Basic Books, Inc.

Siever, L. J. (1987). Role of noradrenergic mechanisms in the etiology of the affective disorders. In H. Y. Meltzer (Ed.), *Psychopharmacology: The third generation of progress* (pp. 493–504). New York: Raven Press.

Snyder, S. H. (1977). Opiate receptors and internal opiates. *Scientific American, 236*, 44–56.

Snyder, S. H. (1984). Drug and neurotransmitter receptors in the brain. *Science, 224*, 22–31.

Squires, R. F., & Braestrup, C. (1977). Benzodiazepine receptors in rat brain. *Nature, 266*, 732–734.

Sulser, F. (1978). Functional aspects of the norepinephrine receptor coupled adenylate cyclase system in the limbic forebrain and its modification by drugs which precipitate or alleviate depression: Molecular approaches to our understanding of affective disorders. *Pharmacopsychiatry Neuropsychopharmacology, 11*, 43–52.

Taylor, D. P. (1988). Buspirone, a new approach to the treatment of anxiety. *The Faseb Journal, 2*, 2445–2452.

Treit, D. (1985). Animal models for the study of anti-anxiety agents: A review. *Neuroscience and Biobehavioral Review, 9*, 203–222.

Watkins, L. R., & Mayer, D. J. (1982). Organization of endogenous opiate and nonopiate pain control system. *Science, 216*, 1185–1192.

White, F. J., & Wang, R. Y. (1983). Differential effects of classical and atypical antipsychotic drugs on A9 and A10 dopamine neurons. *Science, 221*, 1054–1057.

Wilner, P. (1984). The validity of animal models of depression. *Psychopharmacology, 83*, 1–16.

Witkin, J. M., Mansbach, R. S., Barrett, J. E., Bolger, G. T., Skolnick, P., & Weissman, B. (1987). Behavioral studies with anxiolytic drugs. IV. Serotonergic involvement in the effects of buspirone on punished behavior of pigeons. *The Journal of Pharmacology and Experimental Therapeutics, 243*, 970–977.

Wolfe, B. B., Harden, T. K., Sport, J. R., & Molinoff, P. B. (1978). Presynaptic modulation of beta adrenergic receptors in rat cerebral cortex after treatment with antidepressants. *Journal of Pharmacology and Experimental Therapeutics, 207*, 446–457.

Woods, J. H., Katz, J. L., & Winger, G. (1987). Abuse liability of benzodiazepines. *Pharmacological Review, 39*, 251–413.

AN INTRODUCTION TO PHARMACOTHERAPY FOR MENTAL DISORDERS

John R. Hughes is a professor of psychiatry, psychology, and family practice at the University of Vermont. Dr. Hughes has over 100 scientific publications in psychiatry, drug abuse, and behavioral medicine. He is the recipient of a Research Scientist Development Award from the National Institute of Drug Abuse (NIDA) and is the primary or coinvestigator on several NIDA and National Heart, Lung, and Blood Institute (NHLBI) grants. He is also a fellow of Divisions 28 (Psychopharmacology and Substance Abuse), 38 (Health Psychology), and 25 (Experimental Analysis of Behavior) of the American Psychological Association and serves on the Division 28 Prescription Privileges Committee. Dr. Hughes is a board-certified psychiatrist and Medical Director of the University of Vermont Substance Abuse Treatment Center.

AN INTRODUCTION TO PHARMACOTHERAPY FOR MENTAL DISORDERS

B oth psychotherapy and pharmacotherapy are well-accepted treatments for several mental disorders (American Psychiatric Association, 1989). With some disorders, psychotherapy but not pharmacotherapy is the major therapy (e.g., sexual disorders). Other disorders require pharmacotherapy but not psychotherapy as the major therapy (e.g., bipolar disorders). Finally, in some disorders, both treatments are effective (e.g., major depression) and clinicians and patients can choose either therapy or can combine the two treatments.

Psychologists need to be familiar with pharmacotherapies for several reasons. First, some of their patients will already be on medications when first seen. In one survey, 79% of psychologists reported having patients who receive psychoactive medications (Beitman, 1991). Psychoactive medications can influence the assessment and psychotherapeutic treatment of patients. For example, the side effects of certain medications can change the symptomatic presentation (e.g., tremulousness induced by some antidepressants can resemble anxiety and akinesia induced by some antipsychotics can look like depression). Ces-

This chapter was supported in part by Research Scientist Development Award K02–00109 from the National Institute on Drug Abuse (Dr. Hughes) and by D/ART (Depression/Awareness, Recognition and Treatment) Grant MH 19179 from the National Institute on Mental Health (Dr. Pierattini).

sation of such medications can induce new symptoms (e.g., anxiety). Second, psychologists must be familiar with the conditions for which psychoactive medications may be important primary or adjunctive treatments. For example, psychoactive medication for patients with mania or acute psychosis is viewed by many as essential, and referral for medication evaluation would be indicated. Third, familiarity with pharmacotherapy permits psychologists to recognize inappropriate drug therapy. For example, some patients use tricyclic antidepressants on an ad-lib basis and some primary physicians still use antipsychotics to treat anxiety disorders. Finally, psychologists are sometimes asked by patients, families, or social systems to render an opinion about pharmacotherapy for psychological and behavioral symptoms.

There are many existing books on the use of psychoactive medications (American Psychiatric Association, 1989; Baldessarini, 1985; Bassuk, Schoonover, & Gelenberg, 1990; Beitman & Klerman, 1991; Ellison, 1989; Fisher & Greenberg, 1989; Gitlin, 1990; Goldenberg, 1990; Gorman, 1990; Guttmacher, 1988; Hersen, 1986; Julien, 1988; Klein, Gittelman, Quitkin, & Rifkin, 1980; Lader & Herrington, 1990; Lawson & Cooperrider, 1988; Preston & Johnson, 1990; Shader, 1975). A condensation of these books into one chapter can provide only limited coverage of the various disorders, symptoms and medications.

The purpose of the present chapter is to provide a brief overview of the therapeutic use of psychoactive medications. Indications for pharmacotherapy, effects of pharmacotherapy, and appropriateness of medication administration will be considered. This chapter provides several general guidelines. These should not be viewed as standards or rules of expected behavior. As with psychotherapy, the complexity of patient histories and current conditions are such that blind following of a priori rules can be detrimental to the patient. Consideration will be given first to the major disorders and which psychoactive medications might be indicated, how such medications are typically used, and what the major side effects are. Then, the general principles used in prescribing psychoactive medications (e.g., how medications are chosen, monitored, combined with psychotherapy, etc.) will be presented.

Indications for the Use of Psychoactive Medications

Psychoactive medication use is usually based on either diagnostic or symptom-relief indications. A diagnostic indication occurs when a specific disorder is diagnosed and this leads to the selection of a specific

John R. Hughes presented a Master Lecture at the 1991 APA Convention. The lecture was based on this chapter, which was produced in collaboration with Robert A. Pierattini, a clinical assistant professor of psychology at the University of Vermont. Dr. Pierattini is the Director of the University of Vermont's Psychopharmacology Consultation Service.

pharmacological class of medications. The importance of diagnostics to the choice of psychoactive medications is often overlooked. Its importance resides in the fact that the efficacy of many medications is limited to specific disorders. For example, antidepressants improve the mood of patients with major depressive disorders but do not improve the mood of patients whose depressions are due to recent environmental events (i.e., an adjustment disorder). In fact, such diagnosis/medication specificity has been used to argue the validity of certain psychiatric disorders.

There are several disorders in which medications can be indicated (Table 1). The three most important classes of disorders are psychotic, mood and anxiety disorders.

Psychopharmacological Treatment of the Psychoses

The major psychotic disorder in the *Diagnostic and Statistical Manual of Mental Disorders* (*DSM-III-R*; American Psychiatric Association, 1987) is schizophrenia. The acute phase of this disorder is dominated by "positive" symptoms of illogical thought processes, delusions and hallucinations. Between acute phases, the "negative symptoms" of social isolation, markedly eccentric behavior, blunted or inappropriate affect, odd or magical thinking, perceptual disturbances (illusions, etc.), impaired hygiene, and lack of interests and initiative predominate. Often some negative symptoms occur during the acute period and some positive symptoms remain between acute episodes.

Psychoactive medications used to combat psychotic disorders have been referred to as antipsychotics, major tranquilizers, neuroleptics, or analeptics. The first class of antipsychotics were the phenothiazines which were followed by other effective medications, notably haloperidol. The mechanism of action of traditional antipsychotics is blockage of the D_2 dopamine receptor in the mesolimbic system. Antipsychotics are quite effective in treating an acute episode of positive symptoms. Larger doses are used initially to calm patients suffering from schizophrenia and then decreased. Although antipsychotics usually calm patients within 1–3 days, there is often a 2–8 week lag before these medications significantly improve delusions, hallucinations, and illogical thinking. Traditional antipsychotics are either not effective or, if so, minimally effective for negative symptoms of schizophrenia. Antipsychotics vary little in efficacy but do vary in side effects. High potency medications (e.g., haloperidol) have high potential for extrapyramidal side effects and little for anticholinergic and autonomic side effects. Low potency medications (e.g., chlorpromazine) have less extrapyramidal and more anticholinergic effects. Extrapyramidal symptoms are due to dopamine blockade in the niagrostriatal pathways and include dystonias (involuntary contractions of the tongue, neck muscles, etc.), akathesias (motor restlessness) and parkinsonian-like symptoms (akinesia [slow and difficult movement of large muscle groups], rigidity and slow tremors).

Table 1
Commonly Used Medications For The Major Psychiatric Disorders

Disorder	Medication
Disorders first evident in infancy, childhood, or adolescence	
Attention-deficit hyperactivity disorder	Stimulants
Tic disorder	Antipsychotics
Organic Mental Disorders (OMD)	
Dementia	
with delirium	Antipsychotics
with delusions	Antipsychotics
with depression	Antidepressants
Psychoactive Substance-Induced OMD	
Alcohol withdrawal	Benzodiazepines
Nicotine withdrawal	Nicotine agonists
Opioid withdrawal	Opioid agonists
Sedative/Hypnotic/Anxiolytic withdrawal	Benzodiazepines
OMD Associated With Physical Disorders	
With delirium	Antipsychotics
With delusions	Antipsychotics
With depression	Antidepressants
Psychoactive Substance Use Disorder	
Alcohol dependence	Disulfiram
Nicotine dependence	Nicotine replacement
Opioid dependence	Opioid agonists
Schizophrenia	Antipsychotics
Major depression	Antidepressants
Bipolar disorder	Lithium
with mania	Antipsychotics, Benzodiazepines
with depression	Antidepressants
Generalized anxiety disorder	Benzodiazepines
Panic disorders/agoraphobia	Antidepressants
Obsessive-compulsive disorder	Clomipramine

Anticholinergic side effects include constipation, dry mouth, difficulty urinating, blurred vision, and sexual dysfunction. Autonomic effects include postural hypotension (an exaggerated fall in blood pressure upon standing resulting in dizziness and the possibility of fainting or falling) and cardiac arrhythmias. Antipsychotics also cause sedation and weight gain. Abrupt cessation of antipsychotics can cause a withdrawal syndrome of insomnia, gastrointestinal problems, sweating, and extrapyramidal side effects.

The class of side effects that has most influenced the use of anti-psychotic medications is tardive dyskinesia (Cummings & Wirshing, 1989). Tardive dyskinesia is involuntary muscle movements of the face and tongue that can occur with chronic use of antipsychotics. The risk of tardive dyskinesia increases with age, the dose and duration of use of antipsychotics and concomitant organic brain syndrome. Unfortunately, tardive dyskinesia is often irreversible and untreatable. Thus, many psychiatrists will not use antipsychotics unless it is clear they are essential and other medications cannot substitute.

The exception among antipsychotics is the newly released medication clozapine. Clozapine is an effective antipsychotic that does not appear to work via dopamine blockade, produces little or no extrapyramidal side effects, may effect negative as well as positive symptoms and, importantly, improves 30%–50% of schizophrenics who have not responded to traditional antipsychotics. One problem with clozapine is that in approximately 2% of the patients, white blood cell production is inhibited and this can be fatal. Due to this complication, weekly blood work is necessary to detect this problem early on. The second problem is that clozapine is expensive.

Most of the side effects of antipsychotics are dose related; thus, one usually tries to find the lowest effective dose. However, blood levels of the drug do not appear to be helpful, and it is often difficult to dose-titrate patients.

Schizophrenia is typically a relapsing disorder. Patients who have had two or more episodes are usually placed on a lower dose of the antipsychotic for at least 6 months to decrease relapses. Such therapy decreases the chance of relapse in the first year from 60% to 30%. The duration of maintenance therapy of antipsychotics usually increases with the number of prior episodes and the severity of those episodes.

Psychopharmacological Treatment of Mood Disorders

Major depression refers to a prolonged depressed mood that has associated symptoms of diminished interest in or pleasure in activities, fatigue, guilt or worthlessness, difficulty thinking and deciding, and thoughts of death. More importantly, several "neurovegetative" signs or symptoms occur as well: weight loss, insomnia or hypersomnia, and psychomotor agitation or retardation. It is the presence of these latter symptoms, a definite onset and course to the depression, and the all-day every-day mood disturbance that predict a positive response to medication therapy. Because 60% of major depressions reoccur, many patients are placed on 6–12 months of preventive therapy.

Antidepressants are the psychoactive medications of choice for this disorder. Tricyclic (three-ring) antidepressants have traditionally been the mainstay of treatment. Their mechanism of action is thought to be the blockade of reuptake of catecholamines (norepinephrine and serotonin) thereby increasing the amount of catecholamines in the synaptic cleft. Tricyclic antidepressants often take 2–6 weeks to work but are effective in 60%–80% of cases. They can be classified as more serotonergic (e.g., amitriptyline) or more adrenergic (desipramine). The more serotonergic tricyclic antidepressants have more anticholinergic side effects and are more sedating. Other side effects of tricyclic antidepressants include autonomic side effects, weight gain and, when taken in overdoses, especially with alcohol, death. Abrupt cessation of tricyclic antidepressants can produce withdrawal symptoms of rebound insomnia, gastrointestinal problems, nausea, and vomiting. Blood levels are available for several tricyclic antidepressants and these are somewhat related to outcome.

In addition to tricyclic antidepressants, several polycyclic (many-ringed) and noncyclic antidepressants have been marketed in the last 15 years. They appear to be equally efficacious; however, some appear to have fewer side effects (e.g., fluoxetine has less weight gain and anticholinergic effects than tricyclic antidepressants).

Sometimes major depressions include psychotic features (e.g., delusions of having caused some disaster). Antidepressants alone are less effective in these depressions and one must consider the addition of antipsychotic medications. Major depressions that do not respond to tricyclic antidepressants are often treated by adding a second medication such as lithium, thyroid, or amphetamine or by switching to electroconvulsive therapy.

The other class of psychoactive medications effective in major depression is monoamine oxidase (MAO) inhibitors. MAO is an enzyme that breaks down catecholamines in the synaptic cleft; thus, by inhibiting this enzyme, MAO inhibitors increase catecholamines in the cleft. MAO inhibitors require patients to follow a special diet as ingesting tyramine can provoke a hypertensive crisis. This requirement led MAO inhibitors to fall out of favor when tricyclic antidepressants became available. Other common side effects of MAO inhibitors include anticholinergic effects, stimulation, sexual problems, dizziness, insomnia, and agitation. Whether the efficacy of MAO inhibitors for major depression is equivalent to that of tricyclic antidepressants is debatable; thus, MAO inhibitors are often used as a second-line drug. On the other hand, recent evidence suggests MAO inhibitors may be especially effective for "atypical" depressions; that is, those with hypersomnia, hyperphagia, mood swings, rejection sensitivity, and hypochondriasis.

The other major mood disorder is bipolar disorder (manic-depression) which consists of manic states with or without depressive episodes. Manic states are characterized by an elevated or irritable mood plus grandiosity; less need for sleep; loquacity; flight of ideas or tangential speech; distractibility; increased activity; and monetary, sexual, or other indiscretions.

Lithium is the treatment of choice and is effective in 70%–80% of cases. Its mechanism of action is not well understood. Patients typically have blood levels taken daily until lithium blood levels of 0.6–1.2 mEq/l are consistently reached. Often lithium is not completely adequate at first and a sedating medication, which can usually be stopped after 1–2 weeks, is added. The major side effects of lithium are tremors, polyuria, muscle weakness, anorexia, and gastrointestinal problems. Lithium can also induce hypothyroid disorders, conduction defects in the heart, and renal problems but these are rare. Lithium is not a tranquilizer and does not cause sedation. Dehydration with exercise, heat, or other medications, can cause lithium intoxication. Lithium overdoses can be fatal.

Bipolar disorder patients also have depressive episodes that are symptomatically similar to major depression. Although lithium can be used to treat this as well, usually an antidepressant is needed. Lithium is also used as a preventive; thus patients are usually maintained on lithium after their acute episode.

Whether other mood disorders (e.g., dysthymia [chronic depressed mood with fewer vegetative signs]) and organic affective disorders (e.g., from neurological disorders) are responsive to medication therapy is not well documented. Thus, in these disorders it must be decided whether the benefits of a medication trial outweighs its possible costs.

Psychopharmacological Treatment of Anxiety Disorders

Generalized anxiety disorder is characterized in *DSM-III-R* as unrealistic or excessive anxiety or worry accompanied by symptoms of motor tension (e.g., trembling, restlessness, or fatigue); autonomic hyperactivity (e.g., shortness of breath, dizziness, tachycardia, palpitations, tremor and sweating); and hypervigilance (e.g., easily startled, insomnia, difficulty concentrating). Benzodiazepines are quite effective in reducing this type of anxiety. Their mechanism of action appears to be due to interactions at the benzodiazepine/gamma-aminobutyric acid (GABA)/ chlorine (Cl) channel receptor. Prior to the benzodiazepines, barbiturates and other drugs (e.g., meprobamate) were used. Benzodiazepines are far superior to these drugs because benzodiazepines have less abuse potential and are unlikely to result in death in an overdose (unless combined with alcohol and other sedatives).

Benzodiazepines differ in their rate of absorption and elimination. Medications with rapid onset of effects (e.g., diazepam) are useful for quickly sedating patients; however, they are thought to have more abuse liability. Those with a rapid offset and shorter half-lives (e.g., alprazolam) are less likely to accumulate over time but are thought to have more potential to produce withdrawal when stopped. Those with longer half-lives (e.g., prazepam) are able to be used on a daily basis but have more potential for accumulation in the elderly and others unless the dose is appropriately adjusted. Typically, elderly patients require lower doses than do younger patients.

Sedation is the major acute side effect of benzodiazepine. Dizziness, ataxia (balance problems), amnesia, nausea, hypotension and changes in liver function are less common. Another side effect is physical dependence—tolerance and withdrawal. Although significant tolerance occurs in some patients, in most this is not a problem. Benzodiazepine withdrawal may include anxiety, insomnia, tremors, weakness, tachycardia, sweating, hypotension, perceptual disturbances, and, rarely, seizures or delirium. About 30%–50% of patients on benzodiazepine chronically will have significant withdrawal. Since withdrawal symptoms are similar to those of anxiety, it may be difficult to distinguish withdrawal from a return of the anxiety disorder being treated. In addition, a minority of patients cannot stop benzodiazepines despite several attempts, due in part to this withdrawal syndrome. Abuse (i.e., use of benzodiazepine for recreational purposes) is rare among patients unless they have a past history of alcohol or drug abuse.

Whether benzodiazepine should be prescribed chronically for generalized anxiety disorder is controversial. Most physicians try to stop benzodiazepine every so often to verify they are still necessary; however, due to withdrawal symptoms, this is often not accomplished.

Due to the side effects associated with long-term use, many clinicians will try psychological therapies for generalized anxiety disorder before considering benzodiazepines. Others believe the side effects of benzodiazepines are uncommon and cite compliance problems with psychotherapies and use benzodiazepine as a first-line therapy.

Several nonbenzodiazepine medications that have essentially no physical dependence or abuse potential have been tried. Beta-blockers (e.g., propranolol), tricyclic antidepressants, and clonidine are sometimes effective. A new drug, buspirone, may be a significant advance in this area as it appears to be an anxiolytic barren of the side effects mentioned in the previous paragraph. However, many clinicians believe buspirone is less effective than benzodiazepines.

Panic disorder consists of repeated episodes of unprovoked intense anxiety accompanied by autonomic symptoms (see generalized anxiety disorder in the previous paragraph) plus chest pain, fear of dying, et cetera. Tricyclic antidepressents are the mainstay of treatment for panic disorders. Alprazolam and MAO inhibitors have also been recommended but due to their side effect profiles, tricyclic antidepressants are often preferred. The mechanism of action for the tricyclic antidepressants and monoamine oxidase inhibitors in panic disorders is unclear.

Agoraphobia is a fear of being in situations in which it would be difficult to escape from or get help if one suddenly developed embarrassing or incapacitating symptoms. This fear results in a restriction of travel away from home. Panic attacks are often accompanied by agoraphobia but agoraphobia can occur in the absence of panic attacks. Tricyclic antidepressants are also first line medications in this disorder; however, behavioral and other psychological therapies are often effective.

In obsessive-compulsive disorders, obsessions are defined as recurrent, intrusive and senseless thoughts (which are often fears) and compulsions as repetitive behaviors in response to the obsessions (often rituals to neutralize a feared event). Tricyclic antidepressants are also effective in treating obsessive-compulsive disorders; however, unlike other disorders, a single tricyclic antidepressant, clomipramine, appears to be more effective than others. The mechanism of action for clomipramine is unclear.

Pharmacotherapies for other anxiety disorders (e.g., post-traumatic stress disorder and social phobias) have been tested with varying degrees of success.

Symptomatic Treatment

A second indication for psychoactive medication is based on symptom relief. Symptomatic treatment is sometimes thought of as being less scientifically-based or less efficacious; however, several symptomatic treatments have well-documented efficacy. One common, well-accepted symptomatic use is antipsychotic medications for the psychotic behavior that accompanies delirium, bipolar disorder, depression and drug intoxication.

Another important, well-proven symptomatic use is benzodiazepines for insomnia; however, this use is controversial for two reasons. First, effective psychological interventions for insomnia are available. Second, some patients use the benzodiazepine for prolonged periods, become dependent on benzodiazepine to sleep, and develop a rebound worsening of insomnia upon cessation of the benzodiazepines.

A third common symptomatic use is benzodiazepine for situational anxiety. As with insomnia, benzodiazepines appear effective for this problem, but there is concern about dependence and withdrawal if patients use benzodiazepines for a prolonged period.

One common reason for using medications based on symptoms is an unclear diagnosis. For example, if both psychotic and affective symptoms are present and the diagnosis is unclear, a trial with an antidepressant may occur in hopes the patient will not require an antipsychotic (due to the adverse effects of antipsychotics).

Another reason for symptomatic treatment is our lack of diagnostic or therapeutic knowledge in some areas. For example, how to best diagnosis and treat aggression in the absence of a clear diagnosis is unclear. In these grey areas, two types of evidence are used by clinicians to decide on possible pharmacotherapies. The first is scientific evidence (e.g., open, nonrandomized trials) that a psychoactive medication might be helpful. The second is a logical extension of the knowledge of the mechanism of certain medications (e.g., carbamzepine prevents sub-seizure "kindling" and some aggressive episodes have been linked with such kindling). Optimally, psychoactive medication use in this situation is seen as a "therapeutic trial" in which the clinician quantitatively assesses symptom and functional improvement as well as the possible side effects before giving the drug, during drug therapy, and then after the drug therapy has been stopped. Such information can satisfy the patient and clinician that such treatment is working.

A final use of symptomatic treatment is construed by some to be a "fishing expedition." This occurs when a patient or clinician is unwilling to confront the fact that for some conditions or symptoms, there is no good pharmacological treatment. This has three hazards. First, patients are placed at risk for side effects in the absence of any significant prospect of benefit. Second, it might encourage patients to continue to avoid undertaking a psychological treatment. Third, since many behavioral disorders run a time-limited course, if remission occurs while the patient is using an ineffective medication, the patient and clinician may falsely conclude that the medication caused the remission.

Preventive Treatment

As discussed in the previous sections, the three major prophylactic medications are antipsychotics for schizophrenia, antidepressants for major depression, and lithium for bipolar disorder and recurrent major depression. Although the term "preventive" is often used, these medications do not prevent these disorders but rather decrease the probability of a disorder recurring (i.e., increase the time between episodes of the disorder or decrease the number of episodes in a lifetime). Sometimes such preventive treatment appears to be suppressive therapy in that when the preventive medication is tapered, the patient's symptoms quickly return.

Epistemology of Clinicians' and Patients' Beliefs about Psychoactive Medications

Several nonscientific factors may play a role in decisions on whether to use medications or psychotherapy. One possible factor is that both patients and clinicians have biases for or against psychological or pharmacological treatments based on training, clinical experiences or general philosophical grounds. Sometimes a prior experience of the patient or his or her relative or friend (e.g., a failure to respond to a medication) will be the major basis for this belief. It is important to elicit patient beliefs and deal with them early on in the decision to use or not to use psychoactive medication (Bassuk et al., 1990; Beitman & Klerman, 1991; Gorman, 1990; Hersen, 1986; Lawson & Cooperrider, 1988).

Biases that might encourage patients to use medication and avoid psychological treatments include ease of treatment, desire for immediate symptom relief, avoidance of making tough or emotionally taxing decisions, avoiding responsibility for one's problems, and fear of loss of control of emotions in psychotherapy. Biases that might encourage avoiding medications and using psychological treatment include a history of medication sensitivity, fear of side effects, fear of delegating emotional control to medications, reluctance to attribute the problem to biological factors and avoidance of labeling the problem as a psychiatric disorder.

There are at least four instances in which, in the opinion of most psychiatrists, it is critical to refer a patient for evaluation for possible psychoactive medication:

1. acute psychosis,
2. mania,
3. alcohol or sedative withdrawal with a history of delirium or seizures, and
4. depression with significant "neurovegetative" symptoms (psychomotor retardation, terminal insomnia, etc.) which are unresponsive to psychotherapy.

Among the first three of these conditions, there is good evidence that medications are helpful, but well-documented evidence that psychological treatments are helpful is not available. In regard to the last situation, one psychiatrist was recently sued for not instituting pharmacotherapy in a severely depressed patient unresponsive to psychotherapy (Klerman, 1990; Stone, 1990).

The four indications in the prior paragraph should not be construed as a list of the only times medications should be considered. Unfortunately, one cannot depend solely on the Food and Drug Administration's (FDA) list of indications included in the *Prescription Drug Reference* (PDR) (Barnhart, 1991). This list of indications is conservative to protect against careless use. Better sources are the American Medical Association's (AMA) *Drug Evaluations* (1991) or the American Psychiatric Association's *Treatment of Psychiatric Disorders: A Task Force Report of the APA* (1989). However, these texts cannot cover all the possible situations that might occur; thus, it is as difficult to second-guess the appropriateness of pharmacotherapy in a given case as to second-guess the appropriateness of certain psychotherapeutic techniques.

In summary, a patient should be prescribed a medication for a defined psychiatric disorder, for a clear target symptom or for the prevention of a recurrence of a disorder. There are several disorders in which failure to consider medications might be questioned. Psychologists should be aware of the reasoning that patients and clinicians use in deciding on the use of psychoactive medications.

Principles in the Rational Use of Psychoactive Medications

Choice of Medications

Usually medications are chosen by pharmacological class. As described previously, despite the advertisements of pharmaceutical companies, medications within a pharmacological class usually have similar efficacy. The history of most psychoactive medications has been one of claims of therapeutic superiority, followed by a reactionary scapegoating of the medication, followed finally by a more reasonable evaluation of the appropriate indications and realistic benefits and liabilities of the new medication as compared to existing medications. Prescribing practices often follow a similar trajectory. For example, benzodiazpines were first enthusiastically prescribed, then avoided as extremely dangerous, and are now used judiciously.

Since efficacy is typically similar within a class, specific medications are usually chosen for other reasons. First and foremost, medications within a class can vary in side effect profiles. For example, some antidepressants are sedating and others stimulating. When taken at night, the former might be helpful to depressed patients with insomnia whereas when taken during the day, the latter might be more helpful to those who are apathetic or retarded.

Second, psychoactive medications vary by how quickly they are taken up by the blood system and how long effective blood levels are maintained. For example, a benzodiazepine with a long half-life may be preferred so that a patient will have to take the medication only once a day whereas a benzodiazepine with a short half-life may be preferred in an elderly person who might accumulate the drug over time.

Third, sometimes psychoactive medications are chosen because the patient has responded to the medication before or even because a close family member with a similar disorder has responded to the medication.

Fourth, psychoactive medications vary in route of administration. Liquid medication is used sometimes in noncompliant or elderly patients to insure the medication is delivered. Long-acting injectable medication (i.e., one injection every 2–4 weeks) is sometimes used in patients with schizophrenia as they are often noncompliant to oral medication regimens.

Fifth, generic medications are often prescribed. Psychoactive medications have a generic name (the name of the chemical) and a trade (i.e., brand) name. When a pharmaceutical company develops a medication, through patent laws it has sole rights to market the medication for up to 17 years since its discovery. Once this patent expires other pharmaceutical companies can market the chemical equivalent of the drug (i.e., a generic). Although the substitutability of generics is controversial and may vary across types of medications (Strom, 1987), our opinion is that for the large majority of psychoactive medications, generic substitutes are acceptable.

Sixth, combination products (i.e., two medications in one tablet) are typically not chosen as this limits flexibility in dosing and confuses decisions as to which medication to attribute improvement.

Choice of Dose and Schedule

The effects of medications vary by dose, preparation, and other factors. Choosing the right psychoactive medicine but the wrong dose can be equivalent to choosing the wrong medication. In fact, it may be worse, in that an effective medicine is falsely deemed ineffective. This is not unlike stating that the effect of psychological interventions vary by their intensity and duration and that poorly administered psychotherapies can be falsely deemed ineffective.

The effective dose differs greatly across patients. Dose-response relationships often show an inverted U shaped pattern—at doses below a certain level little effect is seen, at moderate levels efficacy is seen, and at high levels side effects interfere with efficacy. Unfortunately, both the relationship between dose and blood levels and between blood levels and response varies widely across individuals. Blood levels from a given dose of medication often vary 10-fold across individuals (Glassman et al., 1985). These differences can be due to differences in the rate of absorption, distribution among body compartments (e.g., fat vs muscle vs organs), protein binding in the blood, metabolism by the liver, and elimination by the kidney. Thus, the existence of certain medical disorders (e.g., liver or kidney disease) can have a profound effect on absorption and elimination. Use of other substances (e.g., cigarette smoking, caffeine) and other medications (e.g., barbiturates) can increase the elimination of several medications such that a patient using these substances will require higher doses. Response to a given dose of a drug is especially idiosyncratic in several populations, including the elderly, the mentally retarded, those with neurological disease, alcohol/drug abusers, and children.

Doses cited in texts should not be taken as rigid standards. These are the doses the "average" patient will require; thus, many patients will require larger or smaller doses than listed. Effective doses of the same medication vary 20-fold across patients. Because many patients and nonphysicians rely on the *PDR*, the *PDR* usually lists conservative dose recommendations and ranges. Effective doses also vary 50-fold across medications within a class. For example, among antipsychotics, 2 mg of haloperidol is similar in effect to 100 mg of chlorpromazine. Patients often think the medication with the higher numerical dose is more toxic and should be avoided. In reality, the relative potency of medications often has little correlation with efficacy or toxicity.

For several medications (e.g., antidepressants and antipsychotics), small doses are prescribed initially and then slowly raised until therapeutic effects or side effects are seen. Sometimes doses are given multiple times per day early on and then switched to single daily dosing. The final dose may be as much as 10 times greater than the initial dose. This dose-titration procedure can be prolonged since the effects of a given dose may not be evident for 2–4 weeks after each dose change.

In contrast, some psychiatric medications (e.g., lithium) are given on a fixed time schedule (e.g., twice a day) and others (e.g., benzodiazepines) are sometimes given ad-libitum (for example, when the patient needs some relief). Interestingly, although ad-libitum dosing is effective with acute dosing, chronic dosing of benzodiazepines and narcotic analgesics may be more effective with fixed-time dosing than with ad-libitum dosing and may be less likely to lead to prescription misuse.

The utility of blood levels of medications varies widely across medications. For example, lithium levels are necessary for its use, whereas the benefits of antidepressant blood levels are more limited (Glassman et al., 1985). At the very least, blood levels can often help determine whether toxic doses are being given and if the patient is taking at least some of the medication.

A common mistake is to use too small a dose for too short a time. For example, many psychiatrists would consider anything short of 4 weeks of an antidepressant at the maximal tolerable dose an inadequate trial. Unfortunately, inadequate treatment is often cited as evidence that a patient will not benefit from a class of medications; thus, falsely denying the patient a possible treatment. A second common mistake is to change doses too quickly. Although some symptoms respond quickly to medication (e.g., acute anxiety), other symptoms have a 2–4 week delay before efficacy is clearly seen (e.g., psychotic and depressive symptoms). A third mistake is to change more than one parameter at a time; for example, lowering the dose of medication and discharging the patient from the hospital the next day.

Whenever possible, medications should be given once daily to improve compliance (Haynes, Taylor, & Sackett, 1979). Medications that are sedating are usually given at night whereas those with stimulant effects are given early in the day. Usually only enough medication to last until the next visit is given in hopes of reinforcing returning for the next visit or preventing prolonged use without appropriate monitoring.

Small amounts of medication (e.g., 1 week supply) are usually given to patients with suicidal ideation or alcohol/drug abuse problems in case the patient attempts to overdose.

Medications are sometimes stopped to determine if the medication is effective or because the period of high risk of relapse has passed. When stopping the use of a medication, it is usually tapered by decreasing the dose over several weeks. This is done for three reasons. First, relapses may occur soon after cessation; thus with a gradual taper, the onset of early symptoms can be detected and medication reinstituted prior to a full-blown relapse. Second, many patients are fearful of stopping medication. A taper is, in effect, a fading procedure for these patients. Third, abrupt cessation can cause withdrawal symptoms.

Withdrawal has traditionally been thought to occur only with dependence-producing drugs; however, as described above, abrupt cessation of several psychiatric drugs that are not abused (e.g., antipsychotics and antidepressants) can lead to a withdrawal syndrome (Dilsaver, 1990). This is probably due to receptor changes responsive to chronic exposure to medication (see Johanson, this volume). Medications are essentially removed after five half-lives. A common misperception is that the absence of blood levels of a substance means the absence of any drug effects. However, changes in CNS receptor activity may take longer.

Patients ultimately determine the dose and duration of treatment. Compliance with nonpsychiatric medications is poor (Haynes et al., 1979). Compliance with psychoactive medications is especially problematic due in part to significant side effects from the medication. In addition, some psychiatric patients exhibit disorganized thinking, chaotic lifestyles, denial of having a disorder, denial that medication is needed, social reinforcement of illness behavior, anger at physician or others, and so on. Thus, when treatment fails, noncompliance is one of the first issues to investigate. Techniques to improve compliance have been outlined elsewhere (Haynes et al., 1979). Techniques that are sometimes helpful with psychiatric patients include long-acting injections of medications, home visits, and use of day hospitals or half-way houses.

Monitoring Medication Effects

In most of medicine, the effects of a medication are readily quantifiable (e.g., physical or laboratory changes). With psychoactive medications, the effects of medications can be harder to quantify. In addition, psychoactive medications often take 2–4 weeks to produce their main effects; thus, poor memory can induce clinicians to under- or overestimate the severity of the disorder initially and thus over- or underestimate the efficacy of the psychoactive medication. Thus, it is best to clearly define target symptoms to be helped by the medications and to quantify these either through standardized rating scales or, when possible, operational definitions (Hughes, O'Hara, & Rehm, 1982). Many times significant others can provide such simple ratings. Also, therapists can complete structured interview ratings at the outset of sessions.

Side Effects

Side effects occur because few medications are so specific that they do not affect several biological systems. Alternatively, even site-specific medications have diverse effects because specific neurochemical systems influence many forms of behavior.

The use of psychoactive medications is a benefit/risk decision that should include consideration of not only the probability, magnitude, and fidelity of benefit but also the probability, seriousness, and reversibility of side effects. Sometimes psychoactive medications with significant side effects are chosen because alternate treatments are not available and the effect of not treating is likely to be quite detrimental. Informing patients of common or significant potential side effects is critical, and a reasoned discussion of these may ameliorate anxiety about the medications and improve compliance.

The side effects of many psychoactive medications often precede therapeutic effects. Most of the side effects common among psychoactive medications have been described in a previous section. Sedation is an especially common side effect that is potentiated by pre-existing insomnia, alcohol use, and the use of other psychoactive prescription, over-the-counter, or illicit drugs. Prescribers typically warn patients to take care while driving and operating machinery and to abstain from or moderate use of alcohol.

Regulatory agencies require a listing of all side effects in package inserts and the *PDR*. Such lists are quite long because the criteria for calling a symptom a side effect are minimal (i.e., a physician notices a symptom after starting the medication). In fact, none of the standard criteria for assessing causality are necessary: for example, the symptom reoccurs upon rechallenge, the side effect fits with the pharmacological profile of the medication, and so on. In summary, the laundry lists of side effects in the package insert and *PDR* are more useful as a list of possible side effects.

Sometimes side effects can be confused with symptoms of the disorder. For example, the restlessness caused by antipsychotics can be confused with the agitation associated with a worsening of schizophrenia. Side effects can also result from medication interactions (e.g., the use of a diuretic can increase lithium levels and cause lithium intoxication symptoms). A common cause of side effects is intermittent compliance. Patients who stop a medication for 2–3 days or more may reexperience side effects upon restarting the medication. In fact, astute clinicians use recurrent side effects as an index of suspicion of non-compliance.

There are four approaches to treating initial side effects. First, most side effects abate with time due to tolerance; thus, and a common response is to simply wait and see if the side effects abate. Second, side effect profiles differ within a class of medications; thus, one could switch to a different medication. Third, because side effects are usually dose related, one can decrease the dose; however, this also may delay or prevent efficacy. A fourth option is to prescribe a medication to treat the side effects (e.g., antiparkinson medications for extrapyramidal symptoms from antipsychotics). Although this latter option leads to polypharmacy, sometimes the need for treatment is great enough and the options limited such that the addition of an extra medication is justified.

Side effects differ from allergic and toxic effects. Side effects usually occur early in therapy, are dose related, and decrease over time. Allergic effects (e.g., rashes) usually occur at very low doses, are not dose related, and tolerance does not occur. Toxic effects usually occur when medication accumulates over time, when too large a dose is given, or with patient-induced overdoses.

Dependence on or abuse of medication is a side-effect about which much confusion exists. Definitions of the terms *abuse* and *dependence* have varied, however, there is some growing consensus (American Psychiatric Association, 1987; Edwards, Arif, & Hodgsen, 1981).

Abuse, which may exist independent of dependence, is usually defined as continuing drug use despite having social or psychological problems from drug use. Dependence can be defined in two ways. The more common way focuses on loss of control of drug use; that is, the drug is used more than was intended, the client is unable to stop using the drug, et cetera. For our purposes we will call this *behavioral dependence*. A second definition focuses on the onset of withdrawal symptoms upon cessation. Tolerance is usually associated with withdrawal and refers to a diminished effect of the drug with repeated dosing. For our purposes, we will call this *physical dependence*.

The probability of abuse and dependence varies greatly across medications. For a given medication, psychiatric patients appear to have a greater probability of abuse and behavioral dependence than general medical patients (Regier et al., 1990; Schneier & Siris, 1987). However, the major factor in predicting abuse and behavioral dependence of prescribed psychoactive medication is a present or past history of alcohol/drug abuse (Portenoy, 1990). In fact, abuse or behavioral dependence on prescribed medication in the absence of such a history is extremely rare.

As discussed in the prior paragraphs, abrupt cessation of several psychoactive medications can induce withdrawal (Dilsaver, 1990). Withdrawal is not the only discontinuation syndrome, and it must be distinguished from rebound symptoms and symptoms indicating a return of the disorder being treated (Pecknold, Swinson, Kuch, & Lewis, 1988). Clinically these distinctions can be quite difficult. For example, consider insomnia after cessation of benzodiazepines. Whether this represents withdrawal, rebound, or reemergence of an anxiety disorder is often unclear. Often only abstaining from benzodiazepines for 4 – 6 weeks can clarify the picture. Unfortunately, this is uncomfortable, difficult and unachievable in many patients. In considering withdrawal, it is important to distinguish the withdrawal from medications that may prompt patients to restart medication (e.g., benzodiazepines) from the withdrawal from other medications that rarely cause patients to restart medication (e.g., antipsychotics).

Although abuse, behavioral dependence, and physical dependence often co-exist with illicit drugs, this is often not the case with prescribed psychoactive medications. To illustrate the possible combinations of abuse and dependence, consider the following scenarios. First, a patient with a past history of drug abuse uses benzodiazepines intermittently, often gets into trouble while intoxicated, but can start and stop such use easily and without withdrawal. This is abuse without behavioral or physical dependence. Second, a patient has been using benzodiazepines for 5 years without any problems, has tried to stop in the past and had no significant withdrawal, but cannot seem to stop benzodiazepine use. This is behavioral dependence without abuse or physical dependence. Third, a patient has been using an antidepressant without problems, is asked by the physician to stop it, has withdrawal but successfully stops. This is physical dependence without abuse or behavioral dependence.

Use of Medication in Special Populations

The diagnosis and treatment of behavioral disorders among children is difficult given (a) the scientific database is small, and (b) there is little data on whether the classic symptom clusters of psychiatric disorders match those of adults (Campbell & Spencer, 1988). However, despite these problems, there is good scientific evidence for the utility of certain psychoactive medications in certain disorders (e.g., stimulants in attention deficit disorder; Kavale, 1982; Rapport, 1984).

One concern with medications in children is that the medication may impede growth, learning, or social development during critical developmental times and, thus, cause what may be irreversible effects. The actual data on this issue is quite mixed (Rapport, 1984). In addition, the very real possibility that the disorder itself is impeding learning and social development is often not considered. Another concern is use of medication leading to illicit drug abuse. Interestingly, this is very rare.

Psychoactive medication is usually used in children when behavioral or psychotherapeutic programs fail. Noncompliance with psychological treatments by children or parents or a lack of resources to implement such treatments often occur. Thus, it is often difficult to decide when to stop trying psychological treatments and add medications.

In children, dosing is often based on body weight. Even so, children vary widely in neurological and intellectual development; thus, idiosyncratic responses are common. In addition, doses for behavioral control and cognitive improvement of children may diverge. For example, low doses of amphetamine improve intellectual performance but not hyperactivity while higher doses of amphetamine improve hyperactivity but worsen intellectual performance (Sprague & Sleator, 1977). Thus, identification of the optimal dose for combined effects is especially important. Finally, "medication holidays" are often used in children to determine if continued medication use is necessary.

Many of the same issues apply to the use of psychoactive medications in the mentally retarded; for example, a poor database, symptom manifestations that may differ from nonretarded adults, noncompliance, and lack of resources for psychological treatments (Aman & Singh, 1988). On the one hand, the mentally retarded often have severe and difficult-to-treat problems, such as self-injurious behavior and physical aggression and failures to respond to behavioral programs do occur. On the other hand, the mentally retarded are at greater risk of developing tardive dyskinesia and other complications (Cummings & Wirshing, 1989). As a result many states have regulations about the indications for and monitoring of medication in the mentally retarded (Rinck, Guidry, & Calkins, 1989).

Mental disorders among the elderly are more difficult to treat with psychoactive medications for several reasons (Jenike, 1989). Physiological changes with aging influence the absorption, binding, distribution, metabolism, and elimination of medications. Many elderly are on several medications, thus increasing the probability of drug interactions. Finally, some elderly have mild symptoms of dementia thereby increasing the probability of noncompliance. All of these can not only impair efficacy but also increase the possibility of side effects. Dosing is usually done cautiously, beginning with very low doses as the elderly often need only half the dose of middle-aged adults.

Women on psychoactive medication may become pregnant (Cohen, Heller, & Rosenbaum, 1989). A clinician should keep this possibility in mind. Almost all psychoactive medications cross the placenta to expose the fetus and are also present in breast milk. Psychoactive medications may cause malformations and perinatal complications (e.g., early delivery). Less well recognized is the possibility that such medications may produce learning and other behavioral deficits in offspring. Thus, when possible, psychoactive medications are discontinued during pregnancy. If continued, the doses of psychoactive medications may be decreased to decrease fetal risk and any resultant increased symptomatology accepted. Two issues arise in stopping or decreasing psychoactive medications during pregnancy. The first is that some patients cannot provide adequate prenatal and self-care without medication and will need to continue medication. The second is that withdrawal effects from too rapid a reduction of medication might harm the fetus.

Legal Issues

Many states have laws regulating the right to refuse psychoactive medication. Much of the confusion around this issue is whether commitment to a facility implies the right to force medications. Usually danger to self or others are the criteria for both commitment and forcing medication (Appelbaum, 1988; Rinck et al., 1989). There is no legal precedent or tradition to determine when written informed consent should be obtained prior to prescribing a psychotropic drug. Two situations in which informed consent has been recommended include the use of a medication for a disorder not formally approved by the FDA, and the long-term use of antipsychotics (due to the risk of tardive dyskinesia). This latter situation is complicated by the fact that many persons who begin antipsychotics are not able to give true informed consent. However, consent can be sought when delusions and other symptoms have cleared enough to indicate informed consent can be given.

The Drug Enforcement Agency (DEA) regulates medications determined to have significant abuse liability and physicians must have a license from the DEA to prescribe such medications. Several states have introduced triplicate prescription pads for some of these medications. With these pads, a copy of all prescriptions are sent to the state agency responsible for drug abuse litigation. Triplicate prescription systems are intended to make physicians give serious review and consideration before writing prescriptions for these medications. Triplicate plans do decrease prescriptions (Sigler et al., 1984). The debate is whether this is a decrease in inappropriate use of these medications or a decrease in appropriate use of these medications with the result of patients being denied adequate pain relief or other symptom alleviation (Street, 1991).

Pharmacological and Psychological Therapies

Whether psychoactive medication and psychotherapy are combined varies widely across disorders (Hollon & Beck, 1987; Hughes, 1991; Klerman, 1989; Rounsaville, Klerman, & Weissman, 1981). Combined treatment improves outcome beyond either treatment alone in several disorders (i.e., anxiety disorders, depression, nicotine dependence, and schizophrenia). In some disorders, such as schizophrenia and severe depression, pharmacotherapy appears to be essential. For other disorders, psychological treatment appears to be essential (e.g., alcohol dependence).

Relative Utility of Pharmacological Versus Psychological Therapies

Several articles have compared the efficacy of psychoactive medication to psychological treatments for anxiety, depression, and other disorders (Hollon & Beck, 1987). However, efficacy is but one criterion to compare treatments. Other important factors are target outcome, acceptability, availability, safety, universality, and cost-effectiveness (Hollon & Beck, 1987). The utility of a treatment is often determined not by efficacy but by its acceptability and availability. An effective treatment that is not acceptable to many patients (e.g., a medication that has a strong negative impact on sexual desires) or a therapy that is not readily available (e.g., psychotherapists in rural areas) is not very useful.

In terms of target outcome, pharmacological therapy often uses symptom relief as a criterion of success whereas psychological treatments often use functional criteria (e.g., return to work, etc.). Pharmacotherapy often assumes that symptom relief removes a barrier to functional improvement. Whether this assumption is true probably varies across disorders and patients with the same disorder. There are no sound data on this issue.

Collaboration With Physicians

Recent surveys indicate that many psychotherapy patients are being simultaneously treated by a physician and a psychologist (Beitman, 1991). Psychologists should ask about the psychoactive medication their patients are receiving. Some basic information that a psychologist should have about a patient's medication is listed below.

1. What medication (brand name and generic name) is being used.
2. Which *DSM* disorder or target symptom is being treated.
3. Whether the medication is being used for a diagnosis, for symptom relief, or for prevention.
4. What the expected dose and duration of treatment is.
5. When the medication should begin to work.
6. When and how the patient is to take the medication.
7. How long the patient is to take the medication.
8. What the patient is to do if a dose of medicine is missed.
9. What are the possible side effects of the medication and what should the patient do about them.

10. What are the medication's possible effects on the patient's driving, work, and other activities and what precautions are to be taken.
11. How the medication interacts with alcohol and other drugs.
12. What are the alternative plans if this medication trial fails.

Although patients should know this information, many times physicians fail to make this information clear. Also, existing biases in patients may result in misinterpretation of such information. For example, consider the possible attitudes toward medications of patients with antisocial, anxiety, compulsive, dependent, and paranoid disorders. In addition, patients are sometimes ashamed about taking psychoactive medication and do not readily inform psychologists about medication use. In some cases this may result from lack of acceptance or lack of understanding of the importance of medications by therapists themselves (psychologists and psychiatrists).

Coordinating treatments between physicians and psychologists requires attention and vigilance (Beitman, 1991; Beitman & Klerman, 1991; Ellison, 1989; Gitlin, 1990; Goldenberg, 1990; Guttmacher, 1988; Lader & Herrington, 1990; Lawson & Cooperrider, 1988). Several procedural details need to be explicitly agreed upon: who does the patient call when symptoms worsen or suicidal thoughts occur, how are joint decisions made, and so forth. Finally, some patients are keen to attribute their problem to either a biological cause or a behavior over which they have no control. If physicians and psychologists are not concordant on their view of the problem, the patient can affiliate with the therapist most sympathetic to his or her cause, use one therapist against the other, and not comply with the alternate therapy.

Summary

A knowledge of pharmacotherapy is more than simply knowing the diagnostic schema, the indications for psychoactive medications and the recommended doses. Pharmacotherapy, no less than psychotherapy, is a complex field where those practitioners who read the literature, see patients, and constantly question their own practices become experts.

The present chapter is written with the hope that the debate over prescription privileges will cause the interaction between the professions of medicine and psychology to increase. This chapter is also written with the bias that the quality of such interactions increases as psychologists and psychiatrists learn more about each other's practices.

References

Aman, M. G., & Singh, N. N. (1988). *Psychopharmacology of the developmental disabilities*. New York: Springer-Verlag.

American Medical Association Drug Evaluations. (1991). Littleton, MA: Sciences Group.

American Psychiatric Association. (1987). *Diagnostic and statistical manual of mental disorders* (rev. 3rd ed.). Washington, DC: Author.

American Psychiatric Association. (1989). *Treatment of psychiatric disorders: A task force report of the American Psychiatric Association*. Washington, DC: Author.

Appelbaum, P. S. (1988). The right to refuse treatment with antipsychotic medications: Retrospect and prospect. *American Journal of Psychiatry, 145*, 413–419.

Baldessarini, R. (1985). *Chemotherapy in psychiatry*. Cambridge, MA: Harvard University Press.

Barnhart, E. R. (1991). *Physicians' Desk Reference*. Oradell, NJ: Medical Economics Data.

Bassuk, E. L., Schoonover, S. C., & Gelenberg, A. J. (1990). *The practitioner's guide to psychoactive drugs*. New York: Plenum Publishing Corporation.

Beitman, B. D. (1991). Medications during psychotherapy: Case studies of the reciprocal relationship between psychotherapy process and medication use. In B. D. Beitman & G. L. Klerman (Eds.), *Integrating pharmacotherapy and psychotherapy* (pp. 21–44). Washington, DC: American Psychiatric Press.

Beitman, B. D., & Klerman, G. L. (1991). *Integrating pharmacotherapy and psychotherapy*. Washington, DC: American Psychiatric Press.

Campbell, M., & Spencer, E. K. (1988). Psychopharmacology in child and adolescent psychiatry: A review of the past five years. *Journal of the American Academy of Child and Adolescent Psychiatry, 27*, 269–279.

Cohen, L. S., Heller, V. L., & Rosenbaum, J. F. (1989). Treatment guidelines for psychotropic drug use in pregnancy. *Psychosomatics, 30*, 25–33.

Cummings, J. L., & Wirshing, W. C. (1989). Recognition and differential diagnosis of tardive dyskinesia. *International Journal of Psychiatry in Medicine, 19*, 133–144.

Dilsaver, S. T. (1990). Heterocyclic antidepressant, monoamine oxidase inhibitor, and neuroleptic withdrawal phenomena. *Progress in Neuro-Psychopharmacology & Biological Psychiatry, 14*, 137–161.

Edwards, G., Arif, A., & Hodgsen, R. (1981). Nomenclature and classification of drug and alcohol-related problems: A WHO memorandum. *Bulletin of the World Health Organization, 59*, 225–242.

Ellison, J. M. (1989). *The psychotherapist's guide to pharmacotherapy*. Chicago: Year Book Medical Publishers.

Fisher, S., & Greenberg, R. P. (1989). *The limits of biological treatments for psychological distress: Comparisions with psychotherapy and placebos*. Hillsdale, NJ: Erlbaum.

Gitlin, M. J. (1990). *The psychotherapist's guide to psychopharmacology*. New York: Maxwell Macmillan International.

Glassman, A. H., Schildkraut, J. J., Orsulak, P. J., et al. (1985). Tricyclic antidepressants—Blood level measurements and clinical outcome: An APA Task Force report. *American Journal of Psychiatry, 142*, 155–162.

Goldenberg, M. M. (1990). *Pharmacology for the psychotherapist*. Muncie, IN: Accelerated Development.

Gorman, J. M. (1990). *The essential guide to psychiatric drugs*. New York: St. Martin's Press.

Guttmacher, L. B. (1988). *Concise guide to somatic therapies in psychiatry*. Washington, DC: American Psychiatric Press.

Haynes, R. B., Taylor, D. W., & Sackett, D. L. (1979). *Compliance in health care*. Baltimore: Johns Hopkins University Press.

Hersen, M. (1986). *Pharmacological and behavioral treatment: An integrative approach*. New York: Wiley.

Hollon, S. D., & Beck, A. T. (1987). Psychotherapy and drug therapy: Comparisons and combinations. In S. L. Garfield & A. E. Bergin (Eds.), *Handbook of psychotherapy and behavior change* (pp. 437–490). New York: Wiley.

Hughes, J. R. (1991). Combining psychological and pharmacological treatment for smoking. *Journal of Substance Abuse, 3*, 337–350.

Hughes, J. R., O'Hara, M. W., & Rehm, L. P. (1982). Measurement of depression in clinical trials: A critical overview. *Journal of Clinical Psychiatry, 43*, 85–88.

Jenike, M. A. (1989). *Geriatric psychiatry and psychopharmacology*. Chicago: Yearbook Medical Publisher.

Julien, R. M. (1988). *A primer of drug action* (5th ed.). San Francisco: Freeman.

Kavale, K. (1982). The efficacy of stimulant drug treatment for hyperactivity: A meta-analysis. *Journal of Learning Disabilities, 15*, 280–289.

Klein, D. F., Gittelman, R., Quitkin, F., & Rifkin, A. (1980). *Diagnosis and drug treatment of psychiatric disorders: Adults and children*. Baltimore: Williams & Wilkins.

Klerman, G. L. (1989). Drugs and psychotherapy. In S. L. Garfield & A. E. Bergin (Eds.), *Handbook of psychotherapy and behavior change: An empirical analysis* (pp. 777–818). New York: Wiley.

Klerman, G. L. (1990). The psychiatric patient's right to effective treatment: Implications of Osheroff v. Chestnut Lodge. *American Journal of Psychiatry, 147*, 409–418.

Lader, M., & Herrington, R. (1990). *Biological treatments in psychiatry*. New York: Oxford University Press.

Lawson, G. W., & Cooperrider, C. A. (1988). *Clinical psychopharmacology: A practical reference for nonmedical psychotherapists*. Rockville, MD: Aspen Publishers, Inc.

Pecknold, J. C., Swinson, R. P., Kuch, K., & Lewis, C. P. (1988). Alprazolam in panic disorder and agoraphobia: Results from a multicenter trial. *Archives of General Psychiatry, 45*, 429–436.

Portenoy, R. K. (1990). Chronic opioid therapy in nonmalignant pain. *Journal of Pain and Symptom Management, 5*, S46–S62.

Preston, J., & Johnson, J. (1990). *Clinical psychopharmacology made ridiculously simple*. Miami, FL: MedMaster.

Rapport, M. D. (1984). Hyperactivity and stimulant treatment: Abusus non tollit usum. *The Behavior Therapist, 7*, 133–134.

Regier, D. A., Farmer, M. E., Rae, D. S., Locke, B. Z., Keith, S. J., Judd, L. L., & Goodwin, F. K. (1990). Comorbidity of mental disorders with alcohol and other drug abuse. *Journal of the American Medical Association, 264*, 2511–2518.

Rinck, C., Guidry, J., & Calkins, C. F. (1989). Review of states' practices on the use of psychotropic medication. *American Journal on Mental Retardation, 93*, 657–668.

Rounsaville, B. J., Klerman, G. L., & Weissman, M. W. (1981). Do psychotherapy and pharmacotherapy for depression conflict? *Archives of General Psychiatry, 38*, 24–29.

Schneier, F. R., & Siris, S. G. (1987). A review of psychoactive substance use and abuse in schizophrenia: Patterns of drug choice. *The Journal of Nervous and Mental Disease, 175*, 641–652.

Shader, R. I. (1975). *Manual of psychiatric therapeutics.* Boston: Little, Brown.

Sigler, K. A., Guernsey, B. G., Ingrim, N. B., et al. (1984). Effect of a triplicate prescription law on prescribing of Schedule II drugs. *American Journal of Hospital Pharmacy, 41*, 108–111.

Sprague, R. L., & Sleator, E. K. (1977). Methylphenidate in hyperkinetic children: Differences in dose effects on learning and social behavior. *Science, 198*, 1274–1276.

Stone, A. A. (1990). Law, science, and psychiatric malpractice: A response to Klerman's indictment of psychoanalytic psychiatry. *American Journal of Psychiatry, 147*, 419–427.

Street, J. P. (1991). Multiple prescription forms don't stop diversion. *American Druggist.*

Strom, B. L. (1987) Generic drug substitution revisited. *New England Journal of Medicine, 316*, 1456–1462.

SUBSTANCE ABUSE: IMPLICATIONS OF A BIOPSYCHOSOCIAL MODEL FOR PREVENTION, TREATMENT, AND RELAPSE PREVENTION

G. Alan Marlatt is currently a professor of psychology and the Director of the Addictive Behaviors Research Center at the University of Washington. He received his PhD in clinical psychology from Indiana University in 1968 and served a clinical internship at Napa State Hospital in California (1967–1968). After serving on the faculties of the University of British Columbia (1968–1969) and the University of Wisconsin (1969–1972), he joined the University of Washington faculty in the fall of 1972.

His major focus in both research and clinical work is the field of addictive behaviors. Professor Marlatt has conducted basic research on cognitive-behavioral factors in addiction, including expectancies for alcohol and drug effects (research using the balanced–placebo design), social facilitation of alcohol use, and the role of stress and coping in substance use. His applied research has focused on the effectiveness of relapse prevention and other self-management strategies in the prevention and treatment of addictive behavior problems, including alcohol dependence, nicotine addiction, and sexual paraphilias (e.g., pedophilia). His most recent work has investigated the "harm reduction" approach to reducing the risk of alcohol problems in young adults (including high-risk college students and Native American youth).

In addition to over 150 published journal articles and book chapters, he has served as editor/author for several books in the addiction field, including *Behavioral Approaches to Alcoholism, Alcoholism: New Directions in Behavioral Research and Treatment, Relapse Prevention, Assessment of Addictive Behaviors*, and *Addictive Behaviors: Prevention and Early Intervention*. He has served on the editorial boards of 15 professional journals, including the *Journal of Consulting and Clinical Psychology*, the *Journal of Abnormal Psychology, Addictive Behaviors*, and the *Journal of Studies on Alcohol*. He is also a consultant with the Veterans Administration, the National Institute of Alcohol Abuse and Alcoholism, the National Institute of Medicine, and the Federal Bureau of Prisons. He has served as President of the Society of Psychologists in Addictive Behaviors (1983–1984), President of the Section for the Development of Clinical Psychology as an Experimental-Behavioral Science (Division 12) of the American Psychological Association (1985–1986), and is the current President of the Association for the Advancement of Behavior Therapy (1991–1992).

His present academic appointment is supported by a Research Scientist Award from the National Institute of Alcohol Abuse and Alcoholism. Professor Marlatt is an internationally recognized psychologist in the field of addiction, and has served as a visiting faculty member at universities in various countries, including Australia, Britain, Canada, Germany, and Scandinavia. His work has been recognized by the following awards: a MERIT Award from the National Institute of Alcohol Abuse and Alcoholism (1989), a Distinguished Psychologist for Professional Contributions to Knowledge Award from the Washington State Psychological Association (1990), and The Jellinek Memorial Award for Alcohol Studies (1990).

SUBSTANCE ABUSE: IMPLICATIONS OF A BIOPSYCHOSOCIAL MODEL FOR PREVENTION, TREATMENT, AND RELAPSE PREVENTION

To many psychologists, the topic of substance abuse is a confusing one. Everyone seems to agree that it is a problem, but what kind of problem is it? We are bombarded on a daily basis with a multitude of terms, both in the lay and professional literature, that seem to describe the same thing. Substance abuse, chemical dependency, drug addiction, addictive behavior—these labels are often used interchangeably, with considerable overlap in meaning.

To gain an understanding of how the public usually understands the meaning of the term *substance abuse*, here is how one popular dictionary (Random House, 1987) defines it: "Long-term, pathological use of alcohol or drugs, characterized by daily intoxication, inability to reduce consumption, and impairment in social or occupational functioning; broadly, alcohol or drug addiction" (p. 1897). There are several problems with this definition. What exactly is meant by the term "pathological use"? By referring to the use of "alcohol *or* drugs," the definition implies that alcohol is *not* a drug, a common misperception among the lay public. Is "daily intoxication" a necessary condition for substance abuse? If so, smoking or tobacco dependence would not qualify as substance abuse. The phrase "inability to reduce consumption," also often known as "loss of control," is a vague and ambiguous concept, suggesting that substance abuse is somehow an involuntary behavior. By limiting impairment to "social or occupational functioning," important other consequences to one's health and self-esteem are ignored. As a final problem, this definition seems to equate substance abuse with alcohol or drug addiction.

Substance Dependence Versus Substance Abuse

Psychologists, along with other mental health professionals, rely on the *Diagnostic and Statistical Manual of Mental Disorders* or *DSM-III-R* (American Psychiatric Association, 1987) for more precise definitions of various disorders. The *DSM-III-R* makes a distinction between (a) psychoactive substance-induced organic mental disorders—disorders associated with the acute or chronic effects of drug use on central nervous system functioning, including intoxication, physical withdrawal symptoms, and delirium, and (b) psychoactive substance use disorders—a diagnostic class that deals with "symptoms and maladaptive behavioral changes associated with more or less regular use of psychoactive substances that affect the central nervous system" (p. 165). This later category encompasses what most professionals consider substance abuse.

In the *DSM-III-R* a critical distinction is made between substance dependence and abuse. *Dependence*, or what most people think of as addiction, is characterized by a cluster of cognitive, behavioral, and physiologic symptoms indicating that the individual has "impaired control of psychoactive substance use and continues use of the substance despite adverse consequences" (p. 166). *Abuse* is a residual category that applies to "maladaptive patterns of psychoactive substance use that have never met the criteria for dependence for that particular class of substance" (p. 169). The diagnostic criteria for psychoactive substance dependence are:

1. At least three of the following:

   - substance often taken in larger amounts or over a longer period than the person intended
   - persistent desire or one or more unsuccessful efforts to cut down or control substance use
   - a great deal of time spent in activities necessary to get the substance (e.g., theft), taking the substance (e.g., chain smoking), or recovering from its effects
   - frequent intoxication or withdrawal symptoms when expected to fulfill major role obligations at work, school, or home (e.g., does not go to work because hung over, goes to school or work high, intoxicated while taking care of his or her children), or when substance use is physically hazardous (e.g., drives when intoxicated)

- important social, occupational, or recreational activities given up or reduced because of substance use
- continued substance use despite knowledge of having a persistent or recurrent social, psychological, or physical problem that is caused or exacerbated by the use of the substance (e.g., keeps using heroin despite family arguments about it, cocaine-induced depression, or having an ulcer made worse by drinking)
- marked tolerance: need for markedly increased amounts of the substance (i.e., at least a 50% increase) in order to achieve intoxication or desired effect, or markedly diminished effect with continued use of the same amount

Note that the following items may not apply to cannabis, hallucinogens, or phencyclidine (PCP):

- characteristic withdrawal symptoms (see specific withdrawal syndromes under heading "Psychoactive Substance-Induced Organic Mental Disorders")
- substance often taken to relieve or avoid withdrawal symptoms

2. Some symptoms of the disturbance have persisted for at least one month, or have occurred repeatedly over a longer period of time.

The criteria for diagnosing substance abuse, as listed in the *DSM-III-R*, are:

1. A maladaptive pattern of psychoactive substance use indicated by at least one of the following:

- continued use despite knowledge of having a persistent or recurrent social, occupational, psychological, or physical problem that is caused or exacerbated by use of the psychoactive substance
- recurrent use in situations in which use is physically hazardous (e.g., driving while intoxicated)

2. Some symptoms of the disturbance have persisted for at least one month, or have occurred repeatedly over a longer period of time.
3. Never met the criteria for psychoactive substance dependence for this substance.

The *DSM-III-R* also lists criteria for severity of substance dependence. Five categories are listed: (a) mild severity, in which few symptoms, if any, in excess of those required to make the diagnosis, and mild impairment in occupational or social functioning; (b) moderate severity, a mid-way category between mild and severe dependence; (c) severe dependency, characterized by many symptoms and marked impairment in functioning; (d) in partial remission, indicating some substance use and dependence symptoms in the past 6 months; and (e) in full remission, where the following criteria are met: "During the past six months, either no use of the substance, or use of the substance and no symptoms of dependence" (p. 168).

These criteria are important conceptually, since they indicate that dependency is represented as a continuum, with severity ranging from mild to severe, depending on the number and intensity of symptoms exhibited. It is also of interest to note that an individual could be diagnosed in full remission even if drug use occurred within a 6-month period, as long as no symptoms of dependence were observed. The distinction between substance abuse and dependence will be maintained and further elaborated in the forthcoming *DSM-IV* (Nathan, 1991).

Psychoactive Substances

What substances are included as psychoactive in this diagnostic classification system? The *DSM-III-R* includes both dependence and abuse of alcohol, amphetamines (including speed and ecstasy), cannabis (marijuana, hashish), cocaine (including crack), hallucinogens (e.g., LSD or lysergic acid), inhalants (e.g., glue sniffing and inhaling other volatile substances such as gasoline), nicotine (dependency only), opioids (including heroin, morphine, methadone, codeine, and buprenorphine), phencyclidine or ketamine, and a final combined category of sedative, hypnotic, and anxiolytic substances (including sleeping pills and other benzodiazepines, methaqualone, and barbiturates). That many of these substances are taken by the same individual is noted by the inclusion of the diagnostic category of *polysubstance dependence*.

It is interesting to note that this list includes both legal and illegal substances, substances that are not usually thought of as drugs (e.g., glue sniffing), and medications usually prescribed by physicians (e.g., sedatives and antianxiety drugs). It may be surprising to some that nicotine dependence is included in the list, since tobacco is a readily available substance that does not produce intoxication effects. Yet in a recent Surgeon General's Report on smoking (U.S. Department of Health and Human Services, 1986) nicotine is described as a highly addictive substance and one that is associated with higher mortality rates than any other drug. Recent government reports show that approximately 400,000 Americans die each year from illnesses linked to the effects of smoking, compared to 150,000 deaths associated with alcohol use, and less than 5,000 deaths attributed to the combined effects of all the other substances in the *DSM-III-R* list.

Models of Addiction

In the substance abuse field, controversy and disagreement often arise as a result of differing conceptual models that attempt to explain both the causes and remedies for these problem behaviors. Competition among the models exists because there is little consensus among those working in this area concerning the relative impact of the various etiological factors involved in the development of substance abuse or addiction. Nor is there consistent agreement as to how to best prevent or treat the problem. Part of this uncertainty and conflict stems from the plethora of experts who claim to have a stake in the field, including the lay public, individuals recovering from addiction problems, paraprofessional substance abuse counselors, professional treatment providers, researchers and educators, politicians, and police.

In order to disentangle and clarify these conflicting theoretical models, it is helpful to understand two basic underlying controversies. The first conflict concerns the cause of substance abuse: Is it due to voluntary or involuntary factors? Is addiction the fault of the individual involved or is it caused by factors beyond the individual's personal control? The second controversy relates to how substance abuse can be changed: Is it possible for people to change a substance abuse problem on their own, or is self-help or professional treatment necessary in order for change to occur? Another important point is the relationship between these two issues. Is it necessary to know the precise etiology of substance abuse in order to prevent or treat it? Are the mechanisms of behavior change with substance abuse problems independent of the initial determinants of these behaviors?

These questions were addressed in an influential paper by Brickman and his colleagues at the University of Michigan (Brickman et al., 1982). Applying attribution theory to address the relationship between the causes (etiology) and solutions (treatment) to clinical problems, these investigators outlined four models of helping and coping. Each of these four models has been applied in the substance abuse field. A modified version of their analysis is presented in Figure 1.

The first model is known as the *moral model* (upper left quadrant in Figure 1). In this approach, people are held responsible for both the development of a substance abuse problem and its solution. Brickman uses drinking problems as an example: "Under the moral model, drinking is seen as a sign of weak character, requiring drinkers to exercise willpower and get control of themselves in order to return to sobriety and respectability" (Brickman et al., 1982, p. 370). The legal sanctions endorsed by the American "War on Drugs" movement is rooted in the moral model. The individual must accept responsibility for both having developed the problem and changing the behavior (e.g., to abstain). One does not get off the hook because of a genetic predisposition or because one comes from a dysfunctional family. The chief limitation is that this

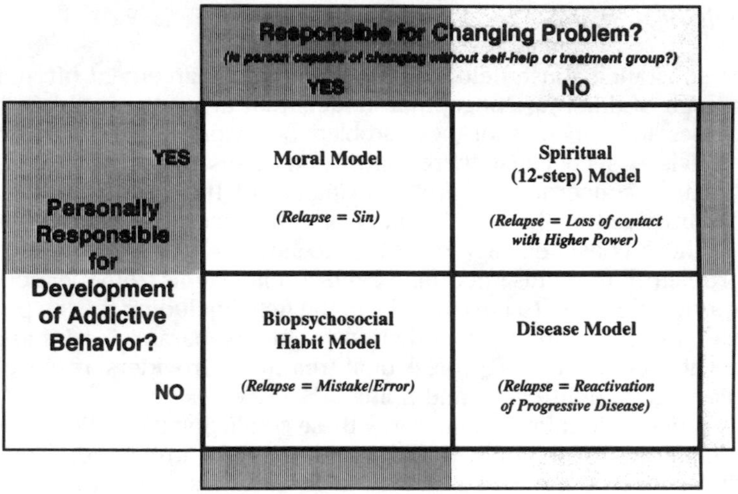

	Responsible for Changing Problem? *(Is person capable of changing without self-help or treatment group?)*	
	YES	**NO**
Personally Responsible for **YES**	**Moral Model** *(Relapse = Sin)*	**Spiritual** **(12-step) Model** *(Relapse = Loss of contact with Higher Power)*
Development of Addictive Behavior? **NO**	**Biopsychosocial Habit Model** *(Relapse = Mistake/Error)*	**Disease Model** *(Relapse = Reactivation of Progressive Disease)*

Figure 1. An attribution model of addiction and relapse: Four alternative models.

model tends to blame the victim: People are made to feel guilty for having a substance abuse problem and are often blamed for their inability to change. In attempts to recover on their own, relapse is tantamount to having committed a sin, often attributed to a lack of willpower or moral fiber.

The second paradigm for understanding substance abuse is the *disease model* (lower right quadrant of Figure 1). First applied to describe alcohol dependence by Jellinek (1960), this model holds that addiction is caused by an underlying disease condition, such as a genetic abnormality or pathological metabolism. Brickman extends the disease model to include "all cases in which people are considered subject to forces that were and will continue to be beyond their control" (p. 372). Under this scheme, people who have the disease cannot change on their own but require specialized medical treatment. If left untreated, the disease is thought to run a progressively deteriorating course, often culminating in death. The symptoms of the addictive disease intensify over time, including increased loss of control, irresistible physical craving for the substance, enhanced physical tolerance to substance effects, and pronounced physical withdrawal upon cessation of use. Although advocates of this approach disagree as to the specific medical cause of the problem and the best way to treat it, all are in strong agreement that the only acceptable treatment goal is total abstinence. Relapse thus implies a return to the progressive disease state, and is presumably triggered by forces beyond the individual's personal control.

The main advantage of the disease model is that it allows people to seek help without being blamed for their weakness; the same symptoms that would be punished under the moral model are entitled to treatment in this approach. One important disadvantage is that it casts the substance abuser into the role of a helpless victim, with no possibility of changing the problem without undergoing specialized medical treatment. Since no medical cure for substance abuse currently exists, no one can ever fully recover or be cured. Even though one has successfully achieved abstinence, one is still recovering since the underlying disease remains active. The chronic disease model remains the most dominant paradigm applied to alcohol problems and other forms of substance abuse in this country.

The *spiritual* or *enlightenment model* (upper right quadrant in Figure 1) is most often associated with Alcoholics Anonymous and other 12-step programs. Often linked to the disease model, this approach relies upon the concept of a higher power as a means of overcoming the spiritual disease of addiction. Just as salvation in the Christian religion cannot occur without the seeker's admission of personal failings and a turning to Christ for redemption, so recovery from a substance abuse problem is impossible unless the abuser admits to personal powerlessness over the substance and turns to a higher power for help. Missing group meetings is considered high-risk for relapse, since one is no longer protected by the divine influence of the higher power.

The advantages of the spiritual model include the renewed sense of spiritual awakening and support members receive from group fellowship. Critics of this paradigm often express concern that any nonbeliever is shunned as a heretic in denial and is rejected by those group members who have already been converted into the fold. Professionals in the substance abuse field who are not themselves in recovery are also sometimes critical because members of anonymous self-help groups operate outside of the realm of the professional treatment arena and downplay alternative, research-based approaches.

The fourth and final model is the *biopsychosocial habit model* (lower left in Figure 1), also known as the behavioral model. Brickman refers to this as the *compensatory model*, since although an individual is not considered personally at fault for the development of the problem, he or she is able to compensate for it by assuming responsibility for change, either on their own or by seeking outside help. The major assumption of the behavioral model is that substance abuse is a learned, maladaptive habit pattern. Addictive behavior becomes maladaptive to the extent that it becomes the person's central means of coping with life's demands. Most habits that become excessive or addictive in nature are those that are rewarded or reinforced by immediate positive consequences, such as the euphoric rush or high that follows when a substance is consumed. In addition, substance use can be rewarding to the extent that it provides relief from unpleasant mood states or the physical distress associated with drug withdrawal (using substances for self-medication).

One advantage of the behavioral model is that the development of a substance abuse problem is thought to be due to the combined effects of biological, psychological, and sociocultural factors, only some of which are under the voluntary control of the individual. The biopsychosocial model does not blame the person for developing a substance abuse problem, but it does hold the individual responsible for doing something to change. Self-initiated attempts to change are accepted, as are attempts to get help from others. Habit change is seen as an opportunity to develop new and more adaptive coping strategies and to establish a newly balanced lifestyle. Goals for change are flexible, and sometimes include moderation or controlled use as an alternative to abstinence (e.g., controlled drinking). Relapse is defined as a mistake or error in the new learning process.

Etiology and Development of Substance Abuse

Multiple Determinants of Substance Abuse: Toward a Comprehensive Biopsychosocial Model

The behavioral model described in the previous section endorses a biopsychosocial definition of substance abuse. Addictive behaviors are acquired through the combined influence of biological, psychological, and sociocultural factors. Such factors may also influence maintenance of drug dependence over time, as well as the cessation of drug use or response to treatment interventions.

Biological factors are important in that they play a role in determining the individual's vulnerability or resistance to substance effects and the associated risk of abuse or dependency. It is well documented in the literature, for example, that sons of alcoholic fathers are at greater risk for developing alcohol problems than sons of nonalcoholic fathers, perhaps because their genetic makeup renders them more sensitive to the rewarding effects of alcohol or less immune to the negative consequences (Crabbe, McSwigan, & Belknap, 1985; Goodwin, 1990; Newlin & Thompson, 1991). But biological vulnerability or a genetic predisposition for substance abuse may not cause a problem unless the person at risk is exposed to an environment that facilitates or brings out the problem behavior. The alcoholic's offspring may not experience a drinking problem unless or until the parent's drinking in the home is observed or he or she experiences social pressure to drink from peers. Exposure to this kind of high-risk environment may augment the impact of biological vulnerability (Zucker, 1987). Alternatively, if the environment is low on these same risk factors, the impact of biological predisposition may be muted or rendered inactive.

The pharmacological impact of substance use on body chemistry and physiology plays a critical role in maintaining a substance abuse pattern over time. Drugs that provide immediate psychoactive effects (e.g., nicotine and cocaine) appear to have a higher addiction potential than substances whose effects are more delayed (e.g., alcohol; Hunt, 1990; Tabakoff & Hoffman, 1991). This may be one reason why many people who drink alcohol do not develop an abuse or dependence problem, whereas those who smoke tobacco or crack cocaine find it extremely difficult to moderate their use. Detailed descriptions of mechanisms of drug action and behavioral pharmacology are beyond the scope of this chapter, since this material is covered extensively elsewhere in this volume.

Biological factors exert a wide range of influence in other related areas. Substance abuse has been found to increase risk of developing chronic physical disorders (e.g., cirrhosis with alcohol dependence, lung cancer with smoking). Drug use during pregnancy may damage the fetus and lead to chronic health problems in the offspring (e.g., fetal alcohol syndrome, and the damage observed in crack babies). Tolerance to the physical effects of a substance can lead to increased frequency and intensity of dose, thereby enhancing the risk of long-term dependence. Finally, physical withdrawal symptoms experienced upon cessation of drug use may increase the probability of relapse.

In addition to biological determinants and effects, substance abuse is strongly influenced by psychological and social factors. Psychological risk for substance abuse is affected by one's personal beliefs, expectancies, and attributions about the effects of various substances (Goldman, Brown, & Christiansen, 1987; Lang & Michaler, 1990). Although there is no evidence to support the notion of an addictive personality, researchers have identified certain personality traits that correlate with substance abuse, including sensation-seeking, impulsivity, and negative affect (Cox, 1988). One's repertoire of coping skills (e.g., relaxation and assertion skills), particularly if they offer functional alternatives to drug use, constitutes another important psychological dimension (Shiffman & Wills, 1985). Motivation for both initial drug use and seeking help to change one's pattern of abuse or dependence is also critical (Cox, 1990).

It is well documented in the literature that both family and peer pressures increase (or decrease) the risk of substance abuse. For those raised in a dysfunctional family setting, especially in the presence of drug and alcohol problems or for children who have suffered from physical or sexual abuse, the risk of substance abuse is high (Jacob, 1987). As children approach their preteen and adolescent years, the major social forces shift from the family to peers. Peer influence and social pressure to engage in risk-taking behaviors are major prompts to engage in a wide variety of antisocial and delinquent behaviors, including substance abuse (White, Bates, & Johnson, 1990). Experimenting with drugs is but one of a cluster of problem behaviors that emerge among adolescents who are involved in conduct disorder problems (Jessor & Jessor, 1975). Lack of parental supervision, as is the case with latch-key children, further increases the risk of substance abuse, as does the lack of alternative recreational activities (Hawkins, Catalano, & Miller, in press).

Participation in gangs or other deviant groups further enhances this risk, because drug use is often part of the ritual of initiation and the rite of passage into group membership (Zoja, 1989). The ritual use of drugs often associated with gang membership in the inner city environment has its parallel in the heavy drinking norms and party animal mentality found in college fraternities and sororities. Perceived group norms, coupled with the direct modeling of these high-risk behaviors among members of the group, may make these activities extremely difficult to resist. How can the individual "just say no" when everyone around them is saying "yes" and rejecting those who decline to participate?

Society as a whole also serves to encourage reliance on alcohol, tobacco, and other drugs as a means of obtaining a quick fix or providing access to the trappings of an exciting lifestyle. Media and advertising portrayals of drinking, smoking, and other drug use often tend to glamorize and sensationalize these behaviors in the eyes of young viewers. American society is caught up in a pattern of immediate gratification and quick relief. Every drug store and convenience market sells substances designed to produce instant remedies for every ailment. A person who uses illegal substances to provide self-medication faces arrest and punishment, whereas others know that they have only to turn to their personal physician to obtain prescriptions for licit medications to provide relief from anxiety and depression. It is no wonder that young people have difficulty knowing where to draw the line when faced with these omnipresent offers of instant gratification.

Approaches to Prevention

From a public health perspective, prevention of substance abuse and dependence involves three major strategies: primary, secondary, and tertiary prevention. An overview of all three prevention strategies is illustrated in Figure 2.

The boxes outlined in Figure 2 designate a series of stages in the development of both substance abuse and dependence. Individuals may or may not progress into each successive stage. The fundamental purpose of all prevention strategies is, of course, to arrest or prevent the progression of problems at the earliest stage possible. The goal of *primary prevention* strategies is to prevent initial use of substances, or if

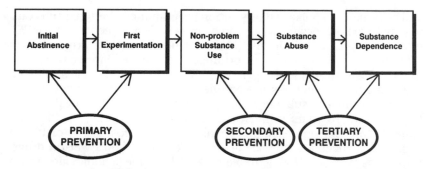

Figure 2. Stages of development of substance abuse and dependence: Prevention strategies.

the individual has already experimented with substances (e.g., has tried the first cigarette or alcoholic drink), to prevent further use that may lead to patterns of abuse or dependence.

Secondary prevention strategies are designed to prevent ongoing use from escalating into substance abuse and/or dependence. For those already exhibiting problems associated with abuse of a substance, the goal is to either return them to abstinence or to reduce the harm of their behavior (harm reduction approach). *Tertiary prevention* is designed to either return the individual who has already developed an ongoing pattern of substance abuse or dependence to a drug-free state or, failing that goal, to prevent the problem from getting worse.

Primary Prevention

Primary prevention programs for substance abuse employ a wide variety of methods and procedures, typically aimed at children and administered in educational, religious, and family settings (Botvin, 1986; Pentz, 1991). Education is the cornerstone of most primary prevention programs. Children and young adults are taught about various substances and their effects, with an emphasis on the personal, social, and health risks involved. Prior programs that emphasized information and values clarification only have not shown to be as effective as programs that combine information on social norms with stress training skills (Hawkins et al., in press). Coping skills include resisting social and peer pressure to experiment with substances, and learning alternative activities that may reduce the risk of substance abuse (e.g., relaxation and other stress-management skills). Training in effective decision making and enhancing self-efficacy are also important components of effective primary prevention.

Despite the absence of evidence documenting effectiveness, social pressure to "just say no" has become the major thrust of many media and government-sponsored prevention programming. National and community-based organizations (e.g., drug abuse resistance education [DARE], mothers against drunk driving [MADD], students against drunk driving [SADD]) and media-based consortiums (e.g., Partnership for Drug-Free America) have targeted the general population with messages to avoid drug use. Legal sanctions are another component of society's overall attempt to prevent substance abuse. Laws governing the legal age for tobacco use (18 years in most states) and for drinking (age 21 in all states) represent one example. Penalties for the possession or use of illegal substances are increasing as part of the nation's war on drugs. Provisions for smoke-free workplaces and drug-free schools (along with penalties for noncompliance) are now commonplace. Decreasing outlets for the sale of tobacco and alcohol is an approach adopted by many communities, as is raising the price of such substances to make them less affordable to youngsters (Single, 1988). The provision of alternative recreational facilities for youth is an example of an environmental engineering approach to primary prevention (McCarty, 1985).

Secondary Prevention

Figure 2 indicates that secondary prevention strategies can influence two stages: nonproblem substance use and substance abuse. Although the term *nonproblem use* may at first appear to be a misnomer, it does apply to both moderate use of alcohol and appropriate use of prescription medications. Although reports have appeared in the literature documenting the nondependent use by some individuals of other substances such as marijuana, cocaine, and opiates (e.g., Zinberg & Harding, 1982), any use of an illicit drug represents a potential legal problem for the user. In the present context, we will therefore limit the discussion of nonproblem substance use to alcohol. The two goals of secondary prevention with alcohol are (a) to prevent nonproblem or social drinking from developing into alcohol abuse and/or dependence, and (b) to reduce the harm of alcohol abuse.

A heavy drinker who is experiencing some problems (e.g., periodic excessive drinking in hazardous situations), yet who does not meet the criteria for alcohol dependence, may benefit from a secondary prevention program designed to inculcate moderate drinking. If abstinence is not a viable goal for such an individual (either because they refuse to accept this goal or have been repeatedly unsuccessful at maintaining abstinence), a return to nonproblem use is preferable to ongoing abuse or the development of dependence on alcohol.

As an illustration of a secondary prevention program with alcohol use and abuse, I will describe an ongoing project we are conducting at the University of Washington (Baer, Kivlahan, Fromme, & Marlatt, 1991). The population we are working with consists of college student drinkers.

Recent reviews indicate that college students are a population at elevated risk of alcohol problems based on high consumption patterns (Berkowitz & Perkins, 1986; Brennan, Walfish, & AuBuchon, 1986). In one national survey, Engs and Hanson (1988) reported that over 20% of college students report drinking six or more drinks at one occasion, and almost half reported driving a car when intoxicated. Alcohol-related accidents represent the leading cause of death in this age range (age 17–25), and alcohol abuse is associated with a wide range of related problems in the college population, including acute alcohol toxicity (which can be lethal), date rape, unsafe sexual practices, vandalism, and impaired academic performance. Despite the fact that most students drink (including those under the legal drinking age), with many meeting the criteria for alcohol abuse (see page 133), few see themselves as having a problem with alcohol.

In response to this concern, many campuses have developed alcohol awareness programs based on a primary prevention philosophy (Braucht & Braucht, 1984). Although these programs typically lead to changes in alcohol-related knowledge and attitudes, few if any such programs have been found to produce changes in drinking behavior itself (Goodstadt, 1986; Moskowitz, 1989). This limitation in effectiveness appears to be due to the fact that these traditional programs have been restricted to providing information about the negative effects of drinking, often coupled with a disease model of alcoholism (Miller & Nirenberg, 1984). Programs with a goal directed toward the prevention of alcohol dependence, however, may be less effective with this population than programs that are directly targeted toward the prevention of alcohol abuse.

Our program, based on cognitive-behavioral principles and self-regulation theory, is designed to reduce the amount of drinking by teaching college students moderation skills and responsible drinking practices. Because students who meet the criteria for alcohol *dependence* are screened out and referred to an appropriate abstinence-based program, the project is specifically aimed at students at risk for alcohol abuse. The underlying philosophy of this approach is consistent with a public health model geared to *harm reduction* (reducing the risks of dangerous drinking practices). Our program for student drinkers is similar to those successfully employed by other investigators working with young adult problem drinkers (e.g., Alden, 1988; Sanchez-Craig, Leigh, Spivak, & Lei, 1989).

To date, we have completed two studies that have evaluated the effectiveness of our secondary prevention programs for high-risk drinkers. In the first study (Kivlahan, Marlatt, Fromme, Coppel, & Williams, 1990), we compared our cognitive-behavioral skills-training program to two control groups: a didactic, information-only program (similar to programs designed for drivers who have been charged with driving under the influence of alcohol), and a wait-list control condition (assessment and follow-up only group). All subjects were college students judged to be at risk because of their current heavy drinking behavior. After completion of the intervention phase (conducted with coeducational groups in both the skills-training and information-only conditions), subjects were monitored during a 1-year follow-up period. Results showed that although all three conditions showed a significant reduction in overall drinking behavior at 1 year, only students receiving the skills-training showed reliable changes over time, including reductions of more than 50% in self-monitored drinks consumed per week and peak blood-alcohol levels (reduction in maximum amount consumed per week), compared to baseline drinking levels. These positive results have been replicated in a second study with a 2-year follow-up period (Baer et al., in press).

In a third, still ongoing project, we are investigating the effectiveness of a *stepped-care* secondary prevention program for high-risk drinkers in the college setting. The stepped-care procedure is as follows. We begin our program by exposing all students to a single session of professional advice. In this hour-long motivational interview (Miller & Rollnick, 1991), students meet one-to-one with a member of our professional staff who provides them with both feedback concerning their alcohol-related risks and advice on how to establish a safer drinking pattern. By assessing students on a regular basis after receiving the advice sessions, we are able to determine who has benefited and who is in need of further intervention. For those who continue drinking abusively, we will bump them up a step and assign them to a group. A further step consisting of individual counseling delivered on an outpatient basis for an ongoing period may also be recommended. Finally, if all other approaches still have not succeeded, as a final step, we will attempt to place the student in a traditional treatment program geared toward abstinence. We are following our cohort of high-risk students over a 4-year period to assess the efficacy of this stepped-care program. Subjects have been randomly assigned to receive either the stepped-care option or to a no-treatment control group. Because most college student drinkers mature out of their heavy drinking patterns as they assume greater family and employment responsibilities (Fillmore, 1988), the overall aim of secondary prevention is to accelerate the development of this natural "maturing out" process.

Modification of Substance Abuse: Self-Help, Treatment, and Relapse Prevention

Stages of Change

One of the most useful advances in understanding how individuals go through the process of changing addictive behaviors is the model illustrated in Figure 3. Clinicians working with addictive behavior problems have found the *stages of change* model particularly helpful in developing intervention strategies (Miller & Heather, 1986). First developed as a method of understanding how smokers have attempted to give up their habit (DiClemente & Prochaska, 1982; Prochaska & DiClemente, 1983), this approach has since been applied to a variety of other addictive behaviors (Marlatt, Baer, Donovan, & Kivlahan, 1988; Marlatt & Gordon, 1985). It applies to both self-initiated change and to changes that individuals experience through participation in self-help groups and professional treatment programs.

The *precontemplation stage* applies to people who are continuing a pattern of substance abuse or dependence and who have yet to actively consider or contemplate changing their behavior. Individuals in this stage do not intend to modify their habits in the foreseeable future. Their lack of intention to change may be due to multiple factors, including attention only to the positive aspects of drug use, often accompanied by ignorance about the risks or costs of their behavior, demoralization about their prospects for successful change, or defensiveness in the face of social pressures to change. Denial that one has a problem that needs changing is a common defense mechanism among precontemplators.

Once a person begins to consider the possibility of change, he or she enters the *contemplation stage*. Here there is an intention to make at least some changes in the future, although many contemplators prefer to just think about the possibility of change without making a firm commitment to action—the "I'll quit tomorrow" syndrome. This stage is usually marked by ambivalence and motivational conflict, in which the pros and cons of the risk behavior are considered about equal. For

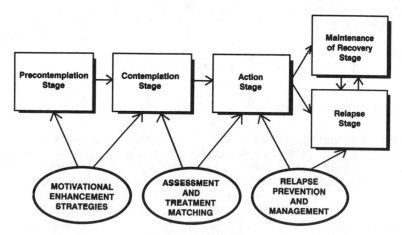

Figure 3. Stages of change in substance abuse and dependence: Intervention strategies.

those contemplators who are able to make a commitment to a plan of action, preparations for change occur such as setting a quit date, obtaining more information about the problem, or investigating self-help or treatment options.

Action is the stage when overt attempts to change first occur. There are three action alternatives: self-initiated change (attempting to change on one's own), participation in self-help groups such as Alcoholics Anonymous (AA), or seeking professional treatment. The goals of change may vary from attempting to reduce or cut down the target behavior (e.g., embarking on a diet or a program of moderate drinking) to a commitment to lifelong abstinence. Detoxification from the effects of substance abuse usually occurs during this period. The action stage is often unstable, marked with mixed advances and setbacks.

The maintenance stage applies to the period from 6 months after the initial habit change has been achieved until the risk of relapse has stabilized at a relatively low level, usually over a period of at least 1 year. The achievement of successful maintenance is also described as the recovery stage in much of the popular addiction literature. Since the risk of relapse never returns to a level of zero probability, many ex-addicts refer to themselves as recovering, rather than recovered or cured. Self-help groups such as AA recommend lifelong membership as a means of preventing relapse in the maintenance stage.

Unstable maintenance or the failure to achieve and maintain successful habit change is associated with the *relapse stage*. This stage is better described as a process marked by fluid and dynamic change. Temporary lapses or slips in maintaining one's goals are often part of recovery and do not necessarily mean that the person has totally relapsed. Although some who experience a relapse give up or drop out of treatment, most recycle back through the contemplation and action stages as they make additional efforts to change. The majority of people who eventually recover from a substance abuse problem report that it took several attempts to change before they achieved success in the long run (Marlatt, Curry, & Gordon, 1988; Schachter, 1982).

Motivation for Change

Motivation and commitment are critical components of changing addictive behavior. Recent research has demonstrated that the strength of one's initial commitment to change is a significant predictor of successful maintenance with a range of substance abuse problems, including smoking, problem drinking, cocaine, and opiate dependence (Hall, Havassy, & Wasserman, 1990, 1991). Motivation includes both intrinsic and extrinsic factors. Although individuals are often shifted from precontemplation into contemplation and action by extrinsic motivating factors (e.g., pressure from family, friends, and employers; being arrested for drunk driving, etc.), intrinsic motives such as health concerns, desire for freedom from addiction, and self-efficacy for change are also important (Cox, 1990). Although the experience of dire consequences or hitting bottom often prompts change in some people, others are motivated to change at an earlier point by recognizing that the costs of substance abuse outweigh the benefits. Often the experience of a critical episode (e.g., being confronted by one's spouse or children) is involved (Littman, 1980), whereas for others it appears that the gradual accumulation of negative effects leads to a final straw that breaks the camel's back experience that pushes one over the threshold of change (Sobell, Sobell, & Toneatto, 1991).

A number of motivational enhancement strategies have been described to promote movement from precontemplation into the contemplation and action stages. Adherents of the traditional disease model of addiction often recommend a confrontational approach in an attempt to break through denial and force the individual to accept the label of an addict or alcoholic and admit to the need for treatment (Trice & Beyer, 1984). Many for-profit inpatient treatment centers use an intervention strategy in which a targeted individual is confronted by family members and employers about his or her substance abuse problem and need for immediate treatment (Johnson, 1986). The confronted individual is forced to choose between accepting treatment or suffering adverse consequences (e.g., loss of employment). Despite the widespread use of coercive motivational procedures, they have not been supported by clinical outcome trials (Institute of Medicine, 1990a; Miller & Rollnick, 1991).

A second, less confrontational approach has recently been advanced as an alternative motivational enhancement strategy. This approach, known as *motivational interviewing*, was introduced by psychologist William Miller and his colleagues (Miller, 1983; Miller & Rollnick, 1991). In this procedure, the interviewer adopts an empathic, nonjudgmental style to engage the interviewee in a discussion of motivational issues. The respondent is given feedback as to the risks involved with the problem behavior, and is asked for suggestions as to potential changes that could be made to reduce these risks. Information is provided about alternative plans of action and treatment options. Instead of confronting the interviewee and relying upon fear-arousing and threatening messages, the interviewer tries to work with the client in helping him or her select the best options for change. Clarification of the decision-making process is encouraged as the pros and cons of change (or failure to change) are discussed. The goal of motivational interviewing is to enhance intrinsic motivation for change and to nudge the interviewee into preparation for action. Research studies reviewed by Miller and Rollnick (1991) provide support for the notion that feedback about risk, given in an empathic, supportive manner, is more likely to induce change than feedback presented in a more confrontational and directive style.

According to social-learning theory, self-efficacy is a critical ante-
cedent for behavior change (Bandura, 1977). Self-efficacy refers to the
individual's subjective expectancy about his or her ability to cope with
an impending situation or task. Self-efficacy has been found to be an
important predictor of recovery from substance abuse problems and is
an essential component of relapse prevention (Marlatt & Gordon, 1985).
Discussion of various change strategies, self-help and treatment options,
and barriers to change may serve to enhance efficacy (Curry & Marlatt,
1987). Commitment to proximal, time-limited goals (e.g., to abstain for
1 month) may be helpful for those individuals who have low self-efficacy
for success in maintaining lifelong abstinence.

Unaided Self-Initiated Change (Spontaneous Remission)

Many people are able to overcome a substance abuse problem without
the assistance of professional treatment. There are two vehicles for self-
change: unaided self-initiated change and involvement in self-help groups.
Unaided self-initiated change refers to habit changes that individuals
carry out on their own, without the assistance of either self-help groups
or professional treatment. The controversy over spontaneous remission
relates to this issue. For those who subscribe to the disease model of
addiction, change is unlikely or impossible without participation in a
formal treatment program of some kind. Similarly, proponents of AA and
other 12-step programs claim that people with substance abuse problems are unable to change on their own; they need the lifelong support
of a spiritual group (and the assistance or belief in a higher power) in
order to change and maintain successful recovery.

Research on addictive behavior change, however, clearly shows that
many people are able to overcome their problems without outside help
(Peele & Brodsky, 1991). The vast majority of smokers who have given
up tobacco have done so on their own initiative (e.g., Cohen et al., 1989;
Marlatt, Curry, & Gordon, 1988; Schachter, 1982). Analyses of the process
of self-change in smokers have utilized the stages of change model (e.g.,
Prochaska, DiClemente, Velicer, Ginpil, & Norcross, 1985), showing that
different change-strategies are employed at each stage (see also Shiffman & Wills, 1985). The results of these studies show that spontaneous
remission is neither spontaneous (since it usually occurs as a result of
specific antecedents) nor best viewed as a remission (since it is often
not a temporary cessation in the natural course of a chronically relapsing
condition).

Only recently has the topic of unaided cessation been studied with
other substance abuse problems. Since most research in this area has
been conducted with clients or patients already in treatment, the topic
of self-initiated change has often been overlooked or ignored. There are
reports showing that unaided change occurs in individuals with alcohol

problems (Sobell, Sobell, & Toneatto, 1991; Tuchfeld, 1981; Vaillant, 1983), opiate dependency (Biernacki, 1986), and other substances (Stall & Biernacki, 1986). The number of people who are able to cure themselves is still largely unknown, but available evidence suggests that it may be quite large: over 90% of ex-smokers (Cohen et al., 1989) and as many as half of problem drinkers appear to have quit on their own (Institute of Medicine, 1990a). These high rates of spontaneous remission raise a challenge for the addiction treatment field: Does treatment improve upon the outcomes obtained by those who are motivated to quit on their own?

Self-Help and Mutual Aid Groups

Self-help groups for overcoming substance abuse problems are readily available in American society. The forerunner of these groups is Alcoholics Anonymous, founded in 1935 (Alcoholics Anonymous World Service, 1955). In 1987, AA membership was estimated to be more than 1.5 million people in more than 730,000 groups worldwide (Alcoholics Anonymous World Service, 1987). The AA philosophy has been adopted by a number of other similar groups for substance abusers, including Narcotics Anonymous, Cocaine Anonymous, and others. Membership in such groups is free and the only requirement to join is a desire to abstain. The demographic characteristics of members varies widely, depending on the location of the group, but one recent survey (Alcoholics Anonymous World Service, 1987) showed that the majority of members (66%) are male, with most in the 31–50 age bracket. The average member attended four meetings a week. In this survey, the average length of sobriety for members was 52 months, with 29% reporting sobriety for more than 5 years, 33% reporting sobriety for 1 to 5 years, and 33% reporting sobriety for less than 1 year. Despite the fact that well-designed studies on the effectiveness of AA are lacking, AA is still considered by many lay people to be the most successful approach to helping people with alcohol problems.

Although AA and other 12-step programs are the most popular self-help groups, a number of alternative approaches have appeared in recent years. Several of these new self-help groups were described in the July 8, 1991 issue of *Newsweek* magazine in an article entitled, "Clean and Sober—and Agnostic." As the title implies, these groups differ from AA in that they do not adopt a spiritual higher power concept in helping their members achieve and maintain abstinence. One such group is the Secular Organization for Sobriety (SOS), founded by James Christopher, with an international membership of 20,000. Another group, founded by Jack Trimpey (1989), is called Rational Recovery (RR), with chapters in 150 cities in the U.S. The RR philosophy is patterned after the approach of Albert Ellis and Rational-Emotive Therapy. Both SOS and RR emphasize taking personal responsibility for kicking the habit, rejecting the AA notion that admission of personal helplessness and reliance on a higher power is necessary for change to occur. Women with alcohol and drug problems have an alternative self-help group known as Women for Sobriety, founded by sociologist Jean Kilpatrick, with a membership of 5,000 women. All three groups do not require lifetime membership as does AA—members are encouraged to attend only so long as they feel they need help or have achieved full recovery.

All self-help groups provide support for individuals in recovery in a climate that is relatively free of guilt and self-blame. Members face their recovery process together, with more experienced members serving as sponsors to assist newer members achieve sobriety. The particular philosophy adopted by the group, whether spiritual or secular, may not be as critical as the social support and encouragement offered by the group itself. The self-help groups are not defined as treatment in the usual sense, because there is no leader or therapist who offers treatment for the afflicted. Most treatment professionals recommend participation in self-help groups as an adjunct to therapy and/or as a source of support during the aftercare period.

Professional Treatment: Settings and Modalities

The treatment of substance abuse is undergoing a period of rapid re-evaluation and change. Before discussing the range of treatment settings and modalities currently available, several critical issues and questions need to be addressed to provide a context for evaluating treatment options.

1. Despite a wide variety of treatment modalities and approaches for substance abuse problems, there is no consensus or agreement among professionals as to the most effective type of treatment. Recent reviews of the treatment outcome literature for alcohol and drug problems by the Institute of Medicine (1990a, 1990b) provide extensive documentation showing that although many types of treatment appear to be effective for at least some substance abusers, no one approach has been found to be uniformly effective. Relapse rates remain high, with many studies showing that the majority of clients in abstinence programs return to substance use within 1 year after the completion of formal treatment.

2. There has been a shift away from treatment programs that focus on a single substance of abuse (e.g., alcohol) toward programs that treat polydrug abuse or clients with mixed drug problems (e.g., combining alcohol and cocaine treatment in the same program). Many drug treatment programs now also offer programs for smoking cessation.

3. Because many substance abuse clients also suffer from psychological problems such as depression, anxiety, and other disorders, many

programs now offer treatment for the dual diagnosis client (Mirrin & Weiss, 1991). Mental health professionals, including psychologists, have become increasingly involved in providing services in combination or consultation with substance abuse counselors and therapists. Many professionals from different disciplines, including physicians (e.g., the American Society of Addiction Medicine), psychologists (e.g., the Society of Psychologists in Addictive Behaviors), social workers, nurses, and paraprofessional counselors, have developed specific training and certification programs in the substance abuse field.

4. Because the costs of treatment are typically paid for by government funds or third-party insurance plans, the scope and duration of treatment is affected by such policies as managed care and restrictions on funds that can be expended for services (e.g., Diagnostic Related Group restrictions). Because of funding limits, there is a move away from long-term inpatient treatment to briefer and less costly approaches such as outpatient treatment and brief interventions.

5. Given the wide range of treatment options available in the public and private domains, coupled with the lack of consensus concerning the best overall approach, many professionals are recommending that clients receive more extensive assessment and diagnostic evaluation so that they can be matched to the most effective form of treatment.

Taken as a whole, the treatment process can be divided into three main stages (Institute of Medicine, 1990a). *Acute intervention*, the first stage, consists of three components: (a) emergency treatment or crisis intervention for resolution of immediate problems caused by excessive substance abuse; (b) detoxification, to manage acute intoxication, overdose problems, and withdrawal, if necessary; and (c) screening, to identify the problem and refer the individual to an appropriate treatment setting.

Stage two, *rehabilitation*, also has three components: (a) evaluation and assessment, for the development of a specific treatment plan based on the individual's problems and resources; (b) primary care, for immediate reduction or cessation of drug use; and (c) extended care, to stabilize and consolidate the effects of initial treatment (e.g., assignment to a transitional, supportive living environment such as a half-way house).

The third stage, *maintenance*, may include up to three components: (a) aftercare, continuing assistance to maintain the gains of rehabilitation (e.g., treatment booster sessions); (b) relapse prevention, designed to prevent a return to drug use or to intervene in the ongoing relapse process; and (c) domiciliary care, placing those who are too disabled by the effects of prior substance abuse to return to independent community living.

A number of recent manuals for the treatment of alcohol and substance abuse problems have documented a wide range of treatment modalities (e.g., Baker & Cannon, 1988; Ciraulo & Shader, 1991; Cox, 1987; Daley & Raskin, 1991; Frances & Miller, 1991; Hester & Miller, 1989;

Lewis, Dana, & Blevins, 1988; Miller & Heather, 1986; Monti, Abrams, Kadden, & Cooney, 1989). Although most treatment programs combine specific intervention strategies, the primary modalities fall into three major categories: pharmacological, psychological, and behavioral therapies.

Pharmacological therapy has yet to produce a "magic bullet" medication to treat substance abuse. Investigators who conduct research to uncover the biomedical substrate of addiction are hopeful that such biological treatment agents will someday be available. Others, such as supporters of self-help groups, are often adamant in their insistence that pharmacological interventions should not be used to treat drug problems. Professional programs, however, often use medications for two adjunctive treatment goals. One goal is to manage withdrawal or detoxification; drugs such as a prescription of benzodiazepines to reduce the anxiety and stress associated with alcohol detoxification, nicotine chewing gum to ease the discomfort of smoking cessation, and an administration of methadone as an alternative to acute withdrawal from illicit opiates are used. In the case of nicotine replacement therapy or methadone maintenance, the continued use of these drugs may be considered an alternative treatment goal to abstinence. Drugs are also used during rehabilitation and maintenance including, for example, the use of disulfiram (Antabuse) in the treatment of alcohol dependence (drinking alcohol when this drug is taken causes an adverse physiological reaction), administration of naltrexone to block the euphoric effects of opiate use, and chemical aversion treatment (e.g., administration of emetic drugs to establish a conditioned aversive response to alcohol cues). In addition, clients are sometimes given antidepressive or antianxiety medications as adjuncts to substance abuse treatment.

Psychological therapies include individual and group approaches as well as marital and family therapy. Individual dynamic psychotherapy has not been widely used as a primary treatment strategy, primarily because it has not proven effective in alleviating substance abuse problems. Recent psychodynamic theories of addictive behavior (e.g., Dodes & Khantzian, 1991) may lead to more effective interventions, however. The majority of contemporary treatment programs rely instead on group therapy techniques (Blume, 1985; Galanter, Castaneda, & Franco, 1991), also the staple of self-help approaches. Group therapy includes both milieu or community-based and insight-oriented approaches. Marital and family therapy has been increasingly utilized as a primary or adjunctive modality, recognizing that substance abuse problems often are influenced by basic interpersonal dynamics (Heath & Stanton, 1991; Koffinke, 1991; McCrady, 1986; Seilhamer, 1991). Popular interests in marital and family issues are prominent in the codependency and ACOA (Adult Children of Alcoholics) movements.

Behavioral treatment methods have also received wide attention (e.g., Cox, 1987; Hester & Miller, 1989; Monti et al., 1989). Behavior therapists have been active in developing and evaluating a variety of empirically based techniques. Aversion therapy (Wilson, 1987), and covert sensitization (Cautella, 1977) have been applied in the treatment of alcohol dependence. Cue exposure, designed to extinguish reactivity or craving to substance-use cues (e.g., exposure to drug-taking paraphernalia) has been explored as a behavioral approach to smoking, drinking, and abuse of other substances such as cocaine and the opiates (Blakey & Baker, 1980; Childress, McLellan, & O'Brien, 1986; Cooney, Gillespie, Baker, & Kaplan, 1987). Other operant procedures, such as contingency contracting (Bigelow, Stitzer, Griffiths, & Liebson, 1981) and community reinforcement methods (Azrin, Sisson, Meyers, & Godley, 1982; Hunt & Azrin, 1973) have also been evaluated. In the community reinforcement method, access to family, jobs, and friends is made contingent upon continued sobriety.

The cornerstone of behavior therapy for substance abuse problems is skills-training (Chaney, O'Leary, & Marlatt, 1978; Monti et al., 1989). In this approach, clients are taught behavioral and cognitive skills such as resisting social pressure, increased assertiveness, relaxation and stress management, and interpersonal communication (Shiffman & Wills, 1985).

Traditional approaches to substance abuse often combine a number of treatment modalities in a composite program. Perhaps the most widely used approach is the 30-day inpatient chemical dependency treatment model first developed by the Hazelton Foundation in Minnesota for the treatment of alcohol dependence (Cook, 1988). The Minnesota model embraces the disease model of addiction and relies on a 12-step approach coupled with training in drug education and group therapy. Another widely used method, first applied in the treatment of heroin addiction is the therapeutic community or TC (DeLeon & Ziegenfuss, 1986). Now applied to both opiate and cocaine dependency, the TC model is based on a residential community experience that emphasizes firm behavioral norms, encounter group sessions, a clearly specified system of rewards and punishments within a communal economy, and a series of hierarchical responsibilities associated with one's progress in the program.

Research on the effectiveness of professional treatment reveals a mixed pattern of results. A recent comprehensive review of the alcohol treatment literature (Institute of Medicine, 1990a) concludes that, "Although no single treatment has been identified as effective for all persons with alcohol problems, a variety of specific treatment methods has been associated with positive outcomes in some groups of persons seeking treatment. Brief interventions have been shown to be effective compared with no treatment and compared with more complex treatments" (p. 149). Other reviews of alcohol treatment studies (e.g., Miller & Hester, 1986) tend to confirm this finding. Reviews of the treatment literature for substance abuse problems other than alcohol reveal a similar pattern of findings. After reviewing the outcome of studies evaluating several treatment modalities (e.g., methadone maintenance, therapeutic communities, and inpatient chemical dependency programs), the Institute of Medicine (1990b) concluded that some individuals do well in each modality but that no one modality is uniformly successful: ". . . the profiles of clients admitted to the major modalities are quite different, and one cannot compare the performance or results of each modality with the others as if they were all simply interchangeable" (p. 12). The simplistic question, "Does treatment work?" is replaced with the following: "Which kinds of individuals, with what kinds of . . . problems, are likely to respond to what kinds of treatments by achieving what kinds of goals when delivered by which kinds of practitioners?" (Institute of Medicine, 1990a, p. 149).

Treatment Matching

That some people with substance abuse problems respond well to certain treatment modalities but not to others has led to the current interest in *treatment matching*. The hypothesis here is that treatment outcome will improve if clients are matched to the most appropriate form of treatment, based on a knowledge of matching criteria. To assist in the matching process, a complete assessment of the client's life situation and personal history is a critical first step. In a recent review of assessment procedures, Donovan and Marlatt (1988) adopt a biopsychosocial definition of substance abuse and recommend a thorough assessment of "factors common to addictive behaviors, those specific to a given addictive experience, the particular response system under consideration, the degree of thoroughness required, the phase of the addictive disorder, and the stage of the change process" (Donovan, 1988, p. 38). A variety of behavioral, cognitive, and physiological assessment procedures for drinking, smoking, and other substance abuse problems are detailed in the Donovan and Marlatt (1988) text.

Treatment matching takes into consideration the client's motivation and beliefs about effective treatment options. Analysis of the client's fit with each of the four models of addiction (described in the section on models of addiction) and his or her current status in the stages of change sequence are important matching criteria. The specific substance or substances of abuse must also be considered, since different treatment modalities are often geared to a particular target behavior (e.g., methadone maintenance for opiate dependence). Although some treatment programs are geared toward specific substance problems such as cocaine addiction (e.g., Wallace, 1991; Washton & Gold, 1987), most adopt an eclectic, polydrug approach to treatment.

Demographic factors are also important in treatment matching. The client's gender may be a factor in selecting either a generic, coeducational program or one that is designed for the particular needs of women or men. Age of the client may dictate assignment to special programs for adolescent or elderly clients. Treatment of minority clients often calls for assignment to programs that respond to the specific needs and values of different ethnic groups. Other possible matching criteria include choice of treatment goals (abstinence vs. moderation), selection of therapist (gender and training), and treatment setting (inpatient vs. outpatient), and concurrent psychopathology (e.g., Cooney, Kadden, Litt, & Getter, 1991). Although research on treatment matching is still in the developmental stage (Institute of Medicine, 1990a; Marlatt, 1988; Miller & Heather, 1986), several ongoing studies will provide further data on the viability of this approach. As one example, the National Institute on Alcohol Abuse and Alcoholism (NIAAA) has funded a major matching study for the treatment of alcohol dependence. In Project Match, patients will be randomly assigned to one of three treatment conditions: cognitive behavioral therapy, motivational interviewing, or a 12-step program; the results should provide information as to who benefits from which type of treatment modality.

Relapse Prevention

Relapse prevention (RP) consists of a variety of prevention and intervention strategies matched to the maintenance stage of recovery (Chiauzzi, 1991; Daley, 1989; Gorski & Miller, 1986; Marlatt & Gordon, 1985; Wanigaratne, Wallace, Pullin, Keaney, & Farmer, 1990). As outlined by Marlatt and Gordon (1985), RP is based in social learning theory and utilizes cognitive-behavioral techniques in the context of self-management training. The goals of RP include (a) training clients to anticipate high-risk situations for relapse and to develop coping skills to prevent relapse; (b) training clients who have experienced an initial lapse (the first slip or violation of treatment goals) how to recover and get back on track before a full-blown relapse occurs; (c) helping clients who have experienced relapse to cope with their setback and to remotivate them to make another attempt to change, before the relapse leads to a state of collapse or giving up (e.g., dropping out of treatment).

RP embraces a wide variety of self-management skills. Clients are trained to identify their unique relapse chain, the chain of events that often culminate in a high-risk situation for experiencing urges or lapses (e.g., negative emotional mood states, social pressure situations, or exposure to substance cues). Assessing self-efficacy for coping with high-risk situations is an important step in formulating intervention strategies (e.g, Annis & Davis, 1989). Clients are taught both behavioral and cognitive coping skills to handle high-risk situations and urges (e.g., mood management, assertive training, and imagery for urge control). Cognitive reframing procedures are used to turn the guilt and self-blame often experienced after a lapse (the *abstinence violation effect*) into a more optimistic set of attributions—a lapse is defined as a mistake or error in the recovery learning process, a temporary setback than can be overcome by renewed coping efforts. A final goal of RP is the development of a balanced lifestyle in which the client learns new and more adaptive ways of coping with stress and to replace the addictive behavior with such positive addictions (Glasser, 1976) as meditation and exercise. Although initial research on the effectiveness of RP is promising (Brownell, Marlatt, Lichtenstein, & Wilson 1986; Chaney, O'Leary, & Marlatt, 1978), further studies are needed to document the overall impact of this approach.

References

Alcoholics Anonymous World Services, Inc. (1955). *Alcoholics Anonymous: The story of how many thousands of men and women have recovered from alcoholism*. New York: Author.

Alcoholics Anonymous World Services, Inc. (1987). AA surveys its membership: A demographic report. *About AA: A Newsletter for Professional Men and Women, Fall*, 1–2.

Alden, L. E. (1988). Behavioral self-management controlled-drinking strategies in a context of secondary prevention. *Journal of Consulting and Clinical Psychology, 56*(2), 280–286.

American Psychiatric Association, (1987). *Diagnostic and statistical manual of mental disorders*. (3rd ed. rev.). Washington, DC: Author.

Annis, H. M., & Davis, C. S. (1989). Relapse prevention training: A cognitive-behavioral approach based on self-efficacy theory. In D. C. Daley (Ed.), *Relapse: Conceptual, research, and clinical perspectives* (pp. 81–104). New York: Haworth

Azrin, N. H., Sisson, R. W., Meyers, R. W., & Godley, M. (1982). Alcoholism treatment by disulfiram and community reinforcement therapy. *Journal of Behavior Therapy and Experimental Psychiatry, 13*, 105–112.

Baer, J. S., Kivlahan, D. R., Fromme, K., & Marlatt, G. A. (1991). Secondary prevention of alcohol abuse with college student populations: A skills-training approach. In N. Heather, W. R. Miller, & J. Greeley (Eds.), *Self control and the addictive behaviors* (pp. 339–356). New York: Maxwell Macmillan Publishing Group.

Baer, J. S., Marlatt, G. A., Kivlahan, D. R., Fromme, K., Larimer, M., & Williams, E. (in press). An experimental test of three methods of alcohol risk-reduction with young adults. *Journal of Consulting and Clinical Psychology*.

Baker, T., & Cannon, D. S. (1988). *Assessment and treatment of addictive disorders*. New York: Praeger.

Bandura, A. (1977). Self-efficacy: Toward a unifying theory of behavior change. *Psychological Review, 48*, 191–215.

Berkowitz, A. D., & Perkins, H. W. (1986). Problem drinking among college students: A review of recent research. *Journal of American College Health, 35*, 1–28.

Biernacki, P. (1986). *Pathways from heroin addiction: Recovery without treatment*. Philadelphia: Temple University Press.

Bigelow, G., Stitzer, M. L., Griffiths, R. R., & Liebson, I. A. (1981). Contingency management approaches to drug self-administration and drug abuse: Efficacy and limitations. *Addictive Behaviors, 6*, 241–252.

Blakey, R., & Baker, T. (1980). An exposure approach to alcohol abuse. *Behavior Research & Therapy, 18*, 319–325.

Blume, S. B. (1985). Group therapy in the treatment of alcoholism. In S. Zimberg, J. Wallace, & S. B. Blume (Eds.), *Practical approaches to alcoholism psychotherapy* (pp. 7–107). New York: Plenum Press.

Botvin, G. J. (1986). Substance abuse prevention research: Recent developments and future directions. *Journal of School Health, 56*, 369–374.

Braucht, G. N., & Braucht, B. (1984). Prevention of problem drinking among youth: Evaluation of educational strategies. In P. M. Miller & T. D. Nirenberg (Eds.), *Prevention of alcohol abuse* (pp. 253–280). New York: Plenum Press.

Brennan, A. F., Walfish, S., & AuBuchon, P. (1986). Alcohol use and abuse in college students: 2. Social environmental correlates, methodological issues, and implications for intervention. *International Journal of the Addictions, 21*, 475–493.

Brickman, P., Rabinowitz, V. C., Karuza, J., Jr., Coates, D., Cohn, E., & Kidder, L. (1982). Models of helping and coping. *American Psychologist, 37*(4), 368–384.

Brownell, K. D., Marlatt, G. A., Lichtenstein, E., & Wilson, G. (1986). Understanding and preventing relapse. *American Psychologist, 41*, 765–782.

Cautella, J. R. (1977). The treatment of alcoholism by covert sensitization. *Psychotherapy: Theory, Research, and Practice, 7*, 86–90.

Chaney, E. F., O'Leary, M. R., & Marlatt, G. A. (1978). Skill training with alcoholics. *Journal of Consulting and Clinical Psychology, 46*, 1092–1104.

Chiauzzi, E. J. (1991). *Preventing relapse in the addictions: A biopsychosocial approach*. New York: Pergamon Press.

Childress, R. F., McLellan, A. T., & O'Brien, C. P. (1986). Role of conditioning factors in the development of drug dependence. *Psychiatric Clinics of North America, 9*, 413–425.

Ciraulo, D. A., & Shader, R. I. (1991). *Clinical manual of chemical dependence*. Washington DC: American Psychiatric Press.

Clean and Sober—and Agnostic. (1991, July 8). *Newsweek*, pp. 63–64.

Cohen, S., Lichtenstein, E., Prochaska, J. O., Rossi, J. S., Gritz, E. R., Carr, C. R., Orleans, C. T., Schoenbach, V. J., Bierner, L., Abrams, D., DiClemente, C., Curry, S., Marlatt, G. A., Cummings, K. M., Emant, S. L., Giovino, G., & Ossip-Klein, D. (1989). Debunking myths about quitting: Evidence from 10 perspective studies of persons who attempt to quit smoking by themselves. *American Psychologist, 44*(11), 1355–1365.

Cook, C. C. H. (1988). The Minnesota Model in the management of drug and alcohol dependency. *British Journal of Addiction, 83*, 735–748.

Cooney, N. L., Gillespie, R. A., Baker, L. H., & Kaplan, R. F. (1987). Cognitive changes after alcohol cue exposure. *Journal of Consulting and Clinical Psychology, 55*, 150–155.

Cooney, N. L., Kadden, R. M., Litt, M. D., & Getter, H. (1991). Matching alcoholics to coping skills or interactional therapies: Two-year follow-up results. *Journal of Clinical and Consulting Psychology, 59*, 598–601.

Cox, W. M. (Ed.). (1987). *Treatment and prevention of alcohol problems: A resource manual*. Orlando, FL: Academic Press.

Cox, W. M. (1988). Personality theory. In C. D. Chaudron & D. A. Wilkinson (Eds.), *Theories on alcoholism* (pp. 143–172). Toronto: Addiction Research Foundation.

Cox, W. M. (Ed.). (1990). *Why people drink*. New York: Gardner Press.

Crabbe, J. C., McSwigan, J. D., & Belknap, J. K. (1985). The role of genetics in substance abuse. In M. Galizio & S. A. Maisto (Eds.), *Determinants of substance abuse* (pp. 13–64). New York: Plenum Press.

Curry, S. G., & Marlatt, G. A. (1987). Building self-confidence, self-efficacy, and self-control. In W. M. Cox (Ed.), *Treatment and prevention of alcohol problems: A resource manual* (pp. 117–138). New York: Academic Press.

Daley, D. C. (Ed.). (1989). *Relapse: Conceptual, research and clinical perspectives*. New York: Haworth Press.

Daley, D. C., & Raskin, M. S. (1991). *Treating the chemically dependent and their families*. Newbury, CA: Sage Publications.

DeLeon, G., & Ziegenfuss, J. T. (Eds.). (1986). *Therapeutic communities for addition*. Springfield, IL: C. C. Thomas.

DiClemente, C. C., & Prochaska, J. O. (1982). Self-change and therapy change of smoking behavior: A comparison of process of change in cessation and maintenance. *Addictive Behaviors, 7*, 133–142.

Dodes, L. M., & Khantzian, E. J. (1991). Individual psychodynamic psychotherapy. In R. J. Frances & S. I. Miller (Eds.), *Clinical textbook of addictive disorders* (pp. 391–405). New York: Guilford Press.

Donovan, D. A., & Marlatt, G. A. (1988). *Assessment of addictive behaviors*. New York: Guilford Press.

Donovan, D. M. (1988). Assessment of addictive behaviors: Implications of an emerging biopsychosocial model. In D. M. Donovan & G. A. Marlatt (Eds.), *Assessment of addictive behaviors* (pp. 3–50). New York: Guilford Press.

Engs, R. C., & Hanson, D. J. (1988). University students' drinking patterns and problems: Examining the effects of raising the purchase age. *Public Health Reports, 103*, 667–673.

Fillmore, K. M. (1988). *Alcohol use across the life course: A critical review of 70 years of international longitudinal research*. Toronto: Addiction Research Foundation.

Frances, R. J., & Miller, S. I. (1991). *Clinical textbook of addictive disorders*. New York: Guilford Press.

Galanter, M., Castaneda, R., & Franco, H. (1991). Group therapy and self-help groups. In R. J. Frances & S. I. Miller (Eds.), *Clinical textbook of addictive disorders* (pp. 431–451). New York: Guilford Press.

Glasser, W. (1976). *Positive addiction*. New York: Harper & Row.

Goldman, M. S., Brown, S. A., & Christiansen, B. A. (1987). Expectancy theory: Thinking about drinking. In H. T. Blane & K. E. Leonard (Eds.), *Psychological theories of drinking and alcoholism* (pp. 181–220). New York: Guilford Press.

Goodstadt, M. S. (1986). Alcohol education research and practice: A logical analysis of the two realities. *Journal of Drug Education, 16*, 349–365.

Goodwin, D. W. (1990). Genetic determinants of reinforcement from alcohol. In W. M. Cox (Ed.), *Why people drink* (pp. 37–50). New York: Gardner.

Gorski, T. T., & Miller, M. (1986). *Staying sober: A guide for relapse prevention.* Independence, MO: Independence Press.

Hall, S., Havassy, B., & Wasserman, D. (1990). Commitment to abstinence and acute stress in relapse to alcohol, opiates, and nicotine. *Journal of Consulting and Clinical Psychology, 58*, 175–181.

Hall, S., Havassy, B., & Wasserman, D. (1991). Effects of commitment to abstinence, positive moods, stress, and coping on relapse to cocaine use. *Journal of Consulting and Clinical Psychology, 59*, 526–532.

Hawkins, J. D., Catalano, R. F., & Miller, J. Y. (in press). Risk and protective factors for alcohol and other drug problems: Implications for substance abuse prevention. *Psychological Bulletin.*

Heath, A. W., & Stanton, M. D. (1991). Family therapy. In R. J. Frances & S. I. Miller (Eds.), *Clinical textbook of addictive disorders* (pp. 406–430). New York: Guilford Press.

Hester, R., & Miller, W. (1989). *Handbook of alcoholism treatment approaches: Effective alternatives.* New York: Pergamon.

Hunt, G. M., & Azrin, N. H. (1973). A community-reinforcement approach to alcoholism. *Behavior Research & Therapy, 11*, 91–104.

Hunt, W. A. (1990). Brain mechanisms that underlie the reinforcing effects of ethanol. In W. M. Cox (Ed.), *Why people drink* (pp. 71–92). New York: Gardner Press.

Institute of Medicine (1990a). *Broadening the base of treatment for alcohol problems.* Washington, DC: National Academy Press.

Institute of Medicine (1990b). *Treating drug problems* (Vol. 1). Washington DC: National Academy Press.

Jacob, T. (1987). Alcoholism: A family interaction perspective. In P. C. Rivers (Ed.), *Alcohol & addictive behavior* (pp. 159–206). Lincoln, NE: University of Nebraska Press.

Jellinek, E. M. (1960). *The disease model of alcoholism.* Highland Park, NJ: Hillhouse Press.

Jessor, R., & Jessor S. L. (1975). Adolescent development and the onset of drinking: A longitudinal study. *Journal of Studies on Alcohol, 36*, 27–51.

Johnson, V. E. (1986). *How to help someone who doesn't want help.* St. Paul, MN: Johnson Institute.

Kivlahan, D. R., Marlatt, G. A., Fromme, K., Coppel, D. B., & Williams, E. (1990). Secondary prevention with college drinkers: Evaluation of an alcohol skills training program. *Journal of Consulting and Clinical Psychology, 58*(6), 805–810.

Koffinke, C. (1991). Family recovery issues and treatment resources. In D. C. Daley & M. S. Raskin (Eds.), *Treating the chemically dependent and their families* (pp. 195–214). Newbury Park, CA: Sage Publications.

Lang, A. R., & Michaler, E. M. (1990). Expectancy effects in reinforcement from alcohol. In W. M. Cox (Ed.), *Why people drink* (pp. 193–232). New York: Gardner Press.

Lewis, J. A., Dana, R. Q., & Blevins, G. A. (1988). *Substance abuse counseling.* Pacific Grove, CA: Brooks/Cole.

Littman, G. K. (1980). Relapse in alcoholism: Traditional and current approaches. In G. Edwards & M. Grant (Eds.), *Alcoholism treatment in transition.* London: Croom Helm.

Marlatt, G. A. (1988). Matching clients to treatment. In D. M. Donovan & G. A. Marlatt (Eds.), *Assessment of addictive behaviors* (pp. 474–483). New York: Guilford Press.

Marlatt, G. A., Baer, J. S., Donovan, D. M., & Kivlahan, D. R. (1988). Addictive behaviors: Etiology and treatment. In M. K., Rosenzweig & L. W. Porter (Eds.), *Annual review of psychology* (Vol. 39, pp. 223–252). Palo Alto, CA: Annual Reviews, Inc.

Marlatt, G. A., Curry, S., & Gordon, J. R. (1988). A longitudinal analysis of unaided smoking cessation. *Journal of Consulting and Clinical Psychology, 56*, 715–720.

Marlatt, G. A., & Gordon, J. R. (Eds.). (1985). *Relapse prevention: Maintenance strategies in the treatment of addictive behaviors.* New York: Guilford Press.

McCarty, D. (1985). Environmental factors in substance abuse. In M. Galizio & S. A. Maisto (Eds.), *Determinants of substance abuse* (pp. 247–282). New York: Plenum Press.

McCrady, B. S. (1986). The family in the change process. In W. R. Miller & N. Heather (Eds.), *Treating addictive behaviors* (pp. 305–318). New York: Plenum Press.

Miller, P. M., & Nirenberg, T. D. (Eds.). (1984). *Prevention of alcohol abuse.* New York: Plenum Press.

Miller, W. R. (1983). Motivational interviewing with problem drinkers. *Behavioural Psychotherapy, 11*, 147–172.

Miller, W. R., & Heather, N. (1986). *Treating addictive behaviors: Processes of change.* New York: Plenum Press.

Miller, W. R., & Hester, R. K. (1986). The effectiveness of alcoholism treatment: What research reveals. In W. R. Miller & N. K. Heather (Eds.), *Treating addictive behaviors* (pp. 121–174). New York: Plenum Press.

Miller, W. R., & Rollnick, S. (1991). *Motivation interviewing: Preparing people for change.* New York: Guilford Press.

Mirrin, S. M., & Weiss, R. D. (1991). Substance abuse and mental illness. In R. J. Frances & S. I. Miller (Eds.), *Clinical textbook of addictive disorders* (pp. 271–298). New York: Guilford Press.

Monti, P. M., Abrams, D. B., Kadden, R. M., & Cooney, N. (1989). *Treating alcohol dependence.* New York: Guilford Press.

Moskowitz, J. (1989). The primary prevention of alcohol problems: A critical review of the research literature. *Journal of Studies on Alcohol, 50*, 54–88.

Nathan, P. E. (1991). Substance use disorders in the *DSM-IV*. *Journal of Abnormal Psychology, 100*, 356–361.

Newlin, D. B., & Thompson, J. B. (1991). Chronic tolerance and sensitization to alcohol in sons of alcoholics. *Alcoholism: Clinical and Experimental Research, 15*, 399–405.

Peele, S., & Brodsky. A. (1991). *The truth about addiction and recovery*. New York: Simon & Schuster.

Pentz, M. A. (1991). Primary prevention of adolescent drug abuse. In C. B. Fisher & R. N. Lerner (Eds.), *Applied developmental psychology*. Cambridge, MA: McGraw-Hill.

Prochaska, J. O., & DiClemente, C. C. (1983). Stages and processes of self-change of smoking: Toward an integrative model of change. *Journal of Consulting and Clinical Psychology, 51*, 390–395.

Prochaska, J. O., DiClemente, C. C., Velicer, W. F., Ginpil, S., & Norcross, J. C. (1985). Predicting change in smoking status for self-changers. *Addictive Behaviors, 10*, 395–406.

Random House dictionary of the English language (2nd ed.).(1987). New York: Random House.

Sanchez-Craig, M., Leigh, G., Spivak, K., & Lei, H. (1989). Superior outcome of females over males after brief treatment for the reduction of heavy drinking. *British Journal of Addiction, 84*, 395–403.

Schachter, S. (1982). Recidivism and self-cure of smoking and obesity. *American Psychologist, 37*, 436–444.

Seilhamer, R. A. (1991). Effects of addiction on the family. In D. C. Daley & M. S. Raskin (Eds.), *Treating the chemically dependent and their families* (pp. 172–194). Newbury Park, CA: Sage Publications.

Shiffman, S., & Wills, T. A. (1985). (Eds.) *Coping and substance abuse: A conceptual framework*. New York: Academic Press.

Single, E. W. (1988). The availability theory of alcohol-related problems. In C. D. Chaudron & D. A. Wilkinson (Eds.), *Theories on alcoholism* (pp. 325–352). Toronto: Addiction Research Foundation.

Sobell, L. C., Sobell, M. B., & Toneatto, T. (1991). Natural recovery from alcohol problems: A controlled study. In N. Heather, W. R. Miller, & J. Greeley (Eds.), *Self-control and the addictive behaviors* (pp. 198–242). New York: Maxwell Macmillan Publishing.

Stall, R., & Biernacki, P. (1986). Spontaneous remission from the problematic use of substance: An inductive model derived from a comparative analysis of the alcohol, opiate, tobacco, and food/obesity literatures. *International Journal of Addictions, 2*, 1–23.

Tabakoff, B., & Hoffman, P. L. (1991). Neurochemical effects of alcohol. In R. J. Frances & S. I. Miller (Eds.), *Clinical textbook of addictive disorders* (pp. 525–527). New York: Guilford Press.

Trice, H. M., & Beyer, J. A. (1984). Work related outcomes of the constructive confrontation strategy in a job based alcoholism program. *Journal of Studies on Alcohol, 45*, 393–404.

Trimpey, J. (1989). *Rational recovery from alcoholism: The small book.* Lotus, CA: Lotus Press.

Tuchfeld, B. S. (1981). Spontaneous remission in alcoholics. *Journal of Studies on Alcohol, 42,* 626–641.

U.S. Department of Health and Human Services. (1986). *The health consequences of involuntary smoking.* Rockville, MD: Author.

Vaillant, G. E. (1983). *The natural history of alcoholism.* Cambridge, MA: Harvard University Press.

Wallace, B. C. (1991). *Crack cocaine.* New York: Brunner/Mazel.

Wanigaratne, S., Wallace, W., Pullin, J., Keaney, F., & Farmer, R. (1990). *Relapse prevention for addictive behaviors.* Oxford: Blackwell Scientific Publications.

Washton, A. M., & Gold, M. S. (Eds.). (1987). *Cocaine: A clinician's handbook.* New York: Guilford Press.

White, H. R., Bates, M. E., & Johnson, V. (1990). Social reinforcement and alcohol consumption. In W. M. Cox (Ed.), *Why people drink* (pp. 233–262). New York: Gardner Press.

Wilson, G. T. (1987). Chemical aversion conditioning as a treatment for alcoholism: A re-analysis. *Behavior Research Therapy, 25,* 503–516.

Zinberg, N. E., & Harding, W. M. (1982). *Control over intoxicant use.* New York: Human Sciences Press.

Zoja, L. (1989). *Drugs, addiction and initiation.* Boston, MA: Sigo Press.

Zucker, R. A. (1987). The four alcoholisms: A developmental account of the etiologic process. In P. C. Rivers (Ed.), *Alcohol and addictive behavior* (pp. 27–84). Lincoln, NE: University of Nebraska Press.

BERNARD WEISS

BEHAVIORAL TOXICOLOGY: A NEW AGENDA FOR ASSESSING THE RISKS OF ENVIRONMENTAL POLLUTION

B ernard Weiss received his BA in psychology from the New York University and his PhD in psychology from the University of Rochester. During the 1950s, Dr. Weiss worked as a research associate at the University of Rochester and the U.S. Air Force School of Aviation Medicine. He then went on to become an instructor and assistant professor at the Johns Hopkins University School of Medicine, Pharmacology and Experimental Therapeutics. He was also an assistant professor at the Johns Hopkins University School of Medicine, Psychiatry. Dr. Weiss is currently at the University of Rochester School of Medicine, where he is a professor of toxicology in the Department of Environmental Health Sciences, and holds appointments in Pharmacology and Psychology.

Dr. Weiss has served on a number of committees and panels, including the National Academy of Science/National Research Council (NAS/NRC) Committee on Neurotoxicology and Risk Assessment, the Science Advisory Board of the Environmental Protection Agency (EPA) and other EPA panels, the Board of Scientific Counselors of the National Institute of Environmental Health Sciences (NIEHS), the NAS/NRC Safe Drinking Water Committee, the NAS/NRC Complex Mixtures Committee and the New York State Advisory Board on Municipal Waste Incineration. In addition, he has served on the editorial boards of *Neurotoxicology*,

Science of the Total Environment, and *Toxicology and Applied Pharmacology.*

Professor Weiss has received several awards including the Association for Children and Adults with Learning Disabilities' Scientist of the Year (1986), Burroughs-Wellcome Visiting Professor award (1986), and the Stokinger Award of the American Conference of Governmental Industrial Hygienists (1990). He is also the author of sections in books such as the *Advances in Clinical Child Psychology, Handbook of Psychopharmacology,* and *Behavioral Toxicology.* In addition, he has written and published articles in *Toxicology and Applied Pharmacology, Fundamental and Applied Toxicology* and other journals.

BERNARD WEISS

BEHAVIORAL TOXICOLOGY: A NEW AGENDA FOR ASSESSING THE RISKS OF ENVIRONMENTAL POLLUTION

The leading toxicology textbook (Klaassen, Amdur, & Doull, 1986) defines *toxicology* as *The Science of Poisons*. Think of the images that such a definition evokes: Lucretia Borgia in her kitchen, hunters dipping arrowheads in curare, preparations to defend against chemical warfare. It conjures up visions of lethal incantations like the opening scene of *Macbeth*.

Contemporary toxicology presents another, contrasting, visage. Its context has become indivisible from risk assessment. Supplanting death, the ultimate endpoint, we now discuss probability: How many cancers would be expected at some specific exposure level? Our concerns have veered toward questions about the impact on health of low environmental exposures whose outcomes may lie quiescent over much of a lifetime. In parallel, we now accept the significance of functional consequences, such as those embodied in behavioral measurements. Behavior, in fact, is gaining increasing power as an arbiter of health threats from environmental contamination and as the source of questions about the adequacy of regulatory decisions. This chapter surveys that role; it

Preparation of this chapter was supported in part by Grants ES05433 and ES01247 from the National Institute of Environmental Health Sciences and Contract 90-8 from the Health Effects Institute.

describes both how it developed, and its current scope. It also demonstrates how it calls upon the skills of many different kinds of psychologists.

Historical Roots

The *Federal Register* is the government's daily newspaper. Its pages record regulatory decisions, requests for proposals, meetings of committees and advisory groups, and other functions. It is printed on paper that deteriorates quickly, like newsprint, giving it a transient quality— perhaps reflecting the longevity of most governmental endeavor. Even so, on March 14, 1991, it proclaimed an elevated status for psychology. That issue described a new test rule proposed by the Environmental Protection Agency (EPA) under the Toxic Substances Control Act (TSCA, pronounced "Tosca") of 1976. The proposed test rule would require manufacturers of 10 high-volume solvents to provide data on the neurotoxic properties of these chemicals. It specifies four endpoints: a functional observation battery, motor activity, neuropathology, and schedule-controlled operant behavior. Although the EPA had taken a few less ambitious steps earlier, the new rule represented a firm, unambiguous stride. (The background for the proposed rule will be discussed in the section on commercial and industrial chemicals.)

Legislation is a slowly-simmering process, perhaps inevitable when so many cooks take turns stirring the pot. So, even before TSCA finally became law, the EPA began to design a response to its emerging outline. Because TSCA was being framed primarily to guard against health hazards arising from environmental pollution, its authors surveyed the entire landscape of health issues and wrote a preamble of special significance to psychology: Here, embedded in Congressional mandate, is the requirement that health assessments rely not just on cancer, reproductive impairment, and developmental deformities, but, as well, upon behavior. With TSCA's imminent passage, the National Academy of Sciences, at the request of the EPA, convened a workshop to address the implications of the forthcoming law (National Academy of Sciences, 1983). The report outlined why behavior is an essential measure of adverse health potential and how we proceed to ask behavioral questions.

In 1972 the first meeting wholly devoted to behavioral toxicology (Weiss & Laties, 1975) was organized as one of a series of Rochester Conferences on Environmental Toxicity. At that time, the discipline represented no more than a handful of investigators. Now, anyone dedicated to collecting frequent flier mileage can choose from a constantly churning menu of meetings, workshops, courses, and cruises devoted to the topic. Neurotoxicology is a recognized specialty in the Society of Toxicology. Two journals are directed specifically to the subject, and the leading general journals of toxicology routinely review and publish articles that contain such exotic artifacts as cumulative records.

Despite the clubby atmosphere of the 1972 meeting, however, behavioral toxicology did not arise through spontaneous generation in that year. Like other new scientific disciplines assembled from the fragments of older enterprises, it reflects its multiple origins: behavioral pharmacology, workplace exposure standards, the environmental movement, and the courts.

Behavioral Pharmacology

With the introduction in the 1950s of drugs for the chemotherapy of behavioral disorders, behavioral research assumed three important roles. The first was drug discovery; to find chemicals capable of modifying behavior, they must first be assayed for behavioral effects. The second took root in the first: Which behaviors should be chosen for such assays, and how do they respond to different chemical classes? This question swept the discipline into a broader scientific stream, because, then, questions arose about neurochemistry and its coupling to behavior. The third set of questions was eminently practical: How is therapeutic outcome measured other than by psychological testing and behavior?

It was a mere sidestep to toxicology for those researchers who had worked in pharmacology. After all, much, if not most of the phenomena studied under the banner of pharmacology amounted to selective toxicity anyway. The main difference? The framework of safety, now formalized in the tenets of risk assessment. Unlike drugs, environmental contaminants do not offer health benefits in exchange for health risks. Rather than simply searching for chemicals that act on the nervous system, behavioral toxicologists, like other toxicologists, are being asked to judge a much more subtle and complicated question: How much is safe? How low a dose or exposure level of a chemical is sufficiently free of adverse effects to pose an acceptable level of risk?

Workplace Exposure Standards

Worksites are notorious repositories of highly toxic substances. The index of chemicals carcinogenic to humans amount mostly to a list of agents whose hazards first engaged attention in workers. Testicular cancer in chimney sweeps and bladder cancer in analine dye workers are two notable examples.

Neurotoxic agents are even more prominent in the workplace of today than possible carcinogens. Anger and Johnson (1985) identified 750 chemicals or chemical groups offering evidence of neurotoxicity, then matched them against a list of 200 chemicals to which one million or more workers are routinely exposed, according to the National Institute of Occupational Safety and Health (NIOSH). Overlap between the two lists indicated that 65 of the 200 high-volume chemicals gave evidence of neurotoxic risk. NIOSH also publishes reviews of workplace chemicals; the reviews are designed to provide the basis for exposure standards. Anger (1990a) noted that standards for about 40% of the chemicals reviewed stem from their nervous system actions at low exposure levels.

Even before behavior and toxicology became formally connected, however, the workplace linkage had been established. The American Conference of Governmental Industrial Hygienists (ACGIH; 1974) pioneered workplace exposure standards long before passage of the Occupational Safety and Health Act of 1970. For airborne exposures, it prescribed *Threshold Limit Values*, defined as concentrations to which the bulk of workers may be exposed chronically without suffering adverse effects. It also recommended what it called *Short Term Exposure Limits*, or concentrations that are limited in duration. Note their definition: "The maximum concentration to which workers can be exposed for a period up to 15 minutes continuously without suffering from . . . narcosis of sufficient degree to increase accident pronenes, impair self-rescue, or materially reduce work efficiency . . ." (p. 2).

Although the ACGIH definition does not use the term *behavior*, its criteria are wholly behavioral. The same is true of many of the classics of occupational medicine and industrial hygiene. It remained for explorers such as Helena Hanninen, who began her work at the Finnish Institute of Occupational Health in the 1960s, to translate these observations into psychological methods and practices (Hanninen, 1971). Now, 20 years after that propitious beginning, psychological testing of workers is itself a flourishing industry, with both experimental and epidemiological branches (Anger, 1990b).

The Environmental Movement

Rachel Carson (1962) reminded us that with stewardship comes responsibility and a tuning of our sensitivities to the less dramatic and conspicuous evidence of environmental degradation. Progressively eroding bird populations do not crash into newspaper headlines with the same jolt as a huge oil spill, but they tell us more about where threats to our own welfare may be lurking.

Thousands of new chemicals are introduced every year, and at a rate that still seems to be ascending. The total volume of chemical production also continues its inexorable rise (Figure 1). At the same time, the accumulating waste products of our society have barely been stemmed by proliferating laws and regulations, with alarming conno-

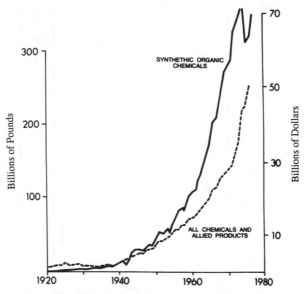

Figure 1. Historical trends in the production of commercial and industrial chemicals (courtesy of Dr. Thomas Clarkson).

tations. Figure 2 depicts the projected burden of waste collected over a century on the basis of different annual rises in pollutant discharge. Some further measures of control, or, at least, restraint, were seen as necessary if the planet were not to be inundated by the products of its own ingenuity.

Projections such as these sensitized many individuals and groups to their implications. They stimulated reflections about the impact on health of such long-term trends, especially those consequences whose actions remain imperceptible until they emerge as disease, much like a latent infection. Environmental catastrophes such as Mexico City and Eastern Europe are compelling illustrations of the perils of inaction.

Toxic Torts

The courtroom is becoming a crucible for venting the lessons of behavioral toxicology. Workers exposed to volatile organic solvents, heavy metals, insecticides, and other neurotoxic chemicals argue that they have suffered lasting effects arising from inadequate protection. Their claims rely on testimony from neurologists, psychiatrists, and psychologists. The debates hinge on the means for ascertaining damage. A worker who inhaled asbestos fibers for years can argue effectively for its role in the etiology of his or her lung cancer. How firmly can you connect complaints of chronic fatigue, depression, and nervousness to

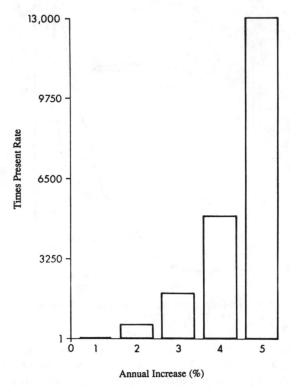

Figure 2. Projected accumulation of pollutant discharge based on different annual increases over a 100-year period (courtesy of Dr. Thomas Clarkson).

employment as a worker in a plant that manufactures pesticides? How compelling is an argument about disability that is based on psychological test scores, especially when the historical record of exposure is an equivocal retrospective reconstruction? The argument can be transformed into a debate about the value of psychological testing, so that psychologists who testify in such cases must be prepared to argue about the validity of their own technology as well as its conjunction with the toxic exposure.

Equivalent debates about the technology erupt when psychological test scores are thrust forward as the basis for setting exposure standards. Here is one instance where the coupling between research and practice is being vetted by lawyers.

The Soviet Tradition

Pavlovian tradition asserts the primacy of the central nervous system (CNS) in physiology. Soviet scientists extended the role of the CNS to toxicology. In departing from the Western practice of relying on tissue damage as the ultimate criterion of adverse responses, the Soviets established function, particularly indexes of CNS performance, as the standard against which toxic potential would be measured.

Exposure standards for both the workplace and the communal environment are typically more stringent in the former USSR than in Western countries. For some agents, the differences amount to ratios of 100:1 or even more. Soviet specialists ascribe the disparities to their reliance on functional criteria rather than pathology (Pavlenko, 1975). Because of these discrepancies, the US–USSR Environmental Health Exchange Agreement, arranged in 1972 in the glow of détente, included a behavioral toxicology component. Its inclusion became an opportunity to familiarize ourselves in detail with Soviet practices. The scenes in Figure 3 are examples of work performed at the Institute for General and Communal Hygiene in Moscow.

It is now obvious to the rest of the world, if it was not before, that Soviet standards reflected what might gently be termed an optimistic imagination. Soviet communities and workplaces expose people to toxic substances at levels far above Western standards. The Soviet standards were political statements, even though many of us concur with the methods proclaimed to have engendered them. But the application of these methods suffered from inadequate investment in technology such as computers, and from rather loose interpretations of scientific rigor. In the laboratory of one Moscow researcher involved in the program, for example, exposures to inhaled materials were based on dial settings calculated at the beginning of the experiments months earlier instead of being continuously monitored. Technicians who were forced to record manually the responses of animals to various conditions (because of the lack of automation) also knew which animals had been exposed to which doses. Most scientists would regard such knowledge as a source of data contamination.

The Current Scene

Eight years ago (Weiss, 1983b) I described behavioral toxicology as a fledgling science. During the intervening time, it has managed to attain a remarkable degree of maturity. I attribute such a rise in status to a convergence between the public's apprehensions and the issues that have engaged the energies of behavioral toxicology's leading investigators. One example is the public's sensitivity to developmental deficits. These have always aroused its concerns, but a continuing flow of media articles about educational crises, low scores on achievement tests by American children, high rates of infant mortality, and associated themes directed attention to sources and remedies. The thalidomide disaster

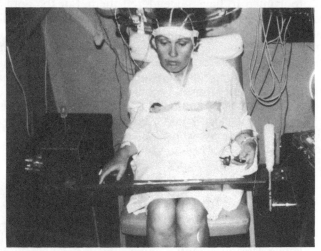

Figure 3. Scenes from the Institute for General and Communal Hygiene (Sysin Institute) in Moscow. Top: Measurement of reaction time in a laboratory devoted to studies of the influence of temperature and illumination on performance. Bottom: Subject in a laboratory devoted to studies of gases and vapors. Exposures occur via a dome above the subject's head. Measures of performance are taken concurrently with electroencephalographic (EEG) and electrocardiographic (EKG) activity.

in the 1960s heightened fears about maternal exposure to chemicals during pregnancy. Stories about the fetal alcohol syndrome and lead poisoning (featuring discussions about mental retardation and intelligence test scores) helped to hone such concerns into a sharpened awareness of the possible risks to normal development posed by toxic chemicals in the environment.

The concept of risk, despite the emotions aroused by the term itself, is inexplicable without an appreciation of the concept of probability. A public that swarms to Las Vegas and Atlantic City and that invests in lottery tickets is not an easy audience to communicate with on the subject. It is no trick to arouse it by pronouncements that a particular chemical used to protect apples will increase cancer by a few cases in a million. Explaining the uncertainties in the statistical model that forms the basis for such a statement strains the expository skills of most scientists. Recall how difficult it is to convey the hazards of tobacco and sunlight effectively enough to alter behavior.

Risk analysis and assessment is viewed with skepticism by many scientists. It is a natural response; scientists are wary of journeying too far from the neighborhood of their data. Risk assessment in toxicology often requires a suspension of skepticism because it may traverse long distances as it leaps across a chasm of extrapolation from high experimental doses to low environmental exposures. For behavioral toxicology the chasm is usually narrower, but still does not relieve us of the responsibility to formulate an answer that is applicable to policy decisions.

Because risk has assumed such a central role in policy decisions by entities such as EPA, it will guide my description of the current status of behavioral toxicology. Such a framework offers another virtue: It aptly highlights the contributions of both laboratory psychologists and those engaged in psychological practice. Think of psychological assessments as predictors of likelihood and the connection leaps out at you. The neurotoxicity of heavy metals, pesticides, and selected industrial chemicals offers a plethora of recent examples that exemplify our evolving perspective.

Metals in the Workplace

The chemist's periodic table consists mainly of metals. They cannot be expunged from our environment by regulations. We can curtail industrial contamination of the environment, of course, but doing so requires that we prescribe levels on the basis of acceptable risks; zero levels are not attainable. For psychologists, the main point to grasp is that many metals may induce deleterious effects (Weiss, 1983a). Table 1 is a partial list. The effects, moreover, may range from pronounced neurological impairment to vague, subjective complaints. I have assembled from clinical

Table 1
Metals Associated With Neurobehavioral Toxicity

Aluminum	Mercury
Arsenic	Nickel
Bismuth	Selenium
Boron	Tellurium
Cadmium	Thallium
Lead	Tin
Manganese	Vanadium

Table 2
Symptoms Ascribed to Metal Toxicity

Anosmia	Jitteriness, irritability
Appetite loss	Mental retardation
Convulsions	Paralysis
Depression	Paresthesias
Disorientation	Peripheral neuropathy
Dizziness	Polyneuritis
Dysarthria	Psychiatric signs
Fatigue, lethargy	Somnolence
Headache	Tremor
Incoordination, ataxia	Visual disturbances
Insomnia	Weakness

and epidemiological reports an inventory of neurobehavioral deficits associated with excessive metal exposure (Table 2).

To complicate things even more, many metals, even those with pronounced toxicity at high levels, are essential nutrients. Selenium is a cogent example. Some parts of China, because of soil conditions, suffer a high prevalence of selenium toxicity (selenosis). Other areas of China, because of inadequate soil concentrations, display a high prevalence of selenium deficiency (Keshan disease). How much selenium in the diet is essential and how much is likely to be toxic? Regulators cannot simply request that it be reduced to the lowest practically achievable level in foods. They have to strike a delicate risk–benefit balance.

Manganese is an essential metal. It is required for cartilage development and participates in many biochemical activities. At high atmospheric levels, workers in manganese mines and in ore-crushing and ferro-manganese processing plants, have often developed severe neurological signs that some observers classified as Parkinson's disease. Barbeau (1984) argued that the disorder is more correctly diagnosed as a dystonia; his arguments seem to have swayed many observers. The other component of manganese neurotoxicity is behavioral in character. In the South American communities where manganese is mined, the disorder is labelled *locura manganica*, or manganese madness. Afflicted miners may display hysterical laughing and weeping, complain simultaneously about insomnia and lethargy, and report sexual dysfunction. Table 3 lists the symptoms of manganese neurotoxicity.

Debates about manganese as a potential source of health problems recently took on a new intensity. Manganese tricarbonyl (MMT), a compound used in Canada as a fuel additive, has been proposed as a replacement for lead in gasoline in the United States. Lead's demise as a fuel additive was partly triggered by its incompatibility with catalytic converters. With accumulating evidence of its contribution to the amount of lead absorbed by children, its final elimination became inevitable.

MMT, when burned in gasoline, is transformed into inorganic manganese compounds like those identified as the source of manganism. Although population exposures, were MMT to be adopted as a replacement for lead, might pose little risk of overt neurotoxicity, some scientists remain cautious. First, they cannot help but recall the chronicle of lead, introduced with little awareness of the quandries it later would generate. Why take a chance of repeating that dismal narrative, they ask? Second, do we really know enough about the less overt risks of manganese exposure—those that require psychological testing to expose? Two recent examples support such prudence (Iregren et al., 1990; Roels et al, 1987). Workers exposed to manganese in industrial settings were studied. Even though both groups of workers displayed no overt signs or symptoms, both investigations detected significant differences between exposed workers and controls on measures such as reaction time, scores on components of the Wechsler Adult Intelligence Scale, and subjective complaints.

A further cause for prudence is our knowledge of how manganese is distributed and disposed of in the body. At Rochester, Newland, Cox,

Table 3
Manganese Neurotoxicity

Major signs	Major symptoms
Abnormal gait	Weakness
Retropulsion, propulsion	Difficulty walking
Diminished leg power	Somnolence
Impaired coordination	Clumsiness
Abnormal laughter	Bradykinesia
Expressionless face	Lack of balance
Dysarthria	Muscle pains

Hamada, Oberdörster, and Weiss (1987) traced the fate of inhaled radioactive manganese, [54]Mn, in monkeys. As with certain other neurotoxicants, typical laboratory species such as rodents offer only remote models of human susceptibility. In these monkeys, however, we found that after a single exposure, radioactivity in the head area, presumably representing brain uptake, declined at a sluggish pace. The half-life (the time required for levels to fall to 50% of their values immediately after exposure) approximated nearly 1 year. Five half-lives span the period required to reach negligible values, so it would take nearly 5 years before almost all of the original [54]Mn would disappear from the brain. A mathematical model of this process indicated that after the original inhalation the lung served as a reservoir of manganese, slowly releasing it for transport to the brain.

To speak of the brain as though it were a homogeneous medium like a bowl of gelatin is absurd, of course. Earlier literature (e.g., Suzuki et al., 1975), based on chemical analyses, indicated that manganese concentrated in the basal ganglia (the collection of subcortical structures assumed to underlie motor control). Technology offers us a much more elegant and precise answer. We took advantage of magnetic resonance imaging (MRI) to localize the accumulation of manganese in the primate brain (Newland, Ceckler, Kordower, & Weiss, 1989). Manganese possesses a special virtue for this purpose; it is a paramagnetic ion, and nuclear magnetic resonance spectropscopy is based on the angular displacement and restoration of protons responding to an oscillating signal superimposed on a static magnetic field. An experimental MRI device, just large enough to contain a monkey, provided access to this technology.

Figure 4 (Newland et al., 1989) contrasts MRI images from a control monkey and one exposed daily, for 6 months, to a manganese chloride aerosol. The difference is striking, almost as though we had inserted a light bulb inside the head. Relevant structures are identified on the right. Later analyses, which quantified aspects of these images, indicated that the globus pallidus retained manganese longer than the other basal ganglia structures. This finding supports the hypothesis that pallidal damage accounts for the dystonias of manganism and is consistent with neuropathological evidence detailed in the earlier literature.

Two questions emerge from our current understanding of manganese neurotoxicity and illustrate the questions about hazard and safety posed by almost any toxic substance. The first is focused on populations: Are workers exposed to manganese from industrial processes distinguishable by psychological tests from unexposed workers? Such questions are answerable only by studies comparing samples differing in exposure histories. The second focuses on individuals: How is it possible to determine that a particular individual is a victim of excessive manganese exposure? The latter question, like most other diagnostic choices, is not wholly a statistical issue, but a judgment based on the integration

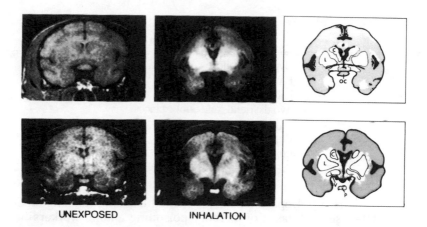

UNEXPOSED   INHALATION

Figure 4. Magnetic resonance images of brain in *M. fascicularis* monkeys. Right: control monkey. Left: monkey exposed to a manganese chloride aerosol for 2 hours daily over a period of 5 months. Coronal sections are displayed at the level of the optic chiasm (top) and pituitary gland (bottom). Abbreviations: L = lentiform nucleus, C = caudate, OC = optic chiasm, V = ventral pallidum, and P = pituitary gland. Note the bright regions in the exposed monkey brain. They indicate pronounced increases in manganese concentrations. From "Visualizing Manganese in the Primate Basal Ganglia With Magnetic Resonance" by M. C. Newland, T. L. Ceckler, J. H. Kordower, and B. Weiss, 1989, *Experimental Neurology, 106*, p. 254. Copyright 1989 by Academic Pess, Inc. Reprinted by permission.

of many sources of information, including exposure history as well as the match between the individual's pattern of test results and that characteristic of a population with a documented exposure history.

Like manganese, mercury exposure engenders a collection of toxic responses that include both behavioral and neurological features. Elemental mercury is notoriously treacherous because it is a liquid at room temperature. When spilled, it can disperse into minute droplets, meander into surface cracks, or seep into carpets. Because of its volatility, any site containing mercury poses a danger of excessive inhalation exposure. Inhaled mercury has a special affinity for the brain.

Tremor is the defining neurological trait of mercury poisoning. In the old felt hat industry where mercury salts were used to process the animal fur, workers would become so disabled by severe tremors that they needed assistance even in getting to the job where they continued to be exposed. The psychological component of mercury poisoning is even more intriguing and goes by the label *erethism*. Its components are listed in Table 4. The extreme shyness of mercury vapor poisoning, described in German mirror workers in 1861 by Adolph Kussmaul, was described in New Jersey hatters in 1912 (Wedeen, 1989).

Table 4
Symptoms of Erethism

Hyperirritability
Blushes easily
Labile temperament
Avoids friends and public places
Timid, shy
Depressed, despondent
Insomnia, fatigue

An Ohio Health Department nurse named Dorothy Benning (1958) encountered several cases of mercury poisoning among workers in a plant that produced carbon brushes for generators. A tamping powder containing 22%–24% mercury was baked on the brushes at high temperatures, a process that released high concentrations of mercury vapor into the workroom atmosphere. One of the women workers described her symptoms in graphic detail:

> I got a sore mouth and had dizzy spells, and I began to be so weak and tired that at night when I got home from work it was hard to even get my supper and do my work. I got so grouchy and nervous I would cry at nothing ... I often would awaken suddenly and have a fluttery feeling like I was scared or floating in space ... I kept feeling worse and getting trembly and nervous and my eyes bloodshot and I seemed to forget things so easily .... (p. 335)

The disparity between flagrant poisoning and incipient toxicity and how it enters into the calculation of worker risk duplicates for mercury the same considerations that I described for manganese. For most substances, exposure standards are erected to provide safety margins broad enough to insulate most workers from adverse effects. Whether they have succeeded in doing so continues to stir debate, partly because such calculations tend to be founded on impressionistic observations rather than on firmly established scientific data.

Research that is based on quantitative testing suggests that the current exposure limits may be too generous to protect all workers. Superficially asymptomatic workers (as defined by clinical medical examinations) may nevertheless display impairment on selected performance measures. One such measure is tremor. Clinical neurologists rate tremor by visual inspection. But irregularities in tremor may be present below amplitudes detectable by unaided observers. Overt tremor is a crude indicator of dysfunction. In a study of women exposed to mercury vapor in the course of calibrating pipettes, we discovered that advanced methods such as power spectral analysis, which require computer processing, are necessary to depict fully the characteristics of abnormal tremor (Wood, Weiss, & Weiss, 1973). Subsequent investigations by other investigators have confirmed this finding, and, moreover, have extended it to show that abnormalities in the frequency spectrum of tremor may be apparent in chronically exposed workers whose blood and urine mercury levels indicate relatively moderate ambient mercury concentrations (e.g., Langolf, Chaffin, Henderson, & Whittle, 1978).

Psychological testing suggests other kinds of deficits as well, some of which resemble components of erethism (reviewed in Anger, 1990a). Complaints of memory difficulties were noted by Rochester investigators in a survey of mercury miners in Spain (Marsh, unpublished report, 1982). Smith, Langolf, and Goldberg (1983) and others, on the basis of short term memory tests, confirmed such complaints. Psychomotor tests (Roels et al., 1985) also pointed to differences between exposed, asymptomatic workers and controls. Such differences, however, are not enough to make the exposed workers dysfunctional. They merely indicate that the exposure controls in place may not offer complete protection. Furthermore, the workers themselves may be unaware of any problems, an aspect noted by Uzzell and Oler (1986) in a neuropsychological study of auxiliary dental workers, and by Albers, Cavender, Levine, and Langolf (1982) in a study of polyneuropathy among chlor-alkali workers. Chlor-alkali processing plants use immense vats of mercury as electrodes to decompose brine into chlorine and caustic soda, and some vapor inevitably escapes.

Although toxicologists think of mercury mostly as an industrial hazard, we are now in the midst of a recurrent debate about its safety for the general population. The latest debate has been incited by claims that silver amalgam dental fillings, which contain elemental mercury, release enough mercury during chewing to provide a dangerous level of exposure. Patient testimonials report miraculous cures of many afflictions following removal of amalgam restorations. Neuropsychologists will surely become entangled in the argument. They must remain aware, however, that dose is the crucial variable in toxicology. On the basis of calculations comparing mercury vapor uptake from amalgams with industrial exposure at the Threshold Limit Value (TLV) of 50 $\mu g/m^3$, Clarkson, Friberg, Hursh, and Nylander (1988) estimated that absorption at the TLV exceeded absorption from amalgams by about 50:1. The anti-amalgam forces will have to find another set of arguments.

Manganese and mercury are prototypes for my argument that the clinical and medical definitions of neurotoxicity are vulnerable to a dangerous degree of imprecision; as I noted in discussing amalgams, they can easily lead to exaggerated estimates or underestimates of toxic potential. They do not protect, set the boundaries of risk, allow any estimate of risk at all, or render patterns, the crucial concomitant of a diagnosis. These deficiencies are why, in the workplace, neuropsychological testing is displacing clinical medicine as the standard by which adverse exposures are gauged.

Pesticide Hazards

Contemporary agriculture is synonomous with pesticides. Even in less developed countries, where agriculture is not practiced on an industrial scale, these chemical treatments have become indispensable. Unhappily, the transfer of pesticide technology has not been accompanied by what might be termed the transfer of toxicological technology (Weiss & Clarkson, 1986). User populations, mostly rural and uneducated, suffer a high incidence of poisonings. Estimates that are derived from World Health Organization data suggest that as many as 500,000 cases of acute poisonings occur annually. As many as 9,000 of these result in death. Wearing contaminated clothing and failure to protect against dermal exposure account for some of this toll. An outbreak of poisoning resulting from the malathion treatment of an area in Pakistan infested with malaria induced toxic signs in 2,800 of the 7,500 applicators. (Malathion is the insecticide that California depends on to keep the Mediterranean fruit fly under control.) The toxic signs included blurred vision, giddiness, and nausea—prime indicators of poisoning by insecticides of the organophosphorous class. Typical acute signs also include weakness and difficulty in breathing, a result of the potent anticholinesterase activity of these compounds.

Massive episodes of this kind occur only rarely in the United States and the other industrialized countries that consume about 80% of world agrochemical production. Yet the developed world suffers only about 1% of all the fatalities ascribed to pesticide poisoning. With such a margin of safety we have moved, as with our other health concerns, from imperiled survival to uneasiness about whether we are functioning as well as we might be. In parallel, the questions that investigators from advanced nations ask about pesticide toxicity have shifted from overt poisoning to incipient dysfunction, which is defined primarily by actions on the nervous system. Nervous system function is a focal question because so many of the pesticides are neurotoxicants (Weiss, 1988a).

The organophosphate (OP) insecticides serve as model compounds with which to illustrate the direction these questions have taken. Levin, Rodnitzky, and Mick (1976) compared farmworkers engaged in OP application with unexposed farmworkers and found significant differences between the groups on the Taylor Manifest Anxiety Scale. Table 5 lists the items distinguishing the responses of the two groups. The exposed workers were free of clinically discernible signs.

Another source of concern is now beginning to emerge. Ishikawa and Miyata (1980) at the 11th International Rochester Conference on Environmental Toxicity in 1978 reported a correlation between areas of

Table 5
Items on the Taylor Manifest Anxiety Scale Sensitive to
Organophosphate Insecticide Exposure

1. I work under a great deal of tension
2. My sleep is fitful and disturbed
3. I have periods of such restlessness that I cannot sit long in a chair
4. I believe that I am no more nervous than most other people
5. I feel anxiety about something or someone almost all the time
6. I am usually calm & not easily upset
7. It makes me nervous to have to wait
8. I practically never blush

Note. Modified from "Anxiety Associated With Exposure to Organophosphate Compounds" by H. S. Levin, R. L. Rodnitzky, and D. L. Mick, 1976, *Archives of General Psychiatry, 33,* p. 227. Copyright 1976, American Medical Association. Reprinted by permission.

high pesticide use in Japan and the incidence of myopia among school children. Between 1957 and 1973, Japan increased its application of pesticides by an astounding 500%, a rise paralleled by a rise of 250% in the prevalence of myopia. They also noted that the amount of OP insecticides applied in any single year was correlated with the incidence of myopia the following year. Experimental studies established that changes in corneal curvature could be produced in dogs treated with OPs over a 2-year period. At the time of the 11th Rochester Conference meeting, U.S. and European scientists had not undertaken such studies. Currently, however, the EPA is beginning to manifest some concern over this issue. Confirmation that visual disturbances may ensue from insecticide exposure would not be surprising. It would simply repeat a pattern already noted with other substances.

Certain OPs can inflict profound structural damage on the nervous system. The first intimations of that possibility loomed in 1930. Large quantities of an alcoholic soft drink flavoring called "Ginger Jake," popular in the South because it was legal during Prohibition, had been contaminated with an extremely potent compound, triorthocresylphosphate (TOCP), which produces a syndrome known as organophosphorous-induced delayed neuropathy (OPIDN; Cranmer & Hixson, 1984). Table 6 lists the main characteristics of this syndrome. Thousands suffered lower extremity weakness, sensory loss, and even paralysis, after consuming the tainted drinks (Morgan, 1982), because TOCP induced axonal damage. Because of this and other episodes, untested OPs are assayed for OPIDN potential by being administered to hens, one of the susceptible species.

The axonopathic properties of certain OPs may need to be considered in evaluating their possible visual neurotoxicity. Merigan and his colleagues have conducted an instructive series of experiments with two other axonopathic agents, acrylamide monomer (Merigan, Barkdoll,

Table 6
Manifestations of Organophosphorous-Induced Delayed Neuropathy

Insidious onset
Progressive distal weakness
Sensory loss in extremities
Ataxia and slapping gait
Altered pain, vibration, and position sense
Altered deep tendon reflexes
Muscle weakness
Normal clinical laboratory tests
Depression, psychotic reactions, anxiety, hallucinations, increased sweating and
    salivation, miosis and blurred vision, nausea, vomiting and diarrhea, tremu-
    lousness

Maurissen, Eskin, & Lapham, 1985) and carbon disulfide (Merigan, Wood, & Zehl, 1985). Acrylamide monomer is a versatile chemical used for stiffening cardboard, for grouting, and as an intermediate in chemical production. Carbon disulfide is a venerable neurotoxicant that finds its most prominent use in the viscose process for manufacturing rayon. Both of these agents, like TOCP, can damage peripheral nerves, but they also act centrally.

Merigan's laboratory at Rochester has trained monkeys to perform several kinds of visual discriminations such as detecting sine wave gratings appearing on a video display as a measure of contrast sensitivity or detecting stimuli of different wavelengths to detect impaired color vision. Monkeys administered acrylamide or carbon disulfide show impaired visual function on such tasks. In pursuing the anatomical correlates of this impairment, Merigan and his co-workers discovered evidence of damage in the lateral geniculate nucleus, a component of the visual pathway, and traced it to destruction of a certain class of retinal ganglion cells. No evidence had appeared earlier to suggest that, in humans, these two agents could produce this kind of neurotoxicity, but the degree of impairment observed by Merigan was probably not detectable by most common clinical examinations or by self-report.

One crucial question about OP neurotoxicity remains unresolved: Are there lasting consequences to an episode of acute poisoning? The question is important because 2–3 thousand poisoning cases severe enough to require hospitalization occur each year in the United States. By clinical criteria, the signs and symptoms fade completely after a few days or weeks. By more sensitive criteria, the aftermath may not be quite as benign. Duffy and Burchfiel (1980) reported enduring electroencephalographic (EEG) changes in both humans and monkeys at least 1 year after the last exposure to the OP sarin, a potent nerve gas. These changes were not apparent simply by inspecting the EEG tracing; as in studies of hand tremor (Wood, Weiss, & Weiss, 1973), they required analyses of the power spectrum, which is the distribution of variance by component frequency. The study was undertaken because of complaints by workers employed in the manufacture of sarin. The symptoms included excessive dreaming, loss of libido, memory loss, and irritability. Other investigators have reported similar results as well as neuropsychiatric disturbances, but several publications have failed to find supporting evidence.

The absence of complete exposure documentation in the earlier studies coupled with their lack of neuropsychological measures led Savage et al. (1988) to attempt a much more detailed assessment of the question. They reported on 100 individuals with carefully documented histories of an episode of OP poisoning and an equal number of matched controls. They standardized their assessment procedures, excluded participants with chronic diseases, and conducted detailed interviews with both the workers and their relatives.

The physical examinations and clinical chemistries in both groups fell within normal bounds, and only the neurological examination suggested possible cognitive impairment. The neuropsychological test battery, which included elements of the Wechsler Adult Intelligence Scale and the Halstead-Reitan battery, revealed marked differences between the groups. Table 7 summarizes these differences. The authors argue the importance of their findings as follows: "The results clearly indicate that there are chronic neurological sequelae to acute organophosphorous poisoning. However, these sequelae are sufficiently subtle that the clinical neurological examination, clinical EEG, and ancillary laboratory testing cannot discriminate poisoned subjects from controls" (Savage et al., 1988, p. 43).

Table 7
Chronic Neurological Sequelae of Acute Organophosphate Pesticide Poisoning

Test name	100 cases	100 controls	p-value
WAIS verbal IQ	105.40	111.86	.001
WAIS performance	108.41	110.13	.242
WAIS full scale	107.5	111.77	.001
Impairment rating	1.07	0.91	.001
Halstead Index	0.30	0.23	.020
Pegboard	148.34	137.96	.002
Card sorting	17.07	12.91	.001

Note. From "Chronic Neurological Sequelae of Acute Organophosphate Poisoning" by E. P. Savage et al., 1988, *Archives of Environmental Health, 43,* p. 42. Reprinted with permission of the Helen Dwight Reid Educational Foundation. Published by Heldref Publications, 1319 18th Street, NW, Washington, DC 20036-1802. Copyright 1988.

Commercial and Industrial Chemicals

The test rule proposed by the EPA on March 14, 1991, stems from a property, neurotoxicity, shared by a group of chemicals known as organic solvents. Although chemically heterogeneous, many of them are highly volatile and lipid soluble. Volatility implies inhalation, a route of exposure that brings these chemicals into contact with the extensive surface area of the lung, from where they enter the blood and are then transported to body tissues. Its high regional blood flow and fat content make the brain a magnet for these agents.

Organic solvents find their way into numerous products and processes. The *Federal Register* announcement lists uses such as solubilizer, diluent, and dispersant, and products such as protective coatings, adhesives, plastics, and inks. Dry cleaning is based on solvents. Degreasing is performed by solvents. They appear in consumer products such as waxes, perfumes, and paint removers, and are manufactured in immense volumes. The 10 chemicals targeted by the test rule are produced in quantities ranging from 12 million to 1.8 billion pounds annually and each entails the exposure of at least 172,000 workers.

Acute exposure to elevated concentrations produces incoordination and drowsiness. Extreme concentrations can induce unconsciousness and, if prolonged, death by respiratory arrest. Repeated episodes of solvent abuse or glue-sniffing may cause permanent brain damage and neurological impairment. These neurotoxic properties are universally recognized. Disagreement flourishes about another issue: the ability of volatile organic solvents at low exposure levels to interfere with complex psychological functions.

Reported associations between chronic solvent exposure, usually in workplace settings, and performance on psychological tests have burgeoned in the past 2 decades (Baker & Fine, 1986; Cranmer & Golberg, 1986). Scandinavian investigators are responsible for many of these reports, which have been disputed for a variety of reasons; lack of appropriate histories and inadequate matching of exposed and control samples elicit the most objections (Grasso, Sharratt, Davies, & Irvine, 1984). Enough consistency had developed, however, especially from recent studies designed explicitly to overcome such criticisms, to provoke the tentative test rule.

Seven of the ten solvents, at some concentration, are proven neurotoxicants in either humans or animals. The other three are also likely to reveal neurotoxic potential. Then why, it is fair to ask, require further confirmation from additional animal testing? The EPA argues that the available data are haphazard; little information is available about the consequences of prolonged exposure and, especially, those reflecting alterations in behavior. The rationale for specifying schedule-controlled operant behavior is particularly revealing. In the past, such data were required only as a second-tier test, after preliminary screening had indicated neurotoxic properties. The March 14, 1991 *Federal Register* notice advised that, "it is proposed as a first-tier test in this rule because of EPA's desire to obtain data on the effects of solvents on learning, memory, and performance" (p. 9112).

Kulig (1990) commented that investigators working at the human level have received little help from their counterparts in the animal laboratory in resolving the effects of solvent exposure on cognitive functioning. The proposed test rule, which even specifies multiple schedule performance, is designed ultimately to redress this imbalance. Properly designed studies, such as that of Wood and Cox (1986), demonstrate that operant techniques can fulfill such a role and even be used to predict human risks without dose extrapolation.

Early Legacies

Teratology describes the scientific study of birth defects. Thalidomide turned teratology into a focus of toxicity testing because the children disfigured by it were the most innocent of victims. Their mothers, early in pregnancy, used the drug as a sedative, convinced, as were their physicians, of its apparent safety. Both were deceived by the German pharmaceutical firm that concealed mounting evidence of its embryotoxicity. The repercussions of that episode triggered a new body of regulations and a swift expansion of research on developmental toxicology.

Recapitulating the domain of general toxicology, developmental toxicology evolved with an emphasis on structure. In the 1960s, however, Jack Werboff introduced the term *behavioral teratology* to describe the functional aftermath of drugs administered during gestation. His own studies largely tested drugs prescribed as psychopharmacological preparations. Despite objections to the term, based on the argument that terata mean deformities, it entered the lexicon of toxicology and has been anointed by widespread use (Riley & Voorhees, 1986). It even has been adopted as a regulatory standard. Great Britain and Japan require that new drugs be tested for functional deficits arising from exposure during gestation.

We now can cite many substances whose effects on the developing brain may be translated, after birth, into behavioral disturbances. The one most familiar to the general public is ethanol, because of the widely-cited research carried out on the Fetal Alcohol Syndrome (FAS) by Ann Streissguth and her collaborators (e.g., Streissguth et al., 1986) and by books and articles directed at the public. Although the public is acquainted with the syndrome in the form of a characteristic pattern of facial abnormalities and mental retardation, the broader significance of the work of the Streissguth group lies elsewhere. It derives from its careful evaluation of the ethanol dose–response relationship, and its demonstration that, even at maternal doses too low to induce facial dysmorphology and overtly retarded development, children may have been victimized by failure to reach what otherwise would have been their full potential.

We are certain to encounter the same kind of invisible deformities in the offspring of mothers who abuse other drugs, notably cocaine. These children, now surging into the primary grades, display an aggregation of behavioral disorders that teachers have begun to identify as characteristic of cocaine. Like FAS children, they merely represent the most easily identifiable vanguard of a much larger population. These other children will divulge no visible scars; only careful epidemiological studies and longitudinal experiments in animals will allow us to grasp fully the scope of the damage inflicted on them.

Lead offers one of the most compelling examples of what we may expect. Its original recognition as a poison lies entombed in history because it was one of the first metals processed and exploited by humans. Some writers attribute the disintegration of the Roman Empire to the nobility's penchant for storing grape syrup, added to wine, in leaden casks. Roman water transport systems depended on lead pipes; the origin of plumbing is the Latin word for lead. Even in this century, industrial processes expose countless workers to lead poisoning. Investigations of factories engaged in lead production, by Dr. Alice Hamilton, a pioneer in occupational medicine, instigated a debate about worker safety that elevated industrial hygiene to a valued discipline (Lippmann, 1990).

Clinical signs of lead poisoning in workers, such as wrist-drop and colic, gave little hint of the more obscure adverse effects associated with more modest exposures. Some of the keener observers, however, glimpsed their outlines, as in this passage from a paper by Rieke (1969, p. 521):

> Severe, classically described symptoms are infrequent. More commonly symptoms are vague; these metal burners are a little achey, dyspeptic, mentally sluggish, and moderately fatigued. Anemia is mild or absent. If symptoms are noted, they are attributed to other causes and the condition remains undiagnosed and untreated. Although denying illness, these workers do not feel fit; they drink too much palliative alcohol, age more rapidly, and are often tested for wrong ailments. Because of a dulled sensorium, they make errors which lead to an increased number and severity of accidental injuries.

Only with the maturing of behavioral toxicology as a discipline was the wider spectrum of deficiencies arising from moderate occupational lead exposure revealed. Compared to unexposed controls, workers with moderately elevated blood concentrations (20–40 μg/dl, say) scored lower on a variety of psychological tests and also presented a higher incidence of subjective complaints. Anger (1990a) provides a useful summary of occupational studies.

Lead in the communal environment elicits the gravest concerns. Adults in occupational settings, where lead sources are readily identified and controlled, can be protected against excessive exposures by adopting recognized safety practices. Children exposed to a diversity of environmental lead sources, such as flaking paint, street dust containing the combustion products of leaded gasoline, and drinking water are not so easily shielded. The problem is compounded because no single authority or agency is empowered to deal with all potential sources. Such diffusion of responsibility is partly to blame for the number of children calculated to be at risk for adverse effects.

Behavioral teratology grew out of the sometimes exquisite vulnerability of the developing brain to chemical disruption. Despite a surfeit of clues that somehow remained interred, as with FAS, lead escaped close scrutiny as such a chemical until a burgeoning of research that commenced about 20 years ago. Although it had long been recognized as a potent poison and public health menace, lead toxicity was still framed as the problem of lead poisoning. The final sundering from that archaic definition occurred with the publication of a seminal paper by Herbert Needleman and his colleagues (Needleman et al., 1979). It clothed the issue in its current guise: a question of exposure standards dictated by performance on psychological tests.

The usual measure of lead exposure is its concentration in blood. Blood lead, however, only reflects recent exposure. The investigator seeking to study the impact of excessive lead exposure during early brain development on how school children perform is stymied without a prospective experimental design. Needleman's detour around this barrier took the form of tooth analysis. Because teeth, like bone, accumulate and retain lead, he and his colleagues collected deciduous teeth from school children in two Boston suburbs and determined their lead concentrations. These analyses yielded an index of cumulative lead exposure. The investigators then performed extensive psychological testing on children from the highest and lowest deciles and also collected teacher ratings for all the children. None of the children displayed any evidence of lead intoxication, but the upper and lower deciles differed substantially on Wechsler Intelligence Scale for Children—Revised (WISC–R) scores and other indices. In addition, scores on the teacher rating scale, which assigned numbers to behaviors such as inability to concentrate, showed a remarkable correspondence with the amount of lead in the children's teeth.

These results triggered a volley of criticisms. Some came from industry. Others came from academic and governmental sources. Most objected to the findings because, they asserted, the Needleman group had not controlled or compensated fully for certain important social, economic, or educational variables on the part of the parents, even though the statistical analysis had included a plethora of such variables.

Despite their hostile reception in some quarters, these findings transformed the terms of the debate, and underscored the need for prospective studies. Several were launched in various parts of the world. Their findings supported and extended the original Needleman data. One of the most revealing was also conducted in Boston. It began with 12,000 analyses of cord blood, collected at birth, in two hospitals. On the basis of these data, the investigators recruited over 250 mothers and children to participate in a longitudinal study. They were divided into three groups: low (1.8 μg/dl), medium (6.5 μg/dl), and high (14.5 μg/dl) cord blood leads. At the ages of 6, 12, 18, and 24 months of age the children underwent testing, with the main instrument consisting of the Bayley Scales of Infant Development (Bellinger, Leviton, Waternaux, Needleman, & Rabinowitz, 1987).

As the children matured, differences among the groups widened. At 24 months of age, the children in the high lead group scored about 8% lower on the Bayley Scale's Mental Development Index than the children in the other two groups. This is especially notable for two reasons. First, the definition of high lead in this study. The Centers for Disease Control (CDC), an agency of the Public Health Service, until late in 1991, listed a blood level of 25 μg/dl or above as warranting clinical intervention. It now views 10 μg/dl as a potential threat. That value is just the latest trough in a steady decline, much of it occurring since Needleman et al. (1979). The downward movement has been propelled by a steady accumulation of data indicating adverse effects of lead at low exposure levels. Not very long ago, a value of 14.5 μg/dl would have been viewed as moderate, if not low. The second reason is the population from which Bellinger et al. drew their sample. Most previous studies reflected the performance of samples from poor, inner-city populations confronting many other hazards and disadvantages besides lead. The multiplicity of hazards confronting such children, in fact, is used to support critics who assert that the results ascribed to lead are hopelessly confounded with all the other variables. Bellinger et al., in contrast, drew their sample from a mainly White, upper-middle-class population consisting of intact families. Even the high-lead group scored above average, like the children in Garrison Keillor's *Lake Woebegon*. There were no instances of mental retardation or lead encephalopathy, no "cases" to fit into the typical epidemiological investigation.

Other prospective investigations support Bellinger et al. Dietrich et al. (1987), in a sample of children from Cincinnati's inner city, also noted relationships between gestational exposure to lead and developmental deficits. A risk model formulated to model a dose-response function based on Bellinger et al. indicated that even cord blood levels as low as 5 µg/dl represented a significant hazard (Wyzga, 1990). Such findings find further confirmation from studies of postural sway and hearing thresholds (reviewed in Lippmann, 1990). The avalanche of evidence from groups both in the United States and abroad (see, also, the collection in Smith, Grant, & Sors, 1989) is disturbing enough to have provoked a large federal effort to severely restrict lead exposure. It also provoked EPA's listing of 10–15 µg/dl as an "area of concern."

It may strike some observers (not psychologists, of course) as peculiar that the value of laboratory animal research in resolving debates about human risk may be clearer in the case of lead and behavior than in the case of such apparently direct biological extrapolations as carcinogenic potential. Extremely high doses are administered in lifetime animal studies to identify carcinogenic properties. Statistical models are then invoked to estimate the risks to humans typically exposed to environmental levels lower by several orders of magnitude. Different models yield vastly different risk estimates and clangorous debates. To the surprise of many (not psychologists, of course), experiments with animals exposed to lead yield the same conclusions cited by most human studies. Cory-Slechta and her coworkers studied rats (e.g., Cory-Slechta, Weiss, & Cox, 1985). Rice and her coworkers studied monkeys (e.g., Rice & Karpinski, 1988). They, as well as investigators from other laboratories, have noted significant behavioral differences between untreated animals and animals exposed to lead at levels sufficient to elevate blood leads into the range of 15 µg/dl. Those critics who repudiate the human studies because of all the possible impurities confounding epidemiological research seem impervious to laboratory data. Perhaps the animal experiments should have included information on maternal education and socioeconomic status.

The critics also dismiss the importance of "a few I.Q. points" attributable to lead exposure. But the implications of such a shift have to be defined in population, not individual, terms. Figure 5 (Weiss, 1988b) depicts two distributions. The one at the top describes a distribution of IQ scores with a mean of 100 and standard deviation of 15 (as for the Stanford-Binet). For a population of 100 million, such a distribution yields 2.3 million individuals scoring above 130. If the mean is shifted by 5%, to 95, the number of individuals scoring above 130 falls to 990 thousand. In addition, the number of children requiring remedial education, defined by scores below 70, sharply expands. Such a shift could be viewed as a societal disaster, and is not merely a hypothetical outcome. Bellinger et al. (1987) found a difference of 8% between the high lead and two lower groups. Furthermore, IQ surely is not the sole index of toxicity. Needleman, Schell, Bellinger, Leviton, and Allred (1990) traced the subsequent history of many of the children in the original 1979 study. Eleven years later, and in their late teens, those children with the highest tooth levels exhibited lower academic achievement, dropped out of school more frequently, and displayed a variety of behavioral distur-

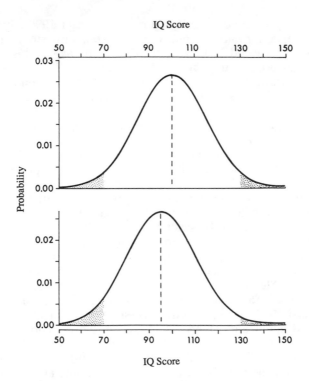

IQ Score

Figure 5. IQ distributions showing the effect of a 5% shift in the mean. Top: Standardized distribution based on a mean of 100 and SD of 15, as exemplified by the Stanford-Binet. In a population of 100 million, 2.3 million, as shown in the shaded areas, will score above 130. Bottom: With a mean of 95, 990 thousand will score above 130. From "Neurobehavioral Toxicity as a Basis for Risk Assesment" by B. Weiss, 1988, *Trends in Pharmacological Sciences, 9*, p. 61. Copyright 1982 by Elsevier. Reprinted by permission.

bances. Even at modest exposure levels, lead imposes a burden that is difficult to cast off.

Methylmercury is an organic compound of mercury. Its toxic focus is much narrower than that of lead, and it is a more destructive poison than elemental mercury. It was responsible for one of the largest mass chemical disasters in history. It is also responsible for much of the perspective and knowledge we have gained about developmental neurotoxicity.

First synthesized in the middle of the 19th century, methylmercury enjoyed widespread adoption as an effective fungicide. Correctly applied to seed grain, it dissipates into the soil and presents no health hazard. Its neurotoxic potency, though, was clear from the time of its original synthesis and was further confirmed in a bleak series of accidents extending into the 1970s. It was recognized as a broad ecological threat only with the solution to a mystery originating in the early 1950s. Then, inhabitants of a remote fishing village in Japan found themselves assaulted by a strange neurological disease whose source resisted detection until a visit by a British scientist who noted the similarities between what came to be known as "Minamata Disease," named for the village, and the Hunter-Russell syndrome, the label for methylmercury poisoning. The methylmercury came from fish and shellfish in Minamata Bay, the almost exclusive protein source for the fishermen and their families. Its ultimate source proved to be the effluent from a factory that used mercury as a catalyst in the manufacture of acetaldehyde and that, apparently inadvertently, had converted it into the highly poisonous methyl form (Tsubaki & Irukayama, 1977).

Methylmercury is a powerful nervous system poison. It destroys brain tissue. It particularly targets tissue deep in sulci, and its victims may suffer visual field narrowing (tunnel vision) to the point of complete blindness, somesthetic disturbances severe enough so that the shape of objects cannot be distinguished by touch, and motor disturbances as gross as ataxia. But severity is a function of dose. Limited exposure produces less blatant signs, such as mild paresthesias manifested as numbness and tingling around the mouth and fingertips.

The Hunter-Russell syndrome is based on adult poisoning, and most cases arose from occupational exposures (Hunter, 1975). Minamata provided the first intimations that the developing brain might be more sensitive than the adult brain. In Minamata, some mothers who showed only minor signs of neurotoxicity during pregnancy delivered children who were severely afflicted. The population was too small, however, and the documentation of intake too vague to create more than an impression of fetal vulnerability. That impression hardened into certainty in Iraq.

Wheat is Iraq's major crop, still produced in fields where it may first have been domesticated. But the wheat harvest of 1971 succumbed to a searing drought. To compensate for the disastrous harvest, and to reduce the impact of future droughts, the Iraqi government ordered about 80,000 tons of seed grain, mostly of the more robust and resistant Mexipak variety. Because of a transmission error, we believe, the order stipulated that the grain be treated with a methylmercury fungicide rather than a more innocuous form of organic mercury. Although the sacks came with Spanish and English labels warning against consumption, and were accompanied by precautions issued by the authorities, they arrived after the planting season. Hungry rural families, naive about handling toxic materials, ground the wheat into flour and baked it into bread (Bakir et al., 1973).

Methylmercury is not an acute poison. Its effects emerge insidiously. By the time unmistakable signs erupt, it already is too late to reverse the underlying brain damage. In Iraq, early symptoms, such as paresthesias, surfaced weeks or months after the victims began to consume the tainted grain. For those ingesting larger quantities, such symptoms were the precursors of more severe effects, including death. Only 450 hospital deaths occurred, but a later survey of the countryside shows that an estimate of 5,000 would be more accurate. As many as 50,000 individuals may have suffered serious toxicity.

The consequences of prenatal exposure began to emerge even more gradually. Researchers from Rochester, led by Dr. Thomas Clarkson, had established a laboratory in Baghdad to investigate potential therapies designed to accelerate methylmercury excretion from the body. With their discovery that scalp hair closely mirrored methylmercury levels in the blood, which reflect intake, they established the perfect exposure metric. Because scalp hair grows at a nearly uniform rate of one centimeter per month, the history of exposure is engraved in the hair shaft. Acquiring samples of scalp hair from mothers who were pregnant during the course of the episode allowed the investigators to trace complete exposure histories (Clarkson et al., 1981).

Responding to indications of magnified fetal susceptibility, Rochester scientists and their Iraqi colleagues traveled to rural villages to obtain hair samples. These provided the foundation for neurological assessment of Iraqi children exposed during gestation and marked the first mass chemical disaster permitting a clear dose–response relationship to be established. Children exposed to the highest levels before birth tended to be those most seriously affected, showing a syndrome of deficits that would be classified by pediatric neurologists as cerebral palsy. Those exposed to more modest levels seemed superficially indistinguishable from unexposed children. But careful neurological examinations revealed latent deficits, such as delays in the achievement of developmental milestones. Furthermore, some of these deficits remained silent until the children reached 5 years of age, when developmental delays could be seen with adequate clarity (Marsh et al., 1987). Even with these relatively cursory clinical measures, we calculate that the fetal brain is perhaps 10 times as vulnerable to methylmercury as the adult brain.

Methylmercury fungicides are banned in the United States. In fact, the ban took effect the year before the grain shipment to Iraq, so that supplies were plentiful when the order arrived. Our primary source of exposure is fish. Inorganic mercury deposited in waterways by a global mercury cycle or by industrial activity is converted by microorganisms in bottom sediment into the potent methyl form. As methylmercury ascends the food chain, the process of bioconcentration exposes the higher levels of the chain to gradually increasing amounts. The flesh of predators at the apex, such as pike, tuna, snapper, swordfish, and shark contains the highest levels. With fish consumption increasing in the United States, and with fish the main protein source in many countries, the question that always nags at toxicologists is inevitable: How much is safe? The question has taken on additional urgency because of high levels of fish from the Great Lakes and from inland lakes menaced by acid rain; acidification, by a process that remains obscure to researchers, promotes metal uptake by fish. Some fish-eating species are threatened; panthers in the Florida Everglades are dying, some believe, because of methylmercury contamination.

Cox, Clarkson, Marsh, and Amin-Zaki (1989) conducted an extensive analysis of the data from Iraq. The results are depicted in Figure 6. They plotted the relationship between maternal hair level and the incidence of retarded walking in the offspring. The dose–response function shows little evidence of a threshold. The relationship can also be modeled by what some statisticians term a hockey-stick function, which is comprised of a horizontal component equivalent to a threshold, and a second, intersecting, line whose slope represents the dose–response function above threshold. Even with a model that forces such a threshold, the intersection occurs at a hair level of about 10 parts per million. Such a level can be attained by consuming just a few meals of shark meat in a period of several weeks.

Concern about the impact of fish consumption on fetal brain development led Kjellstrom, Kennedy, Wallis, and Mantell (1986) to un-

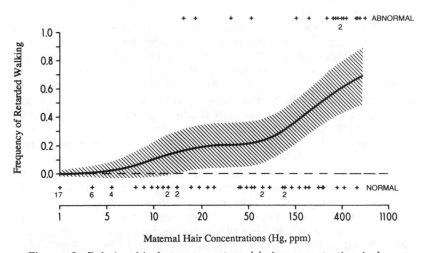

Figure 6. Relationship between maternal hair concentration in Iraq, reflecting methylmercury ingestion during pregnancy, and frequency of retarded walking (after 18 months of age) in offspring. The function was fitted on the basis of normal and abnormal cases shown by the labeled + signs. From "Dose-Response Analysis of Infants Prenatally Exposed to Methylmercury: An Application of a Single Compartment Model to Single-Strand Hair Analysis" by C. Cox, T. W. Clarkson, D. O. Marsh, and L. Amin-Zaki, 1989, *Environmental Research, 48*, p. 326. Copyright 1989 by Academic Press, Inc. Reprinted by permission.

dertake a study in New Zealand, where they identified 1,000 mothers who made fish and shark a major element in their diet and who consumed three such meals per week during pregnancy. The results indicated that maternal hair levels as low as 6 parts per million may produce significant developmental retardation as measured by the Denver Developmental Screening Test. A second study, carried out when the children reached 6 years of age (Kjellstrom et al., 1989) relied on the WISC–R and the Test of Language Development (TOLD) as measures. Maternal hair levels of 10 parts per million or more accounted for 2.5% of the variance in WISC scores and 2% of the variance in TOLD scores.

The methylmercury saga is reminiscent of lead. It begins with recognition of overt poisoning; then, with increasingly detailed examinations, increasingly subtle answers materialize to the question of risk and safety. To provide more definitive data, Rochester investigators have embarked on a study in the Seychelles, an island nation in the Indian Ocean. There, because the sea provides almost the sole source of animal protein, mostly in the form of predatory species such as shark and swordfish, maternal hair levels can reach 20 parts per million or more. That study will include assessments by psychological tests such as the Bayley scales. In parallel with contemporary lead research, gross effects, even at the highest intake levels, are not expected. Again, the issue of risk will be framed on the basis of shifts in the performance of a population, not as number of cases.

Laboratory experiments, again offering a parallel with lead, form a solid footing for risk estimation unencumbered by the inherent uncertainties of epidemiological surveys. Unlike lead, however, methylmercury produces a distinctive pattern of structural aberrations even at relatively low exposure levels. Inhibition of cell division and migration is evident (Rodier, Aschner & Sager, 1984; Sager, Doherty, & Rodier, 1982). Even in the absence of detectable neuropathology, special histological methods reveal diminished branching of dendrites in cells in the cerebellum (Peckham & Choi, 1988). Such morphological abnormalities are accompanied by functional disturbances. For example, infant monkeys exposed during gestation displayed impaired performance on visual recognition memory tasks similar to the Fagan test (Mottet, Shaw, & Burbacher, 1985). Also working with monkeys exposed during development, Rice and Gilbert (1990) noted impaired spatial contrast sensitivity, a sensitive measure of visual discrimination. Except for a few studies, such as those by Bornhausen, Müsch, and Greim (1980), explorations of low prenatal doses remain rare. These investigators found performance deficits in rats on an operant schedule requiring the emission of high response rates. Although major gaps in the methylmercury story, due to a paucity of experiments at low doses, still exist, the information we now possess is certainly sufficient to buttress the human data. It is especially sufficient if conventional safety standards were to be calculated.

Carcinogenesis is presumed to be a process without a threshold. For substances not classified as carcinogens, exposure standards are calculated from what are called effect levels. For example, the no observed adverse effect level (NOAEL) is defined as the highest dose or concentration producing no detectable adverse health effect. A NOAEL based on experimental animal data is typically divided by 100 to yield an acceptable daily intake (ADI) or reference dose (RfD; the term preferred by EPA) for humans. The factor of 100 is termed an uncertainty factor and embodies a factor of 10 for species differences and a factor of 10 for variation among individuals. A lowest observed adverse effect level (LOAEL) would be divided by 1,000 to yield an ADI. We can calculate a value close to a NOAEL or LOAEL from the brain concentrations in animals required to produce structural aberrations or functional disturbances. Were those values transformed into corresponding human intakes, It might be necessary to label tuna fish as a potential hazard for the developing brain. We seem to deliberately violate policies proclaimed by the Food and Drug Administration (FDA) and the EPA because the consequences of adhering to them would prove so disruptive in the cases of methylmercury and lead.

Another cogent example of the ambiguities thrust on regulators by behavioral toxicity is the case of polychlorinated biphenyls or PCBs. These substances, used for over 40 years as insulators and other applications, became a major pollution problem because of their environmental persistence and accumulation in the food chain. Two mass poisonings, both resulting from contaminated cooking oil, identified PCBs as a potent developmental neurotoxicant (Tilson, Jacobson, & Rogan, 1990). One occurred in Japan and the other in Taiwan. In these episodes, the mothers, ill themselves, delivered babies who, in addition to developmental delays, revealed additional evidence of toxicity, such as hyperpigmentation of skin. In U.S. children, exposed to much lower levels during early brain development through maternal consumption of contaminated fish, the effects proved more subtle. PCB levels, as measured in cord blood, correlated with abnormalities on the Brazelton Scale, with scores on the Bayley Scales, and with performance on the Fagan test of visual recognition memory.

Tilson, Jacobson, and Rogan calculated RfDs from breast milk values; because PCBs are stored in fat, and excreted extremely slowly, breast milk concentrations can be extrapolated to estimate PCB ingestion. RfDs calculated in this manner can be extrapolated to PCB dietary intakes eliciting reduced cognitive functioning. Dietary surveys indicate that some U.S. consumption patterns bring exposures close to those critical doses. Here is an instance in which the protective buffer of the uncertainty factor retains, at most, a narrow margin for conserving the integrity of psychological development.

A Retrograde Perspective

Connections with toxic exposures earlier in life are difficult enough to establish even in childhood. The difficulties are infinitely more formidable if the aim is to trace a connection with neurodegenerative diseases in advanced age. Given the massive increase in health costs looming as the U.S. population ages, a search for such connections is essential. Nor would it be a quixotic pursuit. Several discoveries have released a flood of speculation. Some of it followed the discovery (Langston, Ballard, Tetrud, & Irwin, 1983) that a contaminant in what addicts called synthetic heroin, 1-methyl-4-phenyl-1,2,3,6-tetrahydropyridine or MPTP, had provoked an epidemic of Parkinson's disease among drug abusers. Subsequent experiments then revealed that MPTP damages cells in the primate substantia nigra, a subcortical structure whose cell population is severely depleted in parkinsonism (Langston, Langston, & Irwin, 1984). Because the etiology of idiopathic Parkinson's disease remains a mystery, MPTP intrigued neurologists and neuroscientists; it pointed to an environmental cause. Calne, McGeer, Eisen, and Spencer (1986) argued that other neurodegenerative diseases might also originate from exposure to neurotoxicants in the environment.

One of the diseases they discussed is known as ALS-PD, or amyotrophic lateral sclerosis-parkinsonism dementia, a syndrome prevalent in at least three sites in the Western Pacific. The most famous is Guam. ALS is the medical term for Lou Gehrig's disease; the PD component exhibits aspects of both Parkinson's disease and dementia such as that seen in Alzheimer's disease. The disease on Guam evoked enough interest shortly after World War II for the U.S. Public Health Service to establish a research station on the island, but the question finally leaped to prominence with a report by Peter Spencer (1987). It indicted a plant, *Cycas circinalis*, sometimes called the Sago false palm, as the cause. Cycad seeds have been used for generations as a food source by the Chamorros, the native people of Guam. They prepared them for food, however, by a lengthy process that apparently removed the toxic principle. During the Japanese occupation, however, other food sources diminished, and the preparation process was compressed. Spencer holds the short cuts responsible for the high incidence of ALS-PD in the years following the war, and the adoption of a diet more like that of the mainland for its subsequent decline.

Two striking features of this story claim attention. One is histopathology. The brains of afflicted persons carry the hallmarks of Alzheimer's disease. The accumulations of neurofibrillary tangles that pathologists rely on to diagnose Alzheimer's are readily visible. The other is latency. Decades may pass before clinical signs irrupt. In one case, 45 years elapsed between migration from Guam, with no Cycad seeds consumed in the interval, and the emergence of ALS-PD. Spencer speculated that what he called a "slow toxin," conceptually similar to a slow virus, may have initiated the process. Calne et al. (1986) presented another possibility. They hypothesized that earlier damage, whose functional consequences lie dormant, is finally unmasked with aging, when the brain no longer retains enough reserve capacity to compensate. They applied the term *abiotrophic process* to the gradual erosion of functional capacity with aging.

Spencer's arguments are contradicted by other scientists, who claim that ALS-PD arises from a form of metal toxicity attributable to a coupling of calcium deficiency with excessive exposure to manganese, aluminum, or other heavy metals. In fact, high concentrations of aluminum have been detected in the neurofibrillary tangles of ALS-PD victims (Perl, 1985). Furthermore, together with evidence suggesting elevated aluminum concentrations in the brains of Alzheimer patients, some epidemiological data suggest that aluminum exposure in the workplace may also be associated with signs of incipient dementia. Rifat, Eastwood, Crapper-McLachlan, and Corey (1990) studied miners treated decades before, by inhalation, to aluminum compounds because it then was believed to protect them against pulmonary disease. Table 8 summarizes their findings, based on several assessment instruments.

Whatever the sources of ALS-PD, Parkinson's disease, or other neurodegenerative diseases, environmental sources merit exploration because of their potential significance. Furthermore, data from laboratory animals confirm the notion that early damage may remain silent until the reserve capacity of the brain is compromised in senescence. The best documented data come from studies by Joan Cranmer. She adopted the strategy of administering neurotoxic agents to mice during gestation, then tracing the aftermath in the offspring until advanced age. An early methylmercury study (Spyker, 1975) illustrates her findings. Here, some treated mice began to show neurological deficits, such as tremor and

Table 8
Late Effects of Exposure of Miners to Aluminum Powder

	Mean adjusted score (three tests)[a]	Proportion impaired (one or more tests)
Exposed (n = 261)	78.6	0.13
Unexposed (n = 346)	82.8	0.05
Differences	6.3	0.08
p-value	0.0001	0.0002

Note. From "Effect of Exposure of Miners to Aluminum Powder" by S. L. Rifat, M. R. Eastwood, D. R. Crapper-McLachlan, and P. N. Corey, 1990, *Lancet, 336*, p. 1164. © 1990 by The Lancet Ltd. Reprinted by permission.
[a] The three tests were the Mini-Mental State Exam, the Raven Progressive Matrices, and the Symbol-Digit Modalities.

ataxia, at 10–15 months of age. Other mice remained free of overt signs until 2.5–3 years of age, when the rate of neurological deficits and other signs of deterioration began to accelerate.

Early developmental damage is superimposed on what might be called natural aging in the examples just cited. Another possibility is that lifetime exposure to a neurotoxicant might accelerate the process of brain aging. Weiss and Simon (1975) offered a model of such a process as a heuristic aid to grasping the implications of even a relatively minute acceleration. The heavy line in Figure 7 traces the decline in oxygen uptake, glucose consumption, and neuronal cell density beginning at age 25. It shows that by age 70 these functional indexes have fallen about 20%. An incremental acceleration of brain aging as little as 0.1% annually, because of compounding, hastens the decline enough so that the 20% decline is reached by age 60. Although Figure 7 is a model, not an experimental determination, it compels attention because of its broad social and medical implications. Simply take the expense of one year of institutionalized care, now estimated as $30,000–$50,000, and calculate how costly it would be for a large population to reach that critical point one year sooner.

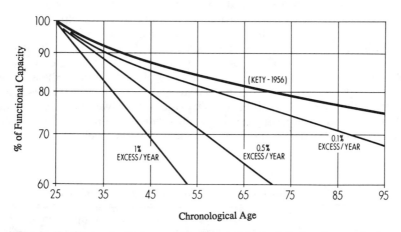

Chronological Age

Figure 7. Chronological age plotted against brain functional capacity, based on neuronal cell density, oxygen consumption, and glucose uptake. Age 25 years is taken as 100%. The heavy line is based on data published by Kety (1956). The lighter lines depict the postulated course of brain aging with superimposed accelerations of 0.1, 0.5, and 1.0% annually due to neurotoxicant exposure. Because of compounding, even slight accelerations, over several decades would produce a substantially earlier decline to an arbitrary value such as 80% of baseline function. From "Quantitative Perspectives on the Long-Term Toxicity of Methylmercury and Similar Poisons" by B. Weiss and W. Simon, in B. Weiss and V. G. Laties (Eds.), *Behavioral Toxicology*, p. 432, 1975, New York: Plenum. Copyright 1975 by Plenum Press. Reprinted by permission.

The Dimensions of Risk

Risk assessment began its penetration of public health and environmental policy with cancer. With only one outcome to consider, a framework for risk assessment and management could readily be devised (National Academy of Sciences, 1983). Mechanistic assumptions about the process of carcinogenesis also helped thrust it into a dominant position. Neurotoxic risk assessment shares some common principles with cancer risk assessment, of course (Weiss, 1991); both must confront extremely long latencies. Both also must share the toxicological principle that response is determined by dose, or, "the dose makes the poison." Neurobehavioral measures are consigned to limbo without some estimate of dose or exposure.

Neurobehavioral toxicology is unique for two reasons: the plethora of possible endpoints or measures, and the scope of possible outcomes. I have discussed both aspects in this chapter, but the realm of potential outcomes is so vast that no single assay, in isolation, is sufficient to characterize neurotoxic risk. Consider the contrast with cancer: a single endpoint (although with many facets) and few debates about biological significance. All of the following possibilities have to be weighed to judge the risks posed by neurotoxic agents (Weiss, 1990):

1. *An elevated incidence or prevalence of some disease or disability.* All young children misbehave at some time. Some children who are challenged by synthetic food dyes respond with disruptive behaviors (Weiss, 1982, 1986; Weiss et al., 1980). Much of the literature has been misinterpreted, even by scientists, because they failed to understand that a low incidence of adverse effects, distributed over a large population, is a serious consequence, exactly as we quantify the risk of cancer.

2. *A shift in the population distribution of scores on a particular measure or test.* Lead exposure, even at moderate levels, attenuates scores on intelligence tests and developmental assays. Small shifts are translated into huge implications for society. Cases cannot be counted; the critical measures are continuous.

3. *Gestational exposure may exert lifetime consequences.* The legacy of methylmercury exposure during pregnancy does not abate with age; in fact, it may remain submerged until senescence. Lifetime animal studies may be necessary to obtain satisfactory answers.

4. *The aging process may be accelerated.* Continual erosion of nervous system function arising from chronic exposure may hasten the emergence of normal age-related deficits.

5. *Toxicity may take the form of reduced compensatory capacity.* Sometimes called silent or latent damage, the result remains imperceptible until some additional demand is imposed on nervous system function. Drug challenges are sometimes used to unmask such latent damage.

6. *Rate of recovery from a reversible effect may be impeded.* Adaptive changes, such as those observed with chronic OP treatment, may be delayed, slowed, or inadequate because of previous exposure or damage.

No one in the profession of psychology ever expected to deal with simple problems and unidimensional answers. Behavioral toxicology provides an even more profuse abundance of complicated questions and multifaceted responses than we thought we had bargained for. But the issues are precisely those that deserve to occupy the front ranks of public health initiatives.

Summary

Behavioral toxicology is a young discipline founded on the heritage of an ancient history. The connection between chemical contaminants in the environment and adverse behavioral consequences has been recognized since antiquity. What has achieved recognition only recently, however, is the need to rely on psychological techniques to detect incipient or covert toxicity and to forecast the potential risks posed by new agents. Such techniques, whether applied to humans or experimental animals, represent a momentous shift from older practices, which depended upon tissue damage or gross morbidity and mortality to signal threats to health. They particularly denote a change in the properties of responses by which adverse effects might be deduced. Instead, say, of a single endpoint, such as cancer, which is the prototype for risk assessment, behavior is characterized by multiple endpoints linked in complex ways to exposure variables. In humans, behavioral toxicity might be expressed as mood changes, impaired memory, slowed motor responses, or population shifts in intelligence test scores. In animals, it might be reflected by changes in spontaneous activity, or impaired learning, or altered response patterns maintained by schedule-controlled operant behavior, or by delays in the appearance of developmental landmarks. Furthermore, the relative prominence or detectability of effects may be a function of exposure pattern; acute exposures often induce markedly different toxic responses than chronic exposures. These attributes of behavioral toxicity are illustrated by heavy metals, pesticides, solvents, and even food additives, and should promote an expanded view of how to design risk assessments for chemical contaminants.

References

Albers, J. W., Cavender, G. O., Levine, S. P., & Langolf, G. D. (1982). Asymptomatic sensorimotor polyneuropathy in workers exposed to elemental mercury. *Neurology, 32,* 1168–1174.

American Conference of Governmental Industrial Hygienists. (1974). *Documentation of the threshold limit values for substances in workroom air* (3rd ed.). Cincinnati: American Conference of Governmental Industrial Hygienists.

Anger, W. K. (1990a). Worksite behavioral research: Results, sensitive methods, test batteries, and the transition from laboratory data to human health. *Neurotoxicology, 11,* 629–720.

Anger, W. K. (1990b). Human neurobehavioral toxicology testing. In R. W. Russell, P. E. Flattau, & A. M. Pope (Eds.), *Behavioral measures of neurotoxicity* (pp. 69–85). Washington, DC: National Academy Press.

Anger, W. K., & Johnson, B. L. (1985). Chemicals affecting behavior. In J. O'Donoghue (Ed.), *Neurotoxicity of industrial and commercial chemicals* (pp. 51–148). Boca Raton, FL: CRC Press.

Baker, E. L., & Fine, L. J. (1986). Solvent neurotoxicity: The current evidence. *Journal of Occupational Medicine, 28,* 126–129.

Bakir, F., Damluji, S. F., Amin-Zaki, L., Murtadha, M., Kahlide, A., Al-Rawi, N. Y., Tikriti, S., Dhahir, H. I., Clarkson, T. W., Smith, J. C., & Doherty, R. A. (1973). Methylmercury poisoning in Iraq. *Science, 181,* 230–241.

Barbeau, A. (1984). Manganese and extrapyramidal disorders. *Neurotoxicology, 5,* 13–36.

Bellinger, D., Leviton, A., Waternaux, C., Needleman, H., & Rabinowitz, M. (1987). Longitudinal analyses of prenatal and postnatal lead exposure and early cognitive development. *New England Journal of Medicine, 316,* 1037–1043.

Benning, D. (1958). Outbreak of mercury poisoning in Ohio. *Industrial Medicine and Surgery, 22,* 354–363.

Bornhausen, M., Müsch, H. R., & Greim, H. (1980). Operant behavior performance changes in rats after prenatal methylmercury exposure. *Toxicology and Applied Pharmacology, 56,* 305–310.

Calne, D. B., McGeer, E., Eisen, A., & Spencer, P. (1986, November 8). Alzheimer's Disease, Parkinson's disease, and motoneurone disease: Abiotropic interaction between aging and environment? *Lancet,* 1067–1070.

Carson, R. L. (1962). *Silent spring.* Boston: Houghton Mifflin.

Clarkson, T. W., Cox, C., Marsh, D. O., Myers, G. J., Al-Tikriti, S. K., Amin-Zaki, L., & Dabbagh, A. R. (1981). Dose-response relationships for adult and prenatal exposures to methylmercury. In G. G. Berg & H. D. Maillie (Eds.), *Measurement of risks* (pp. 111–130). New York: Plenum Press.

Clarkson, T. W., Friberg, L., Hursh, J. B., & Nylander, M. (1988). The prediction of intake of mercury vapor from amalgams. In T. W. Clarkson, L. Friberg, G. F. Nordberg, & P. R. Sager (Eds.), *Biological monitoring of toxic metals* (pp. 247–264). New York: Plenum Press.

Cory-Slechta, D. A., Weiss, B., & Cox. C. (1985). Performance and exposure indices of rats exposed to low concentrations of lead. *Toxicology and Applied Pharmacology, 78,* 291–299.

Cox, C., Clarkson, T. W., Marsh, D. O., & Amin-Zaki, L. (1989). Dose-response analysis of infants prenatally exposed to methylmercury: An application of a single compartment model to single-strand hair analysis. *Environmental Research, 48,* 318–322.

Cranmer, J. M. & Golberg, L. (Eds.). (1986). Proceedings of the workshop on neurobehavioral effects of solvents. *Neurotoxicology, 7*(4).

Cranmer, J. M., & Hixson, E. J. (Eds.). (1984). *Delayed neurotoxicity*. Little Rock, AK: Intox Press.

Dietrich, K. N., Krafft, K. M., Bornschein, R. L., Hammond, P. B., Berger, O., Succup, P. A., & Bier, M. (1987). Low-level lead exposure: Effect on neurobehavioral development in early infancy. *Pediatrics, 80*, 721–730.

Duffy, F. H., & Burchfiel, J. L. (1980). Long term effects of the organophosphate sarin on EEGs in monkeys and humans. *Neurotoxicology, 1*, 667–689.

Environmental Protection Agency. (1991). Multi-substance rule for the testing of neurotoxicity. *Federal Register, 56*, 9105–9119.

Grasso, P., Sharratt, M., Davies, D. M., & Irvine, D. (1984). Neurophysiological and psychological disorders and occupational exposure to organic solvents. *Food and Chemical Toxicology, 22*, 819–852.

Hanninen, H. (1971). Psychological picture of manifest and latent carbon disulphide poisoning. *British Journal of Industrial Medicine, 28*, 374–381.

Hunter, D. S. (1975). *The diseases of occupations* (5th ed.). London: British Universities Press.

Iregren, A. (1990). Psychological test performance in foundry workers exposed to low levels of manganese. *Neurotoxicology and Teratology, 12*, 673–675.

Ishikawa, S., & Miyata, M. (1980). Development of myopia following chronic organophosphate pesticide intoxication: An epidemiological and experimental study. In W. H. Merigan & B. Weiss (Eds.), *Neurotoxicity of the visual system* (pp. 233–254). New York: Raven Press.

Kety, S. S. (1956). Human cerebral blood flow and oxygen consumption as related to aging. *Research Publications of the Association for Nervous and Mental Disease, 35*, 31–45.

Kjellstrom, T., Kennedy, P., Wallis, S., & Mantell, C. (1986). *Physical and mental development of children with prenatal exposure to mercury from fish. Stage 1. Preliminary tests at age 4.* (Report No. 3080). Solna, Sweden: National Swedish Environmental Research Board.

Kjellstrom, T., Kennedy, P., Wallis, S., Stewart, A., Friberg, L., Lind, B., Wetherspoon, T., & Mantell, C. (1989). *Physical and mental development of children with prenatal exposure to mercury from fish. Stage 2. Interviews and psychological tests at age 6.* (Report No. 3642). Solna, Sweden: National Swedish Environmental Protection Board.

Klaassen, C. D., Amdur, M. O., & Doull, J. (Eds.). (1986). *Casarett and Doull's toxicology* (3rd ed.). New York: Macmillan.

Kulig, B. M. (1990). Methods and issues in evaluating the neurotoxic effects of organic solvents. In R. W. Russell, P. E. Flattau, & A. M. Pope (Eds.), *Behavioral measures of neurotoxicity* (pp. 159–183). Washington, DC: National Academy Press.

Langolf, G. D., Chaffin, D. B., Henderson, R., & Whittle, H. P. (1978). Evaluation of workers exposed to elemental mercury using quantitative tests of tremor and neuromuscular functions. *American Industrial Hygiene Association Journal, 39*, 976–984.

Langston, J. W., Ballard, P. A., Tetrud, J. W., & Irwin, I. (1983). Chronic Parkinsonism in humans due to a product of meperidine-analog synthesis. *Science, 219*, 979–980.

Langston, J. W., Langston, E. B. ,& Irwin, I. (1984). MPTP-induced Parkinsonism in human and non-human primates—clinical and experimental aspects. *Acta Neurologica Scandinavica, 70,* 49–54.

Levin, H. S., Rodnitzky, R. L., & Mick, D. L. (1976). Anxiety associated with exposure to organophosphate compounds. *Archives of General Psychiatry, 33,* 225–228.

Lippmann, M. (1990). Lead and human health: Background and recent findings. *Environmental Research, 51,* 1–24.

Marsh., D. O., Clarkson, T. W., Cox, C., Myers, G. J., Amin-Zaki, L., & Al-Tikriti, S. (1987). Fetal methylmercury poisoning. Relationship between concentration in single strands of maternal hair and child effects. *Archives of Neurology, 44,* 1017–1022.

Merigan, W. H., Barkdoll, E., Maurissen, J. P. J., Eskin, T. A., & Lapham, L. W. (1981). Acrylamide effects on the macaque visual system. I. Psychophysics and electrophysiology. *Investigative Ophthalmology and Visual Science, 26,* 309–316.

Merigan, W. H., Wood, R. W., & Zehl, D. N. (1985). Recent observations on the neurobehavioral toxicity of carbon disulfide. *Neurotoxicology, 6,* 81–88.

Morgan, J. P. (1982). The Jamaica ginger paralysis. *Journal of the American Medical Association, 248,* 1864–1867.

Mottet, N. K., Shaw, C. M., & Burbacher, T. M. (1985). Health risks from increases in methylmercury exposure. *Environmental Health Perspectives, 63,* 133–140.

National Academy of Sciences. (1983). *Risk assessment in the federal government: Managing the process.* Washington, DC: National Academy Press.

Needleman, H. L., Gunnoe, C., Leviton, A., Reed, M., Peresie, H., Maher, C., & Barrett, P. (1979). Deficits in psychological and classroom performance of children with elevated dentine lead levels. *New England Journal of Medicine, 300,* 689–695.

Needleman, H. L., Schell, A., Bellinger, D., Leviton, A., & Allred, E. N. (1990). The long-term effects of exposure to low doses of lead in childhood. An 11-year follow-up report. *New England Journal of Medicine, 322,* 83–88.

Newland, M. C., Ceckler, T. L., Kordower, J. H., & Weiss, B. (1989). Visualizing manganese in the primate basal ganglia with magnetic resonance imaging. *Experimental Neurology, 106,* 251–258.

Newland, M. C., Cox, C., Hamada, R., Oberdörster, G., & Weiss, B. (1987). The clearance of manganese chloride in the primate. *Fundamental and Applied Toxicology, 9,* 314–328.

Pavlenko, S. M. (1975). Methods for the study of the central nervous system in toxicological tests. In *Methods Used in the USSR for establishing biologically safe levels of toxic substances* (pp. 86–108). Geneva: World Health Organization.

Peckham, N. M., & Choi, B. H. (1988). Abnormal neuronal distribution within the cerebral cortex after prenatal methylmercury intoxication. *Acta Neuropathologica, 76,* 222–226.

Perl, D. P. (1985). Relationship of aluminum to Alzheimer's Disease. *Environmental Health Perspectives, 63,* 149–153.

Rice, D. C., & Gilbert, S. G. (1990). Effects of developmental exposure to methylmercury on spatial and temporal visual function in monkeys. *Toxicology and Applied Pharmacology, 102,* 151–163.

Rice, D. C., & Karpinski, K. F. (1988). Lifetime low-level lead exposure produces deficits in delayed alternation in adult monkeys. *Neurotoxicology and Teratology, 10*, 207–214.

Rieke, F. E. (1969). Lead intoxication in shipbuilding and shipscraping, 1941 to 1968. *Archives of Environmental Health, 19*, 521–539.

Rifat, S. L., Eastwood, M. R., Crapper-McLachlan, D. R., & Corey, P. N. (1990). Effect of exposure of miners to aluminum powder. *Lancet, 336*, 1162–1165.

Riley, E. P., & Voorhees, C. V. (Eds.). (1986). *Handbook of behavioral teratology.* New York: Plenum Press.

Rodier, P. M., Aschner, M., & Sager, P. R. (1984). Mitotic arrest in the developing CNS after prenatal exposure to methylmercury. *Neurobehavioral Toxicology and Teratology, 6*, 379–385.

Roels, H., Gennart, J. P., Lauwerys, R., Buchet, J. P., Malchaire, J., & Bernard, A. (1985). Surveillance of workers exposed to mercury vapour: Validation of a previously proposed biological threshold limit value for mercury concentration in urine. *American Journal of Industrial Medicine, 7*, 45–71.

Roels, H., Lauwerys, R., Buchet, J. P., Genet, P., Sarhan, M. J., Hanotiau, I., deFays, M., Bernard, A., & Stanescu, D. (1987). Epidemiological survey among workers exposed to manganese: Effects on lung, central nervous system, and some biological indices. *American Journal of Industrial Medicine, 11*, 307–327.

Sager, P. R., Doherty, R. A., & Rodier, P. M. (1982). Effects of methylmercury on developing mouse cerebellar cortex. *Experimental Neurology, 77*, 179–193.

Savage, E. P., Keefe, T. J., Mounce, L. M., Heaton, R. K., Lewis, J. A., & Burcar, P. J. (1988). Chronic neurological sequelae of acute organophosphate poisoning. *Archives of Environmental Health, 43*, 38–45.

Smith, M. A., Grant, L. D., & Sors, A. I. (Eds.). (1989). *Lead exposure and child development: An international assessment.* Boston: Kluwer Academic Publishers.

Smith, P. J., Langolf, G. D., & Goldberg, J. (1983). Effects of occupational exposure to elemental mercury on short term memory. *British Journal of Industrial Medicine, 40*, 413–419.

Spencer, P. S. (1987). Guam ALS/Parkinsonism-Dementia: A long-latency disorder caused by "slow toxin(s)" in food? *Canadian Journal of Neurological Sciences, 14*, 347–357.

Spyker, J. M. (1975), Behavioral teratology and toxicology. In B. Weiss & V. G. Laties (Eds.), *Behavioral toxicology* (pp. 311–350). New York: Plenum Press.

Streissguth, A. P., Barr, H. M., Sampson, P. D., Parrish-Johnson, J. C., Kirchner, G. L., & Martin, D. C. (1986). Attention, distraction, and reaction time at age 7 years and prenatal alcohol exposure. *Neurobehavioral Toxicology and Teratology, 8*, 717–725.

Suzuki, Y., Mouri, T., Suzuki Y., Nishiyama, K., Fujii, N., & Yano, H. (1975). Study of subacute toxicity of manganese chloride in monkeys. *Tokushima Journal of Experimental Medicine, 22*, 5–10.

Tilson, H. A., Jacobson, J. L., & Rogan, W. J. (1990). Polychlorinated biphenyls and the developing nervous system: Cross-species comparisons. *Neurotoxicology and Teratology, 12*, 239–248.

Tsubaki, F., & Irukayama, K. (Eds.). (1977). *Minamata disease.* New York: Elsevier Science Publishers, Inc.

Uzzell, B. P., & Oler, J. (1986). Chronic low-level mercury exposure and neuropsychological functioning. *Journal of Clinical and Experimental Neuropsychology, 8*, 581.

Wedeen, R. P. (1989). Were the hatters of New Jersey "mad"? *American Journal of Industrial Medicine, 16*, 225–233.

Weiss, B. (1982). Food additives and environmental chemicals as sources of childhood behavior disorders. *Journal of American Academy of Child Psychology, 21*, 144–152.

Weiss, B. (1983a). Behavioral toxicology of heavy metals. In I. E. Dreosti & R. M. Smith (Eds.)., *Neurobiology of the trace elements: Vol. 2. Neurotoxicology and neuropharmacology* (pp. 1–50). Clifton, NJ: Humana Press.

Weiss, B. (1983b). Behavioral toxicology and environmental health science. Opportunity and challenge for psychology. *American Psychologist, 38*, 1174–1187.

Weiss, B. (1986). Food additives as a source of behavioral disturbances in children. *Neurotoxicology, 7*, 197–208.

Weiss, B. (1988a). Behavior as an early indication of pesticide toxicity. *Toxicology and Industrial Health, 4*, 351–360.

Weiss, B. (1988b). Neurobehavioral toxicity as a basis for risk assessment. *Trends in Pharmacological Sciences, 9*, 59–62.

Weiss, B. (1990). Risk assessment: The insidious nature of neurotoxicity and the aging brain. *Neurotoxicology, 11*, 305–314.

Weiss, B. (1991). Cancer and the dynamics of neurodegenerative processes. *Neurotoxicology, 12*, 379–386.

Weiss, B., & Clarkson, T. W. (1986). Toxic chemical disasters and the implications of Bhopal for technology transfer. *The Millbank Quarterly, 64*, 216–240.

Weiss, B., & Laties, V. G. (Eds.). (1975). *Behavioral toxicology.* New York: Plenum.

Weiss, B., & Simon, W. (1975). Quantitative perspectives on the long-term toxicity of methylmercury and similar poisons. In B. Weiss & V. G. Laties (Eds.), *Behavioral toxicology* (pp. 429–437). New York: Plenum.

Weiss, B., Williams, J. H., Margen, S., Abrams, B., Caan, B., Citron, L. J., Cox, C., McKibben, J., Ogar, D., & Schultz, S. (1980). Behavioral responses to artificial food colors. *Science, 207*, 1487–1488.

Wood, R. W., & Cox, C. C. (1986). A repeated-measures approach to the detection of the minimal acute effects of toluene. *Toxicologist, 6*, 221.

Wood, R. W., Weiss, A. B., & Weiss, B. (1973). Hand tremor induced by industrial exposure to inorganic mercury. *Archives of Environmental Health, 26*, 249–252.

Wyzga, R. (1990). Towards quantitative risk assessment for neurotoxicity. *Neurotoxicology, 11*, 199–208.

EARN CONTINUING EDUCATION CREDITS THROUGH HOME STUDY PROGRAMS BASED ON THE APA MASTER LECTURES

The Master Lectures, presented each year at the APA Convention, can be used to earn Continuing Education (CE) Credits through the successful completion of a test developed to accompany most volumes of this series. The following Home Study Programs are available:

1993—"PSYCHOLOGY AND THE LAW"

1992—"A CENTENNIAL CELEBRATION—FROM THEN TO NOW: PSYCHOLOGY APPLIED"

1991—"PSYCHOPHARMACOLOGY"

1990—"PSYCHOLOGICAL PERSPECTIVES ON HUMAN DIVERSITY IN AMERICA"

1989—"PSYCHOLOGICAL ASPECTS OF SERIOUS ILLNESS"

1988—"THE ADULT YEARS: CONTINUITY AND CHANGE"

For more information about the Home Study Programs, detach and mail the form below (please print, type or use pre-printed label), or telephone 202/336-5991, 9 a.m.–5 p.m. EST/EDT.

- ✂

Please send me more information about APA's Home Study Programs for Continuing Education Credit.

Name: _____

Address: _____

_____

_____
    (City)   (State)   (Zip code)

Daytime phone: _____ / _____
           Area Code

Mail this form to the following address:

Continuing Education Home Study Programs
American Psychological Association
750 First Street, NE
Washington, DC 20002
202/336-5991